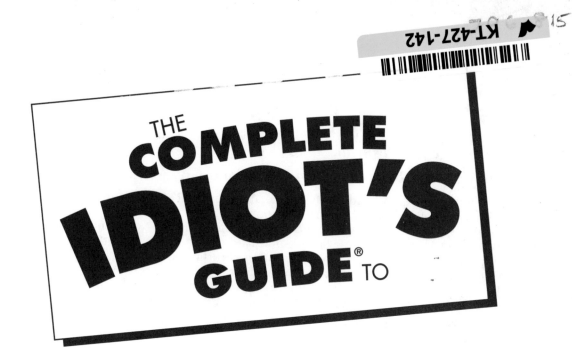

THE **COMPLETE IDIOT'S GUIDE**® TO

Kickboxing

by Karon Karter and Guy Mezger

alpha books

A Pearson Education Company

Karon Karter: To my mother/best friend/confidante, for her unconditional, loving support; and to Janet Harris, for guiding me every step in my career as a writer. A heartfelt thank you goes to my agent, Evan Fogelman, for believing in me as a writer.

Guy Mezger: To my mom.

Copyright © 2000 by Karon Karter and Guy Mezger

THE COMPLETE IDIOT'S GUIDE TO and Design are registered trademarks of Pearson Education, Inc.

International Standard Book Number: 0-02-863175-7
Library of Congress Catalog Card Number: Available upon request.

04   03   02   8   7   6   5   4   3

Interpretation of the printing code: The rightmost number of the first series of numbers is the year of the book's printing; the rightmost number of the second series of numbers is the number of the book's printing. For example, a printing code of 00-1 shows that the first printing occurred in 2000.

Printed in the United States of America

For marketing and publicity, please call: 317-581-3722

The publisher offers discounts on this book when ordered in quantity for bulk purchases and special sales.

For sales within the United States, please contact: Corporate and Government Sales, 1-800-382-3419 or corpsales@pearsontechgroup.com

Outside the United States, please contact: International Sales, 317-581-3793 or international@pearsontechgroup.com

Publisher
Marie Butler-Knight

Product Manager
Phil Kitchel

Associate Managing Editor
Cari Luna

Acquisitions Editor
Randy Ladenheim-Gil

Development Editor
Michael Koch

Production Editor/Copy Editor
JoAnna Kremer

Illustrator
Jody P. Schaeffer

Cover Designers
Mike Freeland
Kevin Spear

Book Designers
Scott Cook and Amy Adams of DesignLab

Indexer
Lisa Lawrence

Layout/Proofreading
Angela Calvert
Cyndi Davis-Hubler
Svetlana Dominguez
Jeanette McKay
Gloria Schurick

Contents at a Glance

Contents

Part 2: Your Secret Arsenal   43

4 Holy Kick-Butt: The Deadly Kicks   45

Part 3: It's Time to Sweat   107

8 Be Your Own Coach   109

Appendixes

Foreword

If you're looking for an introduction to and sound advice on a challenging sport, I can think of no one who is better qualified to write a comprehensive overview of kickboxing than Karon Karter and Guy Mezger. Their talents and expertise cover the full spectrum of kickboxing.

In recent years, kickboxing has become the number one fitness craze. Nationwide, exercise enthusiasts have been searching out a growing number of kickboxing gyms, karate schools, aerobic studios, and other establishments that promise to initiate the curious sports- and fitness-minded into the art and combat of this hybrid sport. With so many gyms and studios vying for your fitness dollars, you need a guide that helps you spot the qualified instructors and gyms among those who merely want to cash in on this fitness craze.

The Complete Idiot's Guide to Kickboxing is a welcome treasure trove of information for aspiring fighters, trainers, or anyone else interested in the art and sport of kickboxing. This book takes you on a whirlwind tour from the origins of kickboxing to current training techniques, while detailing the differences in the fitness and combat aspects of this sport. It shows you how to set up a training and workout regimen, how to diet and spar like a pro, how to prepare for your first fight, and how to make the most of kickboxing in your everyday and professional life. It also helps you identify who is qualified to teach this hybrid sport and what you need to know to avoid unnecessary pain and injury.

If you're looking for one source that will facilitate your entry into this amazing art while educating you on the sport and fitness aspects of kickboxing, look no further.

Derek Panza

Super Heavyweight World Kickboxing Champion
Undefeated Professional Boxer
National Karate Champion

Introduction

Kickboxing is the wave of the future, combining the allure of self-defense with downright cardiovascular fitness; it has tremendous appeal. Now is the time to transform yourself into a kickboxer. Are you a fitness buff eager to retire your body-hugging spandex, give up the mindless climb to nowhere on the Stair-master, and stop counting those trite repetitions to an iron weight bar? Why not try an intense, ongoing challenge that is based on rejuvenation and enlightenment? Kickboxing is what you need—a new way to get your body sweating.

And Here's What You'll Find Inside

This book is divided into six parts. Whether you want to expand your knowledge or try kickboxing for the first time, the pages in this book will be your guide. Here's a quick overview:

Part 1, "Before You Get Your Hands Wrapped," explains why you need to join the kickboxing craze. As you read on, you will pick up interesting facts about kickboxing history and its core concepts and what you need to get started.

Part 2, "Your Secret Arsenal," covers the basic kickboxing terminology and moves. In other words, you'll learn how to punch, kick, and block. Before long, you'll dance just like a fighter—light on your toes. Besides losing weight, staying in shape, and developing those ripped abs and sleek, slender legs, you'll learn how to pace yourself during your workouts and take care to avoid specific kickboxing injuries.

Part 3, "It's Time to Sweat," details three one-on-one workouts that are designed for the beginner, intermediate, and advanced kickboxer, in addition to one fun-filled workout that will help you discover the perfect body.

Part 4, "King of the Ring," chronicles the fighting world. The chapters in this part enlighten anyone who is serious enough to take kickboxing into the ring. What's most exciting is that you can follow a progressive eight week "fight plan" to prepare mentally and physically for the next fight or push yourself to the next fitness level.

Part 5, "Protect Yourself," tells you what to do if confronted by an attacker. You'll learn basic defensive skills as well as countermoves to protect against an attack—both in real life and ringside.

Part 6, "When the Lights Go Out," explores other avenues of kickboxing and the martial arts. Maybe you can be the perfect coach ... or maybe it's time to quit.

Extras

This book also contains a few easy-to-recognize sidebars that offer tips, warnings, and extra information to help you along the way to becoming a kickboxer. Keep an eye out for the following sidebars to enhance your knowledge:

Kick-Tales

These boxes contain stories related to kickboxing, plus interesting tidbits about its history.

Kickboxing Buzz

These boxes contain tips and tid-bits about kickboxing that may be helpful while you perfect your arsenal.

Words for Warriors

These boxes contain kickboxing vocabulary and jargon that may come up while you learn to kick butt.

Warning Warriors

These boxes contain warnings for aspiring warriors to prevent them from getting into a sticky situation.

Acknowledgments

Karon Karter: A special thanks to our friends, who helped with various aspects of this book—especially Peter Robbins, Phree Betoncourt, Susie Grey, Ben Sawyer, and Alex Andrade.

Thanks also to officer Mark Dawson for sharing his self-defense lecture with us.

We are grateful for the entire team at Alpha Books, especially Michael Koch and JoAnna Kremer, who helped get these words into print. We can't thank you enough! Your sharp eyes and penchant for detail makes this a great book.

I can't leave without saying "thank you" to Guy, my co-author, for teaching me how to kick butt.

Guy Mezger: Thanks to my family and friends, my students and staff at the Dojo, and my training partners and teammates on Team Lion's Den who had to persevere through all the trials and tribulations I put them through for many years.

Special thanks to Steve Armstrong and Tonya Parma for always encouraging to live for my dreams, and to my first instructors Tim Kirby and Doc Parker, who took the time to work with a difficult kid.

Thanks also to Evan Fogelmen who brought the idea of the book to life.

My most sincere thanks to Ken Shamrock and "Billye Jack" Jackson, who are my dearest friends and coaches and who have been there for all my world titles—without you guys I could never have been there.

Finally, a very special thank you goes to my coauthor, Karon Karter, who made everything come together. She stayed on me with a determination that would have made a marine drill sergeant proud. Thanks!

Trademarks

All terms mentioned in this book that are known to be or are suspected of being trademarks or service marks have been appropriately capitalized. Alpha Books and Pearson Education, Inc., cannot attest to the accuracy of this information. Use of a term in this book should not be regarded as affecting the validity of any trademark or service mark.

Part 1

Before You Get Your Hands Wrapped

There is a lot of talk about kickboxing these days. Find out why it's the latest craze. Imagine a world where women have no limits; a world where children learn self-respect and fulfill their dreams; a world where people can stay fit and healthy; a world where men can learn the value of competition. It's happening today. Find out why kickboxing is many things to many people. As a hybrid sport, kickboxing combines the power of modern fighting techniques with the roots of ancient wisdom. In this part, we'll introduce you to the different types of kickboxing, share interesting tidbits about the history of kickboxing, and tell you what you'll need to kick butt.

Chapter 1

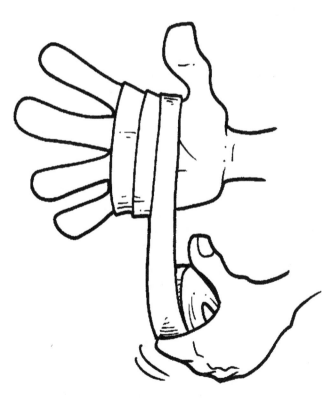

Everyone's Kicking; You Should, Too!

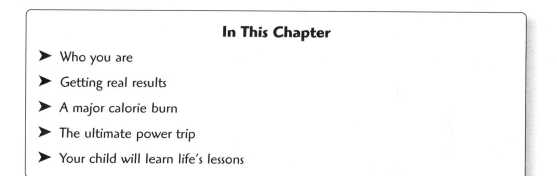

In This Chapter

➤ Who you are

➤ Getting real results

➤ A major calorie burn

➤ The ultimate power trip

➤ Your child will learn life's lessons

Congratulations! You've just taken the first step to learning *kickboxing*—you've picked up this book.

Kickboxing is a hybrid sport. It combines the beautiful hand techniques of American boxing, the thunder-power kicks of hard style karate, the knee strikes and leg sweeps of Thai boxing, and the lightning-fast kicks of tae kwon do. Today, kickboxing is taught like a sport rather than as a traditional martial art; its roots, however, come from ancient Asian wisdom.

Kickboxing is the wave of the future, combining a great workout with self-defense skills. So retire your body-hugging spandex, give up the mindless climb to nowhere on the Stairmaster, and stop counting those trite repetitions to an iron weight bar— you're about to experience an intense, ongoing challenge that is based on rejuvenation and enlightenment. You'll find a whole new way to get your body sweating.

Who Are You?

Chances are you've seen Chuck Norris kickboxing some goon—but that's in the movies. Following are some testimonies from real people who share their reasons for taking up kickboxing; see where you fit in:

➤ The 47-year-old police officer: "I have been in law enforcement for over 20 years and found that the training I have received in kickboxing has made me more confident in my physical abilities to deal with the job. The workout is a mental release from the stress that comes with the job."

➤ The business executive: "I have very little time. In fact, I can't spend hours weight training and then find time to get some cardio in. Kickboxing offers both. I block out three hours a week for fitness, usually at lunch time. I can get in and out and know that I challenged myself physically and mentally. Plus, I get to release the stress of the day by beating up on the bags, and I can take my workout on the road when I'm traveling."

➤ The 20-year-old college student: "I was deathly afraid of the freshman 15-pound gain. I really started to work out hard. Nothing works like kickboxing does … period."

➤ Mom I: "I'm constantly on the go, running from supermarket to malls, picking up this kid and that one. I had to find something for myself. I drop my kids off to a kickboxing class, and then I take a one-on-one lesson. We're a very time-efficient family, trying to squeeze fitness into our hectic life. The whole family can work out together."

➤ Mom II: "After having my baby, I had a hard time losing weight. A friend of mine suggested kickboxing. I've never enjoyed most kinds of training programs, but I really enjoy kickboxing."

➤ Mom III: "I've had my son involved with martial arts since he was five years old. He was always quitting and restarting until kickboxing. He's been training steadily in kickboxing for two years and loves it. I love it because he has been focused; he's sticking with it."

➤ The 60-year-old woman: "Kickboxing keeps me limber. My arthritis doesn't seem to bother me as much. Although I know I'm not cured, I like not having so much pain. I choose this sport for relief; plus, at my age, I'm challenging my mind and my body to do things that I've never done. Women didn't exercise in my day."

➤ The 39-year-old lawyer: "As a former college swimmer, I really missed the hard competitive training. Although I'm not a competitive athlete anymore, I really love the tough workouts of a kickboxing class."

Clearly, kickboxing is many things to many people. Why? Because kickboxing works hand in hand with your real life. So, if you're going to put time and money into a sport, why not learn one that enhances every aspect of your life?

Better than Prozac

Kickboxing as therapy? Why not? You'll feel less cranky after a good sweat, and depression and other unpleasant negative thoughts seem to simply drift away. Kickboxing doesn't require a real opponent—a heavy bag will do. You can go to the gym and hit and kick the heavy bag, and the bag can't hit you back. It's a safe solution for depression and anxiety, emotions that we all experience at some time in our lives. You can get lost in your own thoughts as you punch away. And if you choose to spar with an opponent, you won't have time to feel sorry for yourself because you must stay focused on your opponent—otherwise, he might beat you up.

At some point, we all want to hit someone. Let's face it—we're always being told what to do: our mothers' orders, our bosses' ongoing deadlines, our spouses telling us to do this and that, and the in-laws, who always seem to have something to say. We would love to throttle them, but we can't. However, we can go to the gym and pound out all those frustrations on a heavy bag. Even your trainer will understand; that's the appeal of kickboxing. You can hit someone and get away with it.

Warning Warriors

You can take all your aggression out on a heavy bag because it can't hit you back. But don't hit your trainer as hard—he might remember. Turnabout is fair play in conditioning drills.

The Ultimate Power Trip

Kickboxing offers a complete connection between body and mind. You'll learn lessons in human limits and find the rewards that come with many hours of hard work. If you value hard work; if you want to earn the self-respect, self-confidence, and sense of achievement that comes only with a job well done; and if you want to set goals and work to achieve them, overcoming many obstacles in the process, there is no better workout than kickboxing.

Kickboxing is a metaphor for life: Everyone is scared when they begin, and no one wants to fail at something new or look stupid. Similarly, students don't want to get pummeled or hurt, and fighters surely don't want to lose a fight. But what happens when you start to push yourself a little harder? Pain—or at least mild aches, disappointment, and setbacks—becomes your constant companion.

Let's say you're about to step it up a notch. You train longer and add more conditioning drills—squats, lunges, push-ups, and so on. Muscle soreness sets in. There is also some pain that goes along with sparring with your trainer and hitting the heavy bags. You're scared to death about getting hit, but it's only after the first hard strike that you realize that you're not going to die. On top of all this, you feel fatigue; no doubt that fatigue causes pain.

Your brain tells you to hang in there, yet your weary legs tremble, begging for relief, and you can't hold up your hands any longer. Fatigue initiates the struggle between your mind, which is telling you to keep going, and your body, which is calling it quits.

Most fighters know this struggle all too well. They will endure any amount of pain to win a fight. For you, it's a matter of finishing your lesson, conquering the inner voices that tell you to give up. Just how far will you go to achieve your goals? After 45 minutes of punching and kicking, your legs are shaking. You hear that annoying voice in your head, saying, "I can't do this." But you still have a hundred or so squats, lunges, sit-ups, and push-ups ahead of you, so you tell that voice to go to hell; you can do this despite your exhaustion. You finish fulfilled, and convinced that your trainer is the devil. This physical feat, the merciless workout, proves to you that you can do more for yourself—in your workout and in your life. Pushing yourself when you think you "can't" is a gift to yourself—it's empowering.

Making it through something the first time prepares you for all subsequent times you have to go through it because you now have experience to bring to the table. You'll continually learn new ways to do things, set new goals for yourself, and find ways to overcome setbacks. Take on a *don't quit* attitude—you will probably accept yourself a little more readily and like your body a little more if you don't give up. Perseverance stays with you long after your workout; it spills over into your everyday life.

We fear getting hit; we fear failure. Kickboxing helps overcome the underlying fears that freeze the mind, which in turn impairs the body.

Real Life, Real Results

Kickboxers have incredible bodies because they, unlike most athletes, use all aspects of fitness: muscular strength and endurance, speed of movement, aerobic and anaerobic conditioning, flexibility, body composition, motor skills, and coordination. Let's talk about these training modes because you'll use them later on:

➤ **Your muscles become stronger and stronger as you kickbox.** Not only will you hit the heavy bags, you'll spar with your trainer or use training equipment such as Thai pads, kicking shields, and focus mitts. This, like weight training, adds resistance to your workout. This resistance will help you develop specific muscles that will make you a better kickboxer. As your body becomes stronger, so will you.

➤ **Your endurance will improve.** Muscular endurance equals the amount of reps you can do. Kickboxers throw punch after punch, kick after kick, which is extremely tiring. You'll do push-ups, sit-ups, and lunges so that your body can learn to handle this kind of physical stress.

➤ **Your hand-eye coordination will improve.** Kickboxing helps improve your hand-eye coordination; in fact, that's the purpose of the *speed bag* (the little red bag that hangs from the ceiling).

➤ **You'll train both aerobically and anaerobically.** Whether it's a cardio-kickboxing class or a one-on-one workout, you'll work hard to improve in both areas of fitness. Depending on your goals, your trainer can increase the cardio session by making you jump rope for longer periods of time, or he can make you run sprint after sprint to improve your anaerobic capacity.

➤ **Kickboxing improves your flexibility.** This is important because flexibility is directly related to good kicks. You'll do specific flexibility exercises to improve your kicks.

➤ **Your motor skills will improve.** Your motor skills improve because you have to move in the ring. Your trainer will tell you to move with each kick and punch; kickboxing is not a stand-still sport. You're always on the go, moving from your opponent or trainer. This kind of movement helps better your balance and coordination skills, as does jumping rope. In fact, jumping rope is a lesson in timing and coordinating your legs and arms to work together.

Kickboxing Buzz

Winning and losing aren't just about fighting—they're about life. The drive to win, to be your best, isn't bound to the ring. Kickboxing just gives you a means to test yourself every day. That dedication and drive spill over into the rest of your life. Decide what your life is going to be like, and live every day to succeed.

That's what kickboxing does for you—it trains you for life. Can you think of ways in your everyday life that require you to move in so many training modes?

With all these different kinds of training, your body composition will shift; you'll see less fat and leaner muscles, which will make you a better kickboxer. Overdeveloped muscles get in the way of punches and kicks. For example, body builders often have this kind of inflexibility, sometimes called muscle-bound. Runners, on the other hand, have great endurance, but they may lack the strength to block a sequence of punches. A kickboxer, though, has both strength and endurance—the best of both worlds!

Words for Warriors

A **speed bag** will help you stay alert: It's meant to keep you on your toes, improve speed, develop timing, and sharpen defenses. You have no time to think as the little red bag ricochets back-and-forth as you strike. That's one way in which kickboxers improve their hand-eye coordination; it's like jumping rope for your hands.

No More Sparring with the Weight Scale

We've already talked about having a better body, more strength and endurance, and increased flexibility. You also know that you can use kickboxing to release stress and improve your self-esteem. Is there anything else? You bet!

Kickboxing Buzz

Have you ever seen an over-weight fighter? Probably not! The workout gets them in the best shape of their lives. Kickboxers and martial artists develop their bodies in such a way that they're a perfect blend of fat and muscle.

Kickboxing also helps you win the battle of the bulge, which in turn can improve your sex life. But that's not the whole story .... Exercise in general improves the libido. People who exercise have more energy, less anxiety, more self-esteem, and increased testosterone levels. Kickboxing does all that, *and* it firms and sculpts your body. So, by making you feel better about your body, kickboxing can improve your sex life.

Kickboxing can also increase your immunity, reduce heart disease, and help you fend off signs of old age. You will feel younger because you're doing something healthy for yourself; in addition, there are many scientists who say that exercise can put a hold on growing old.

Just like frequent exercise, kickboxing can enhance your everyday life. The following are the benefits of kickboxing at a glance:

➤ Weight control

➤ Greater energy

➤ Better immunity

➤ Peak mental performance

➤ Stronger bones

➤ Better sex life

➤ Less chance of heart disease

➤ Delayed aging

➤ Reduced stress

➤ Better body image

➤ Greater confidence

➤ More strength

➤ Peace of mind

Blast Away, the Maximum Burn

Throughout this book, you'll learn about two different workouts: an interval *one-on-one* workout and *cardio-kickboxing*.

Cardio-kickboxing is a hybrid form of boxing, martial arts, and aerobics; it can give you an intense total body workout. The one-on-one workout, on the other hand, keeps your heart rate up while you alternate between working and rest intervals. Both give you a killer workout.

Are you bored with jogging or aerobics? Do you find that you're making all kinds of excuses not to exercise? When boredom sets in, sticking to an exercise regimen becomes difficult. You won't get bored kickboxing; it takes a lifetime to perfect this sport. Just imagine … no more dreading your workouts … say good-bye to hated calories.

Kickboxing Buzz

Depending on your workout, you can burn 500–800 calories. In comparison, a typical hour-long step aerobics class burns about 300–400 calories, according to the American Council of Exercise (ACE).

But Mom …

Letting your child kickbox can help him grow up with confidence. Sound like a Nike commercial? It's true; sports can help develop your child's character, and kickboxing is no exception.

Kickboxing is grounded in ancient martial arts wisdom, which teaches self-respect, self-commitment, self-esteem, self-discipline, and self-control. The seeds of ancient wisdom—respect your elders, work exceedingly hard, and be devoted to your family—have filtered into kickboxing. Of course we want to pass such values on to our children. As your child grows up kickboxing, these qualities will soak in. It's sneaky, but because they love the sport, they'll unknowingly absorb the ancient hidden messages that are being passed on to them.

Kids do what's fun. They will continue to play any sport if they enjoy it. The little ones might not understand the lessons and goals you're setting for them, but they might say, "Hey, Mom, I can throw a jab much better than I could last year; I can kick much higher now." Your child will learn how to take on new challenges without dwelling on what he couldn't do last year. Kickboxing keeps him moving up and onward.

Kickboxing Buzz

Most coaches will work to instill good values as your kids train in kickboxing. Look for coaches who practice what they preach.

The focus isn't on whether he's a winner or loser; it's about improving his own skills. His self-esteem will improve as he learns to do things that he couldn't do before. Sure, he'll have to learn how to deal with disappointment on a deeper level—especially if he competes in the ring. He might lose a fight, but he'll learn that if he works hard he'll eventually succeed. With that comes team camaraderie: struggling, winning, and losing as he competes with the same kids throughout his training. Your child will learn that other children matter—it's valuable to care for the other fighters and support them in their dreams (for example, to become a world champion kickboxer).

Good sportsmanship is also taught early: Notice that the referee always says, "Keep it clean," and that a general rule in kickboxing is "Hit someone only as hard as you want to be hit back." Intentionally breaking the rules—especially if it results in injury—in order to win a fight will not only produce an empty victory, it will come back to haunt you. Kids are taught early that cheating steals their self-respect; if you and your opponent respect each other, both of you can aim to be the best you can be. Sometimes you're ahead, and sometimes you're behind.

With integrity comes self-control and discipline. Like everything in life, kickboxing doesn't come instantly. In order to get good, your child will have to follow the rules of this sport; otherwise, he'll risk not practicing or competing. Kids respond to rules; let them know what they can or can't do. Remember that kickboxing is task oriented. Because there are very few natural born stars, your child will have to focus to get good at kickboxing—which means that he might have to give up something else, such as television or hanging out at the mall on a Friday night.

Michael Jordan, You'll Never Know!

A parent's dream: Your child grows up and becomes the next Michael Jordan. Not having the talent to reach super athletic stardom will probably not devastate you, but what if it's your child who is constantly being picked on? If he's not a natural born athlete, it can cause years of teasing by his classmates—a parent's nightmare.

Give your child a head start; it's not easy to comfort your child as he waits for his physical development to catch up with the rest of the kids. Kickboxing can help get your child through elementary school with as little trauma as possible. For one thing, he isn't letting the whole team down if he can't do something. And he doesn't have to compete for the limited space on the team. He is competing against only himself; it's an emotionally safe environment to learn in.

In kickboxing, your child doesn't have to be a natural born star. Most kids start off uncoordinated. He'll be taught that the only way to get good at this sport is to stick it out.

Your child doesn't have to be the one who eagerly sits on the sidelines, waiting to be called to enter the game. Kickboxing teaches him coordination and the connection between body and mind, and how to use this connection in a split second. He won't sit and sit, only to be the last one called as a last resort because he lacks physical strength. Kickboxing will develop his body in amazing ways. No more watching your child's delicate ego dwindle; instead, he'll be excited to get into the game.

Team sports can enhance your child's self-esteem. Soccer, football, basketball, and others can teach your child sportsmanship and team spirit. However, it's the athletically gifted that get to play in the game. You can comfort your child only so much if he doesn't get picked for the team. In kickboxing, he doesn't have to try out for the team; it builds from within. Even though the focus is on his own skill level, he'll still learn to listen to the coach and respect his sparring buddies. It's this confidence that can better prepare your child for team sports.

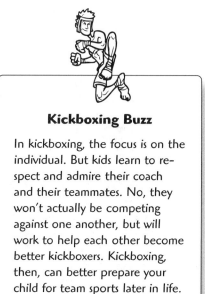

Kickboxing Buzz

In kickboxing, the focus is on the individual. But kids learn to respect and admire their coach and their teammates. No, they won't actually be competing against one another, but will work to help each other become better kickboxers. Kickboxing, then, can better prepare your child for team sports later in life.

As your child conquers his fears, he'll earn self-respect. Most children shy away from being hit. Although they are scared to get in the ring at first, their faces light up when they conquer their fears. Kickboxing teaches your child that self-respect is earned through hard work; it teaches him to go for it and helps to prepare him for life's challenges. With a healthy sense of self-esteem, he'll more readily accept the ups and downs of life. The message in kickboxing is that hard work and determination will create patterns for success. Who knows? He might grow up to be the next Michael Jordan, after all.

Keeping Up with the Boys

Watch it, men—women are taking over kickboxing. Twenty years ago, you couldn't find a female kickboxer. Today, the traditionally male-dominated sport is mostly made up of women. Why?

Maybe it provides women with a sense of empowerment. Whatever the reason, the consensus among women is that kickboxing makes them feel stronger, better, and more courageous than they ever dreamed.

Why not be brave, strong, and sexy, while remaining feminine? That's what kickboxing does for women. Have you ever traveled around the world by yourself? Why not? Are you afraid? Think the world is too unsafe? Your own streets may be unsafe. You shouldn't let fear stop you from doing anything that you really want to do. You can take care of yourself away from home, just as you can when you're in your own territory. Be reasonable, though—no one is suggesting that you travel to a war-torn country. But don't be afraid to see the world.

Kick-Tales

According to the Women's Sport Foundation, women who are involved in sports have higher self-esteem, have a better physical condition, suffer less depression, and are more satisfied with their lives than women who are not involved in sports. So get your girls started early—being physically active reaps big rewards, in and out of the ring.

Be brave, be strong, and be self-reliant. Women are told not to do this or that because it's too dangerous, but you can help dispel that myth by working just as hard as the guys. You'll earn respect by doing as many push-ups, sweating as hard, and sprinting as fast as the men in your class. Use your body, train it, and refine it. Work to develop your inner strength as well as your physical body. Don't forget that you're strong; kickboxing can put you in touch with your strength.

Body size doesn't matter. Kickboxing requires some physical strength, but the emphasis is on good technique. Kickboxing, often called "the equalizer," closes the body-size gap between men and women. Men have more muscle and often are stronger than women. However, a woman can outwit a man using good skill. In a controlled setting, spar against a man. As you become more experienced, you'll be able to take him down through use of good technique. After a while, fighting with a man will be no big deal.

Gaining this experience is important because in real life, you'll almost always have to defend yourself against a man. Why not get an accurate feel for what it takes to win? That's when you'll feel good about yourself, knowing that you can do anything you put your mind to.

Some women may be put off by the violence of boxing; unless you're a fighter, however, kickboxing is typically not a brutal sport—it's mastering the art of self-discipline. You might want to throw in the towel many times. But don't give up. There are many challenges to overcome as you advance, and you'll only discover your own inner strength as you're pushed—a lesson in human power. You'll earn your self-respect if you stick it out. No, you won't be hustling in the ring, but you'll train with as much intensity as a fighter.

Warning Warriors

A cardio-kickboxing class is not a self-defense class—it's a workout. Yes, you're learning to throw punches and kicks. But that doesn't replace common sense, and it doesn't make you immune to crime. If you want to protect yourself, you should learn kickboxing well.

Kickboxing for All

Kickboxing skill is not relative to body size, age, or sex. Men with gray hair can kick butt just as well as the young guys. Remember, along with developing good skills comes power. After working a lifetime, most older people want a new challenge in life. It might take them longer to learn basic moves, but most don't seem to mind. They are doing something to keep themselves feeling young and healthy.

You'll learn to work with what you have. Most coaches will train students with physical handicaps. There are many stories about how kickboxing has enhanced someone's life. Guy, for example, had worked with a hearing-impaired student. To meet his needs, he still taught kickboxing basics, but added some grappling moves to make it fun and interesting. You can always find a way to work with physical limitations.

After all, that's part of the allure—you can do what you want with this sport. You don't have to get in the ring; you don't have to worry about keeping up in class; you'll gain satisfaction from knowing that you're doing something to change your life.

The Ultimate Weapon

What comes to your mind when you hear the words *ultimate weapon?* Nuclear bombs, pit bulls, the IRS? Not yourself, right? That's probably the last thing you would think. In a world of predators, we are at a big disadvantage—no sharp fangs, long claws, or piercing horns to protect us. Why, then, are we the ultimate weapon? Because of our brain.

Nothing happens in the body that the brain does not direct; often it isn't a conscious thought, but some part of the brain is always telling you to take action.

Okay, enough talk about the brain. How does it fit in with kickboxing? In kickboxing, you'll train the brain to become the ultimate weapon by repeatedly going over your technique. That's right—you will read and reread main points.

The subconscious part of the brain recalls actions in a split-second decision better if you've trained it. So you're going to train your brain to react without thinking—that's how you'll learn to kickbox, to get

Kickboxing Buzz

Kickboxing is based on technique rather than muscle power. A woman can take down a 200-pound man if she has good skill. Bigger and stronger males should beware of a skilled female kickboxer.

Kickboxing Buzz

Most coaches will work with children that have a physical limitation. Kickboxing focuses on what you have instead of what you don't have. If you can't kick high, you can always kick low; if your punches lack power, develop the power in your kicks. It's a sport for all!

a great workout, and, most importantly, to protect yourself. Train the brain to react first; the body will follow. To get a great workout, you'll practice kick after kick and punch after punch. Then, you'll put together kicking and punching combos. At the same time, you'll learn how these same kicks and punches can protect you in a life-threatening situation. Or, if you have a competitive spirit, you can learn to use these same moves in the ring to thrash your opponent. It's your choice!

Now let's introduce your weapons: kicks, punches, and knee and elbow strikes.

Long-Range Weapons

You'll use your legs to fire off a variety of kicks. These are your long-range weapons because you can launch an attack even though there's some distance between you and your opponent. You'll learn six different kicks in kickboxing: front kick, rear kick, roundhouse, round kick, side kick, and turn kick. Martial arts are filled with other fancy kicks, but, as kickboxers, we take pride in our kicks because they're simple and effective. Most fancy kicks, such as the flying side kick, can't be used in the ring or the street. So why bother learning? Kickboxing is a practical kind of martial art; you won't use anything unless it can work for you.

Medium-Range Weapons

If your opponent gets a little too close, you can launch a punch. Most of these hand techniques come from the pure science of American boxing. You'll learn six punches: jab, cross, hook, uppercut, overhand punch, and—kickboxing developed its own punch—the spinning back fist.

Kickboxing Buzz

Your legs are your long-range weapons: front and rear kicks, round kick and roundhouse, and side and turn kicks. Punches are your medium-range weapons: jab, cross, hook, uppercut, overhand, and spinning back fist. Use your knees and elbows as your short-range weapons.

Short-Range Weapons

If someone gets in your face, you'll use either your knee or elbow to keep him away. Both strikes are potentially deadly if executed with some power. For fitness purposes, you'll learn how to throw a knee strike; the elbow, on the other hand, will only be taught to you as a self-defense move.

In this book, as you move from Part 2, "Your Secret Arsenal," to Part 5, "Protect Yourself," you'll learn how to use your weapons in a variety of ways. Whether you want a mental challenge, a demanding physical workout, a practical method of self-defense, or the chance to enter the ring in anticipation of a full contact sport, kickboxing has something for everyone. Therein lies its appeal and the reason it's the fastest growing sport today.

It's up to you how far you want to take this sport. Remember, you'll compete against only yourself. We hope to inspire you, give you a new challenge in life. From this point on, you'll train like a born fighter. Don't worry, you don't have to step into the ring—just think like a fighter.

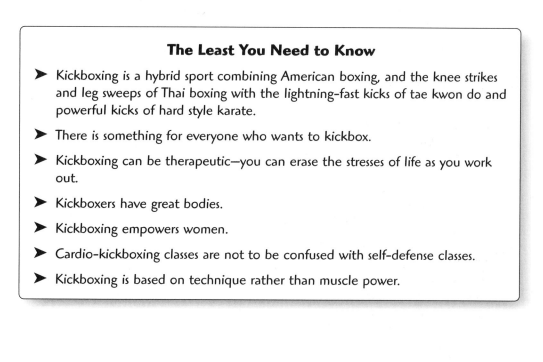

The Least You Need to Know

➤ Kickboxing is a hybrid sport combining American boxing, and the knee strikes and leg sweeps of Thai boxing with the lightning-fast kicks of tae kwon do and powerful kicks of hard style karate.

➤ There is something for everyone who wants to kickbox.

➤ Kickboxing can be therapeutic—you can erase the stresses of life as you work out.

➤ Kickboxers have great bodies.

➤ Kickboxing empowers women.

➤ Cardio-kickboxing classes are not to be confused with self-defense classes.

➤ Kickboxing is based on technique rather than muscle power.

Chapter 2

Ancient Art:
Sport of Today

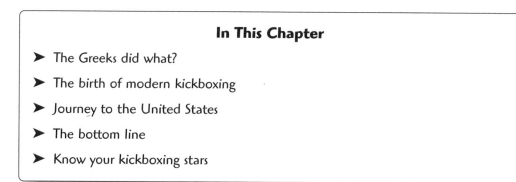

In This Chapter

➤ The Greeks did what?

➤ The birth of modern kickboxing

➤ Journey to the United States

➤ The bottom line

➤ Know your kickboxing stars

Imagine yourself standing upright, head erect, and your left foot forward, poised in a lunge. Your left arm, used for guarding, is extended almost straight with a clenched fist. Your right hand is ready to deliver a strike.

You and your opponent are ready to spar; your eyes lock. You're wondering, "Will he pummel my head, or gouge my eyes out?" Your opponent lands a hard blow to your head, knocking you down to the floor. Even though you are on the ground, he continues to clobber you—there are no rules against hitting a man when he's down.

The crowd chants, "Kill him!" You're fighting to regain your stance, but his powerful punches with leather-bound fists split your head wide open—the blood gushes. "Do I fight to the death, or do I raise my hand and declare defeat?"

Welcome to the classic era of Greek boxing. Could this bloody and brutal sport be the very beginning of the classic martial arts movement? If so, how did kickboxing come about?

Boxing in Ancient Greece

In ancient Greece, the object of boxing and wrestling was to bring an opponent to his knees, sometimes killing him. In the end, fighters used any move to take down their opponent—including grappling, hitting, kicking, leg-sweeping, choking, and joint locking. Some martial art scholars believe that this form of fighting, called *pancration*, evolved into the classic martial arts.

Of course, back then fighters didn't know that some of today's most popular martial arts would employ such tactics. For example, the bloodthirsty kicking that was an essential part of pancration is used in tae kwon do and karate; also, both high-altitude throws, similar to the ones used in the martial art of wrestling, and locks clamped to the limbs or neck, just like the ones used in the martial art jujitsu, were also commonly used during a fight.

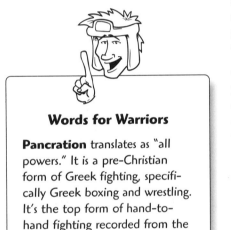

Words for Warriors

Pancration translates as "all powers." It is a pre-Christian form of Greek fighting, specifically Greek boxing and wrestling. It's the top form of hand-to-hand fighting recorded from the Olympic games.

Once upon a time there was a pancratic champion named Dioxippus. He won the Olympic crown by default in 336 B.C.E. because no other fighter would compete against him. Dioxippus's tough-guy reputation caught the attention of Alexander the Great, who loved all fighting sports. As he conquered the world, his followers, including Dioxippus, hauled around elaborate tents in which his soldiers could train and practice athletic games such as pancration. Some scholars believe that in carrying pancration across the Himalayas in 326 B.C.E., Alexander's army laid the groundwork for kung fu in China, which in turn led to the birth of martial arts around the world.

The Motherlands of Modern Kickboxing

Pancration shaped some styles of martial arts; as I stated earlier, moves such as throws, grappling, and kicking were used during a pancration match. Did kickboxing emerge from this bloody barbaric sport? Not exactly. To say that ancient pancration influenced modern-day kickboxing is a stretch. However, pancration *did* pave the way for kickboxing. Odd as it may seem, modern kickboxing was refined by a combination of several martial arts and the sands of time. So, let's travel back about 1,000 years.

Thai kickboxing, or Muay Thai, began in Siam, known today as Thailand. Historians have no definitive clue as to its beginning, but two popular theories exist: that Thai boxing came from the influence of China, and that Thai boxing was mandatory training for the military cadets because of the constant threat of civil war. (Back then, Siam consisted of Thailand, Burma, and Vietnam.)

As you may expect, there are all kinds of legends about famous Thai boxers. Perhaps the most famous story, though, dates back to a sixteenth-century manuscript. The Burmese army was days away from invading Siam. The king of Burma, Bayinnaung, agreed to let his son fight the prince of Siam, Narusun, also known as the Black Prince. A fight was staged between the two princes. After many hours of grueling fighting, the Black Prince won by killing the king's son. That match stopped the Burmese army from invading Siam. To this day, an annual fight called the King's Tournament is held in his memory.

Kick-Tales

Prizefights became a way of settling arguments over just about anything. The goal was to win, so fighters wrapped hemp or rope around their hands to destroy their opponent's face. Depending on the degree of the grudge match, fighters would sometimes glue seashells or glass to the rope to inflict severe damage to the face. Such matches were often fought to the death.

The Big Show

Pretend that you're a famous Thai kickboxer. You've just received notice that you're invited to fight in the King's Tournament; only the elite make it to the big show. A festival is planned in your honor. The city rocks with excitement. Think of the King's Tournament as the Super Bowl of fighting.

Fights are shrouded with tradition and superstition. As you enter the ring, an orchestra of drums, cymbals, and flutes play to honor each competitor. You jump over the ropes. (You never climb between the ropes because they act as a barrier to keep evil spirits out.) You bow to the crowd and your trainer.

As part of the national costume, you wear a headpiece known as mongkon. You show off this headpiece to honor the school in which you train. To keep the evil spirits away, you wear an armband that holds a picture of the God you worship. You pause and say a prayer.

The music drones on. You start a ritual called the Ram Mumi, or boxing dance. A fighter's heart feels nothing but fear; the purpose of this imaginary fight is to conquer your fear. At last, you're ready to fight.

Muay Thai has inspired modern kickboxing, specifically in the Eastern part of the world. By modern kickboxing standards, Muay Thai's tactics and tricks are brutal. For example, elbow strikes, which can be deadly, are allowed during a Muay Thai match, which is one reason why Muay Thai is rarely practiced outside Thailand.

Savate

French foot fighting, known as *savate*, directly shaped modern kickboxing in the Western world. Looking back at the seventeenth century, most historians believe that savate came from Indo-China, where the French had colonies. As it turns out, French sailors were kicking their way out of barroom brawls and the dark alley fights of French seaports—which is how a raw form of savate came to France.

Kick-Tales

The soldiers in Napoleon's army developed a system to punish lazy soldiers: A group of soldiers would hold the lazybones in place while the other soldiers kicked him repeatedly in the butt. The punishment was called "la savate," which translates as "old shoe."

Thanks to a fierce fighter by the name of Casseuse, savate became an overnight success. Casseuse became the country's most sought after master of self-defense. One of his students, Charlie Le Cour, traveled to England to study bare-knuckle boxing. He then had the idea to blend the two styles of fighting together, mixing the wild street fighting style of early savate and the sophisticated style of English boxing.

Words for Warriors

Pugilist is a fancy word for boxer.

Charlie Le Cour thus created a modern form of savate, which became so popular that even restaurant owners in Paris would sponsor savate fights to entertain their guests. Imagine yourself sipping on cognac, puffing on a cigar, and placing a bet on your favorite savoteur. You're stuffed from the rich French meal; now you're about to sit back and enjoy the boxing match. Sounds like a great evening out, doesn't it? Sadly, you won't be able to watch a savate fight here in the United States—savoteurs compete primarily in France. Today, savate is a dying breed of kickboxing, but it's important to remember that modern kickboxing really started with the sailors kicking the butts of their enemies.

And Now ... Modern Kickboxing!

What do you get when you mix punches, kicks, knee strikes, and leg sweeps? Modern kickboxing, of course.

Modern kickboxing is commonly known as a hybrid sport. In other words, this sport has stolen some of the trademark moves from several martial arts. Unlike other martial arts, kickboxing doesn't involve a lot of fancy footwork; it doesn't have long-standing philosophies, or creeds—unless you consider knocking your opponent out a creed. Instead, kickboxing offers a type of no-frills fighting that focuses on power, flexibility, stamina, strength, and a blatant warrior code to win.

Jhoon Rhee is probably the most famous martial artist today. He brought tae kwon do (literally, "way of kicking and punching") to the United States, and specifically to Texas. He is a third-degree black belt who will go down in history for shaping modern kickboxing.

In 1974, he reformed martial arts with the invention of the Safe-T-Chop, a type of foam-dipped protective gear for the hands, feet, and shins. Today, the Safe-T-Chop may not sound like a big deal, but to fighters at that time, it was bonanza.

Kick-Tales

In 1974, Jhoon Rhee invented the Safe-T-Chop. His equipment was revolutionary back then—it was foam-dipped protective gear for the hands, feet, and shins. His invention has evolved into the protective equipment used today, such as the shin and footpads and headgear.

Before 1974, fighters had no way of protecting their bodies, and because of tae kwon do's deadly roots, all competitions were noncontact. In other words, fighters couldn't hit to the face; they could only kick and punch to the body. This was due to the popular belief that a punch or kick to the head could severely damage the body or potentially kill an opponent. By providing bodily protection, the Safe-T-Chop changed the rules.

Let's back up a bit. A noncontact competition consisted of a two-minute continuous round. However, referees could break up a round at their discretion. For example, if they felt a fighter was too rough, they could end the round. That fighter could then be penalized for hitting the opponent too hard or in the face. In other words, if a fighter injured his opponent, he could lose the fight. Think about this: A trained fighter, skilled in delivering powerful punches and snappy kicks, could lose a fight for doing what he did best. Needless to say, fighters desired a more realistic way to fight. The invention of the Safe-T-Chop leveled the field somewhat—fighters suddenly had a fair way to compete against each other and identify the best fighter without getting seriously injured.

Words for Warriors

Tae means to kick or strike with the foot, **kwon** means to punch or strike with the fist, and **do** means philosophy.

In addition, in 1974, the Professional Kickboxers Association (PKA) was established to further that cause. The PKA was the first official kickboxing organization (it invented the term *full contact karate*, which was later changed to *full contact kickboxing*); it set up specific rules and regulations for kickboxers and kickboxing competitions. For example, the PKA decreed that a kickboxing match last twelve rounds, and that each round is two minutes in duration with a one-minute rest. A fighter must execute eight kicks above the waist per round. Boxing gloves, shin and footpads, and groin and mouth protectors became mandatory safety equipment. Kickboxing had turned into an official sport.

Kick-Tales

Prior to 1974, women had no means to compete in full contact sports. Kickboxing was the first full contact martial art to open its doors to women. Interestingly, a woman—Graciela Casillas—became the first world champion of professional full contact karate.

Big Business

The demand for stamina, the colossal need for strength, the delicate balance between kicks and punches, and the everpresent possibility of death define the sport of kickboxing. For centuries this sport has captivated the courageous, rewarded the fearless, and deified the powerful.

Today, kickboxing is big business. Of course, the physical challenge still intrigues and entices warrior types. But what's tempting you? As trainers, we've heard everything from "I want to kick butt" to "Teach me how to defend myself." As they delve deeper into their training, these students become dedicated kickboxers—especially as they see their body become lean and mean.

Of all the martial arts, kickboxing is the most efficient way of fighting. If this system didn't work, fighters would get clobbered in the ring. But the good news is that we're not expecting you to step into a ring any time soon; the bad news is that you have to train like a fighter. That means many hours of sweating, tons of kicks and punches, and grueling conditioning drills. That's how you will get your body in the best shape of your life.

Kickboxing is the hottest workout today because of the great results it produces. Cardio-kickboxing, Tae-Bo, and aerobic kickboxing are catchy names for a high-energy kickboxing workout. But don't worry, the workout is noncontact. In other words, you're not ducking punches and kicks. Later in this book (see Part 2, "Your Secret Arsenal"), or in an aerobic kickboxing class, you will see the best kickboxing moves utilized in an almost dance-like manner.

Indeed, fitness kickboxing has been around for quite some time. In the early 1980s, Gleason's boxing gym in New York City came up with a new fitness program called "White Collar Boxing." The goal of the program was to attract businessmen, and to get them in shape. The class was a hit. Because of its success, fitness kickboxing was born. The idea was to train like a fighter, but without the risk of being knocked out.

Fitness kickboxing came to be highly valued as a tough guy workout. Between the demand for a different kind of workout and one that delivers results, fitness kickboxing has captured the attention of the nation. For example, everyone is talking about Tae-Bo, which was created by Billy Blanks. Blanks, a serious martial artist, developed a series of cardio-kickboxing videotapes. He promises firm abs and thin legs, and the tapes deliver. As a result, fitness clubs everywhere are scrambling to put cardio-kickboxing on their schedules.

Who's Who in Kickboxing

We have all watched with amazement as Chuck Norris fires a perfect flying side kick. Thanks to the movie industry, kickboxing continues to flourish not only in America, but worldwide. Just think about the popularity of action heroes Bruce Lee and Jackie Chan—it's clear that America loves martial artists.

There are a handful of dedicated pioneers who brought the sport of kickboxing its popularity. Indeed, they are the real kickboxing heroes. Sure, they may not be Hollywood-famous, but they are well respected and revered within the fighting world.

For example, Bill "Superfoot" Wallace was kickboxing's first superstar. His flashy kicks and powerful punches—and especially his quick left leg—earned him the name "Superfoot." In 1978, he was voted into the Black Belt Hall of fame as "Man of the Year."

Then there is Benny Urquidez. His claim to fame came when he knocked out the reigning Japanese champion; he's known for beating world-famous Japanese kickboxers at their own game—and remember, Japanese rules are more brutal than those in America. In 1978, he made the Black Belt Hall of Fame as "Fighter of the Year."

Kick-Tales

Bruce Lee had his own style of kicking called jeet kune do. This was a spectacular blend of some of the finest martial arts moves: tae kwon do kicks, wrestling takedowns, and the submission holds of judo. In other words, jeet kune do is a hybrid martial art. Lee was the first to blend several martial arts together to make up his own style. In fact, some historians credit him for jump-starting the modern martial arts movement in the United States.

Finally, there probably isn't a kickboxer alive who wouldn't recognize Maurice Smith. He holds a 15-year reigning world champion title and is the first international kickboxing star to enjoy big success.

Kickboxing Around the World

Japan's two most popular sports are kickboxing and judo. When combined, they basically comprise *shoot boxing:* the explosive punches and kicks of kickboxing mixed with some of the brilliant trips, throws, and tackles of judo. Or, to put it another way, a brand of kickboxing that allows you to toss your opponent to the ground.

The sport of shoot boxing is fairly new, yet it was near extinction shortly after its debut. For one thing, it didn't produce any known stars; for another, the Japanese love a good fight, and shoot boxing was not delivering a good fight. The Association of Shoot Boxers, worried that the sport might not make it, started to recruit fighters from around the world. The strategy was to stage a fight between an internationally known martial artist and a Japanese shoot boxer to gain some notice for the sport. The odds were not in favor of the shoot boxers, but they were winning matches nonetheless. And that's all it took to get the Japanese hooked on shoot boxing. Probably the most famous shoot boxer is Mason Gibson, the first non-Japanese shoot boxing champion. He electrified the Japanese fans with all his flashy moves: He punches and kicks like a tornado. He is now a household name in Japan.

Will we see shoot boxing here in the United States? Quite possibly. A relatively new U.S. organization is

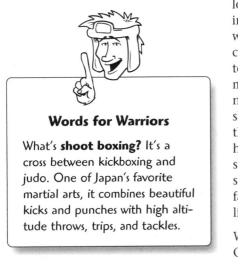

Words for Warriors

What's **shoot boxing?** It's a cross between kickboxing and judo. One of Japan's favorite martial arts, it combines beautiful kicks and punches with high altitude throws, trips, and tackles.

trying to promote shoot boxing as a sport and martial art. Right now, however, competitions are almost exclusively limited to Japan.

Draka

The Russians also have their own form of kickboxing. Although draka is not that popular in the Unites States, you may see more of this sport in the future. For example, it was not too long ago that a Pay-Per-View draka match was featured on cable television.

Draka derived from the hand-to-hand combat of the elite Russian Special Forces. Draka moves are similar to those of shoot boxing. In draka, you can kick, punch, and throw your opponent to the ground. The fundamental difference between the two styles is that a perfectly executed throw will immediately end the round. The fight is over when a perfectly completed throw is delivered within two consecutive rounds. The thrower, of course, is the winner of the fight.

During the 1980s and early 1990s, fitness was about appearance: ripped abs, thong leotards, and buns of steel. Health clubs were the place to be seen. Fitness is now about the quest for personal well-being. Introducing kickboxing. Because of its roots, kickboxing has it all; it's a fighting sport, martial art, fitness workout, and self-defense program. Sure, people are still exercising for the perfect body, but kickboxing for the health of it.

Kickboxing Buzz

Known for its high altitude throws to the floor, shoot boxing is on the rise. The uniform is unique: skintight spandex-type pants with flashy logos and superhero-type shin and footpads.

The Least You Need to Know

➤ The Greeks were ancient martial artists.

➤ Thai boxers have been kickboxing for about 1,000 years; savate influenced modern kickboxing in the Western world.

➤ Jhoon Rhee invented the Safe-T-Chop, the safety gear that revolutionized karate. The sport later became known as full contact kickboxing.

➤ In 1974, the first kickboxing organization in the United States—the Professional Kickboxers Association (PKA)—was established; kickboxing was now an official sport.

➤ Bill "Superfoot" Wallace, Benny Urquidez, and Maurice Smith are kickboxing stars.

➤ Shoot boxing and draka are forms of kickboxing that are growing.

Chapter 3

Kickboxing Wise: Gear Up!

In This Chapter

➤ Finding a gym

➤ Selecting the proper gear

➤ Practicing like a pro

➤ Building your own gym

So, now you're hooked. You can't wait to kick butt. You're willing to take on some soreness and wear the black and blue marks with pride. However, you're not quite sure how to start: where to look for a kickboxing gym, what equipment you will need, how much this sport will cost, and whether you should hire a trainer. These questions will be answered in this chapter.

First, however, you should ask yourself the following questions: What do you expect from kickboxing? How far do you want to take this sport? For example, you may want to take kickboxing to its highest level—a fight. Perhaps your only goal is to develop the perfect kickboxing body. Or maybe you're searching for a way to relieve some serious stress and learn a few self-defense tactics. Whatever your goals, you first need to find a place to work out. A good, reputable gym staff will be able to train you the authentic kickboxing way.

Finding the Right Gym

Safety! Safety! Safety! The number one question you should ask yourself is, "Will I get hurt at this gym?" (The answer should definitely be "No.") The two main causes of kickboxing injuries are incompetent training and defective equipment.

Warning Warriors

Be wary of trainers who advertise that they hold a black belt in kickboxing: Kickboxing doesn't have a belt system. Instead of taking the trainer's words for granted, look for kickboxing trophies, videotapes of competitions, and any kind of memorabilia that indicate a solid kickboxing career.

Some trainers are accomplished martial artists, which is a good start, but make sure they have some kickboxing experience. Your best bet is to ask around. Trainers with good reputations are often recognized in the community. For example, some trainers teach self-defense classes. Others teach kickboxing to children. Some trainers still fight, or they might train aspiring kickboxers. They may have even been world champions at some point in their career. These are all signs that you're choosing a good gym.

You'll also want to drop in to see what's going on. Ask yourself the following questions:

➤ What are the instructors like?

➤ How many classes do they teach?

➤ What kinds of classes do they teach?

➤ How many instructors are there?

➤ What are their qualifications?

Even if you're interested only in the cardio classes, make sure the instructors have some kind of kickboxing experience or, at the very least, some sort of certification. For example, for this book, I started kickboxing with Guy. I also earned certification to teach kickboxing through the Thomas the Promise organization. Even though I have more than 10 years of experience teaching aerobics, I felt that only by adding practical kickboxing experience and earning my certification would I be qualified to teach a cardio-kickboxing class. That's not to say that I couldn't teach, but I didn't feel right doing so. Certification is a great start, but look for instructors who have taken their training a step farther. Keep in mind that you can get hurt if the instructor can't instruct!

Ask the gym owner about the available instructors. Some instructors are former fighters. If they can also dance, you are likely to get a safe workout. However, world champions can sometimes make lousy instructors. That's why it's a good idea to watch a cardio class before you take one. The instructor should take the class through a thorough warmup, workout, and cool down, and he or she should stress proper technique. The floors should be wood or some other material that has the ability to absorb some of the shock from your moves. Also, mirrors should be available so you can watch yourself, which can help you correct your form—it's all about good technique.

In your pursuit to find the perfect trainer, you should watch as he coaches his students. He may be a world champion, yet lack the compassion or empathy to teach. And you'll find a lot of mighty egos out there. You need to be able to trust and admire your trainer, especially if you're training one-on-one. For example, find a coach who can take down a 200-pound-plus fighter, but won't pummel you with his pinky finger when you spar. Often, the coaches are real softies when they teach the kids kickboxing. You want to find a trainer who can teach at all levels. Learning to kickbox takes time, money, and patience. A good coach will know how to pace you, how to train you, and how to encourage and inspire you, so that you'll enjoy kickboxing.

Getting Ready to Enter the Ring

Now that you've found the perfect gym and trainer, you're ready to take the next step. You'll need to invest in some safety equipment to prevent you from getting hurt or hurting someone else. The ultimate weapon is your body. Your goal, then, is to protect your body. Don't worry—you're not signing yourself up for the fight of the century; you're just taking the first step toward becoming a trained kickboxer.

A good kickboxing gym should make equipment available to you. However, keep in mind that everyone else is sweating in the gym's gear as well, so you might want to invest in a few pieces of your own. If you're going to spar or take a series of personal training lessons, think about investing in the highest quality of protective gear out there. Remember that your equipment takes the beating for you, so don't skimp.

As a rule, there are lots of good brands. But your main goal is to buy equipment that's been endorsed or used by professionals. For example, Everlast, Title, Revgear, and Ringside all make catalogs available to the general public. Sometimes, sporting goods stores and martial arts gyms sell safety equipment. At the very least, use them as a starting point and a good reference.

If you're only into aerobic kickboxing, stop reading this chapter now! Aerobic kickboxing doesn't require any fancy gear. All you have to do is trade in your spandex for a few pairs of loose, comfortable shorts. Be sure they are loose enough to execute some snappy kicks.

For the serious workout, think about purchasing handwraps, bag gloves, boxing gloves, headgear, mouthpiece, groin or chest protectors, and foot and shin protection. Protective shoes, such as a wrestling shoe, are optional, but the extra protection helps to keep your toes nice and tight while you kick the bags. For the fitness warrior, I recommend handwraps and bag gloves.

Protecting Your Hands

Let's start with your cheapest investment—your handwraps. Think of the handwraps as the first layer of protection for your hands; they support the bones in your hand by keeping them tight and compact, and they protect your wrist from the shock of repeated punching.

Handwraps are available in both a traditional cotton wrap and in a gauze-type wrap, the latter of which are often referred to as Mexican wraps. Mexican wraps are better for two reasons: First, the hook and loop closures make them easier to wrap; second, because of the light elastic, the wrap clings to your hand like a bandage, providing good hand support.

Your cost: $5 to $12

Kickboxing Buzz

You'll want to wash your wraps after six or seven workouts; otherwise, they'll get really smelly. Use a handwrap wash bag or pantyhose bag to wash your wraps. If you don't, they'll most likely get tangled up around your other clothes or the washer itself. Don't put your wraps in the dryer. After every training session, hang wraps over a door to dry, and then roll them up for the next workout. Retire your wraps after they lose elasticity, or spring.

The Perfect Wrap

If you want to impress your trainer, learn to wrap your own hands. In addition to saving time, you'll show him that you are serious about kickboxing. So let's learn. We'll start by learning the basic beginner wrap (see the following series of figures). As your skill level improves, you can advance into a more technical wrap. There are many ways to wrap your hands, but what's important is that you find a comfortable wrap that stabilizes your fingers, hands, and wrists. The key to the perfect wrap, of course, is practice, practice, practice.

The Basic Wrap

Here's the scoop on the basic wrap:

1. Start by putting the thumb loop over your thumb; wrap across the back of your hand, away from the thumb.

2. Wrap around the wrist two or three times to support the wrist.

3. Bring the wrap around the backside of the hand and wrap the knuckles two or three times; cover the knuckles entirely.

4. Bring the wrap across the back of hand and down. Wrap around the thumb. Go back around the wrist and wrap the thumb the opposite way.

5. Bring the wrap back across the back of the hand and wrap the knuckle area again.

6. Wrap around the hand and wrist area in a figure-eight motion two or three times. Finish by wrapping the rest of the wrap around the wrist.

The basic beginner wrap.

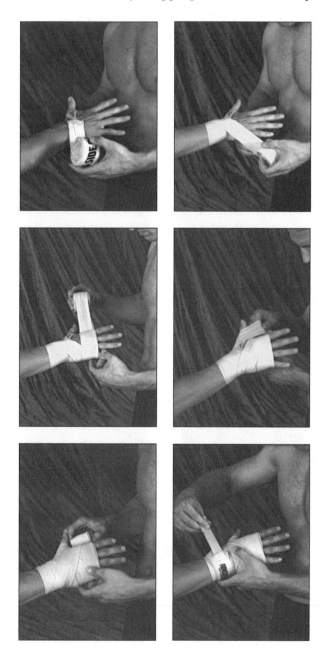

The Advanced Wrap

Here's the scoop on the advanced wrap (see the following series of figures):

1. Put your thumb in the thumb loop and pull the wrap across the back of your hand, away from the thumb.

2. Take the wrap and circle around your wrist two or three times to create a support system for the wrist. Make sure the wrap stays snug and wrinkle free.

3. Work the wrap toward the knuckles. Wrap around from the backside and circle the knuckles three or four times. The wrap should cover your knuckles entirely.

4. Start with the pinky finger. Run the wrap between the pinky and ring finger, straight down the palm of the hand, tightly. Weave the wrap in between each finger.

5. To wrap the thumb, circle the wrist once and then circle the thumb from the backside. Circle the thumb once more.

6. Take the wrap and make a figure-eight around the backside of the hand between the thumb and the forefinger. With the leftover wrap, circle your wrist to secure it and Velcro the wrap shut. The wrap should be snug and firm, without cutting off your circulation.

Kickboxing Buzz

Here's another good reason to train with a pair of heavier bag gloves: You burn more calories. Why? Because you have to hold your arms up to protect your face. After 100 punches or so, your overworked arms feel more like lead weights than your own limbs.

Bag Gloves

There are two different sets of gloves: bag gloves and sparring gloves. Bag gloves have extra padding around the knuckles, and you'll use them during training. Going toe-to-toe with a punching bag is electrifying, but it's important that you have a good set of tough bag gloves with plenty of padding to protect your hands. This padding protects your training partner as well.

Finding the perfect fit may take some time. You'll have to try on a few pairs. You can browse in a martial arts store or sporting goods store to find a comfortable fit. Then, order a pair from a boxing catalog if the martial arts or sporting goods stores don't carry the brand you want. Bag gloves come in many different materials, sizes, and colors—you can even get pink ones!

Kickboxing Buzz

Buy leather bag gloves. In addition to lasting longer, the leather will eventually mold to your hand, providing the perfect fit.

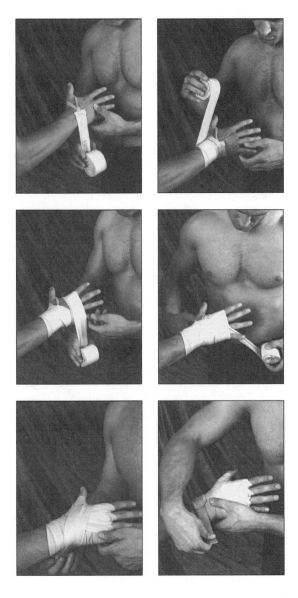

The advanced wrap.

After deciding on the material, size, and color of your gloves, your goal is to find a good weight. On average, bag gloves weigh between 5 and 12 ounces. A 5- or 6-ounce bag glove will do. However, we recommend a 12-ounce bag glove, especially for beginners. You'll get more padding, and therefore more protection. After all, you're just learning to throw punches. A hard hit to a bag may sting a little, mainly because your hands are not accustomed to striking hard surfaces. A heavier glove can absorb the shock so your hands don't. In addition, a pair of 12-ounce bag gloves is more like a real fighter's gloves, which better prepares you for a real fight.

Your cost: $20 to $60

Sparring Gloves

Of course, bag work is vital to your workout. But eventually you'll enter the ring to spar with a real, live person. That is the time to wear a good pair of sparring gloves. You'll find that sparring gloves come in three different sizes: 14-, 16-, and 18-ounce. The 14-ounce glove is worn by female kickboxers and men who weigh less than 130 pounds. The 16-ounce glove is the most common. The 18-ounce glove is used by extremely hard-hitting or super heavyweight kickboxers. Regardless of which you use, a good sparring glove should fit firmly around the wrapped fist. The sizes are usually determined by your weight and the class in which you're fighting. They often come in small, medium, large, and extra large.

Your cost: $45 to $150

Protecting Your Mouth

You're out of luck if you forget to protect your mouth. For example, a powerful blow to the head could cause you to bite down on your tongue. A mouthpiece can prevent you from biting your tongue in half, in addition to keeping your teeth from getting knocked out.

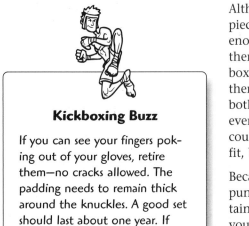

Kickboxing Buzz

If you can see your fingers poking out of your gloves, retire them—no cracks allowed. The padding needs to remain thick around the knuckles. A good set should last about one year. If you're using them twice a week, your gloves may last two to three years.

Although a vital piece of protective gear, the mouthpiece is often overlooked. Mouthpieces are cheap enough that you can keep an extra supply handy, and there are many varieties to choose from. The basic boxing-type fits the upper level of the teeth. Then there's the double-layered mouthpiece, which covers both the top and the bottom set of teeth. You can even have your dentist custom-make a mouthpiece; of course, an exact mold of your teeth provides the best fit, but it's also a pretty pricey way to go.

Because you'll be biting down hard as you take a few punches, you want the best possible fit. And you certainly don't want a mouthpiece that interferes with your breathing. That's why the dental type is best. But because it's expensive, you might want to have a few of the cheaper mouthpieces around just in case you lose the more expensive dental type.

Your cost: $2 to $7 (off the shelf); $75 to $100 (dental)

Protecting Your Private Parts

There isn't a man alive that would dispute the necessity of a groin protector. The moment you get kicked in the groin, you're oh-so grateful that you didn't forget to wear your "cup." There are several kinds of groin protectors—too many, in fact, to list here.

As far as finding the right fit … well, let's just say that's a matter of opinion. Some fighters feel very comfortable wearing the Thai-type groin protector—the cup is made from steel. It is covered with leather and held in place by leather straps, which are uncomfortable at first. The truth, though, is that any groin protector takes some getting used to. Your goal is to make sure your cup doesn't interfere with your kicks.

Groin protectors are also available to women. Most women don't wear them, however. Rather, a chest guard is mandatory for professional female kickboxers. If you're sparring on a regular basis, please consider wearing one to buffer the pain from a hit to the chest, and to protect you from potential serious medical problems. It's very painful to be kicked in the chest, so wear a chest guard. The body-contoured plastic fits inside an average training sports bra.

Your cost: $15 to $40

Kickboxing Buzz

To break in your mouthpiece, wear it while warming up. For example, try jumping rope with your mouthpiece. Can you breathe through your nose while keeping your mouth shut? That's your goal.

Protecting Your Legs and Feet

We've all banged our shins on the coffee table. Do you remember the excruciating pain and the stifled obscenities that followed? Well, that's only a fraction of the pain created by a full-powered round kick to the shin. Shin pads block the pain, prevent serious injury, and help stifle all those rants that follow a kick to the shin.

Shin Pads

Shin guards are pretty popular and come in many varieties. We use Thai shin pads. When picking out a pair of shin guards, make sure that the entire front part of your shin, extending down to the instep of the foot, is covered.

Your cost: $25 to $40

Foot Pads

If your shin pad doesn't have an instep protector, buy a set of footpads. The pad covers the entire top of portion of the foot and toes, leaving the bottom of your the exposed.

Ideally, you want to use the lower part of your shin, not your foot, to strike. Beginners should buy a pair of footpads; there are natural mistakes that come with learning to kick, and the extra padding keeps you from getting seriously injured. To secure a good fit, take one size larger than your foot size.

Your cost: $10 to $30

Protecting Your Head

Don't skimp on your headgear. It protects your head from cuts and your brain from damage, both immediate and potential damage that may not show up until later in life. You'll find that headgear comes in a variety of types; your choice will depend on your needs. Some even have nose and chin protectors. Purchase headgear that is designed for sparring and training; it has more padding to absorb the shots to the head.

Headgear designed for amateur competition has less padding. In other words, you'll feel the heavy blows to the head more. Also, don't buy a head protector that blocks your vision or prevents your head from moving freely.

Your cost: $65 to $150

Words for Warriors

Pugilistic dementia, often called the boxer's disease, is a slow deterioration of the mind caused by being hit in the head too much. Headgear keeps the brain from rattling around after a powerful blow to the head.

Kicking Like the Pros

You got your stuff—finally! Now you're ready for the big kickboxing moment. You're thinking, "Maybe I'll take a one-on-one lesson, a noncontact kickboxing class, or a light sparring workout." But you're not sure what's going to happen. That makes you anxious. Relax; here's everything you need to know before starting your first lesson.

Mirror, Mirror, on the Wall

Most serious kickboxers will spend most of their time looking at themselves in the mirror. So will you. The mirror is the best training mode for correcting stances, guarding techniques, and kicks and punches. Besides watching yourself, you can practice shadow kickboxing.

In other words, you can watch your reflection as you fight an imaginary opponent in the mirror. Even in the cardio class, you should always watch yourself to correct your form—nobody will think you're vain.

Talk About Abs: The Medicine Ball

You'll use a medicine ball to build strength. A medicine ball is a weighted leather ball that resembles an oversized basketball. They vary in size and weight (9 to 18 pounds). Are you having a hard time figuring out how a weighted basketball helps your kickboxing? The ball helps toughen up the stomach for sparring. For example, you and your training partner can throw it back and forth while you do a series of sit-ups. He can drop the ball on your stomach as you crunch up. In return, you'll have to catch it as you curl up. Insanity? Nope—it doesn't hurt, and you'll get strong abs.

Just Jump: Jumping Rope

You'll also have to jump rope. Okay, maybe you haven't jumped rope since elementary school, but there's not a fighter alive that doesn't do it. And if they can jump rope, so can you. Make sure your gym has a good variety of jump ropes, in all sizes and weights. Most trainers will make you jump rope to help build timing and conditioning. In other words, you'll be better able to pace your kicks and punches, and to coordinate your upper and lower body.

Kickboxing Buzz

To find a perfect fit, stand on the jump rope. Your legs should be shoulder width apart. Pull the handles up to your hips. They should sit directly above your hipbones.

Gym Time

Now the fun begins. You get to practice your kicks and punches with a trainer or training partner. You'll be throwing punches, kicks, knee and elbow strikes, and kickboxing combinations to pads. You'll be hitting focus mitts, kicking shields, and Thai pads. These pieces of equipment are used to fake a moving target or create a fighting atmosphere.

Focus Mitts

Focus mitts, or AKA pancakes, are round pads about the size of a human head. Your trainer wears them on his hands to help you refine your boxing techniques. The training is meant to keep you moving while striking the pads. Depending on your trainer, he'll usually call a series of combinations and make you hit from all angles.

Kickboxing Buzz

Focus mitts cost about 30 to 60 dollars. If you have a partner that's willing to hold them while you punch, they will make a nice addition to your home gym.

Thai Pads

Thai pads are thick, heavy-duty pads used to practice your punches and kicks. These pads stand up to the rough beating from the combination work—kicks and punches strung together. The name is a dead giveaway as to their origin, Thailand. The pads are rectangular in shape and anywhere from 18–20 inches long and 8–10 inches wide. The thick padding is actually designed to protect the person holding the pad. Straps and handles are sewn on the back, so your coach or training partner can hold the pad in place while you kick it.

As you kick, your trainer will move around, changing the angles and positions in which you must kick to hit the target. In this way, you can learn kicks from all angles, plus focus on areas in which you need to improve your kicks.

Kicking Shield

With a kicking shield, you'll again be practicing your kicks at full power. These pads are rectangular in shape and are used to gauge how hard you can kick. The pad can be used to create different angles and levels, so you can become more flexible with your kicks. The pad is ideal for practicing your front kicks, side kicks, turn back kicks, and round kicks.

Bag Work

Your kickboxing training is intended to toughen you up, to get you ready for the ring. To prepare you for the big win, you'll be working on all types of bags. That's how you will gain strength, develop power, and create a fighting rhythm that outwits your opponent. Think of these bags as your imaginary enemy. The good news is that they can't hit you back!

Heavy Bags

Heavy bags come in many sizes and lengths, and in different materials such as vinyl, leather, and canvas. Try not to work on a canvas bag, though, because it tears up your hands and equipment.

A six- or seven-foot bag, sometimes called a banana bag, extends to the floor. The extra length, designed specifically for kickboxing, helps hone your lower kicks (such as round kicks and leg sweeps). Because this 200-pound bag doesn't move much when you strike it, it helps you build power in both your punches and kicks.

Finally, what you'll find in most gyms is the 70-pound bag; it's there so you can practice your punching and kicking combinations.

Kick-Tales

Before the invention of the heavy bag, in Thailand, fighters used rubber trees to throw kicks. Rubber trees are fairly soft as far as a tree goes, and the bark helped toughen the skin and tissue.

On Your Toes—Staying Alert

There are several types of bags designed to help you stay alert: If you're not alert, you'll get clobbered as they spring back. Smaller punching bags are meant to keep you on your toes, improve speed, develop timing, and sharpen defenses.

The Head Hunter Bag

The head hunter bag is about the same size as your opponent's head. The bag whips around and around while you practice your jabs and hooks. Timing is essential with this type of bag; otherwise you'll miss the bag as it swings around.

The Chaser Bag

Next is the 40-pound bag, also called the chaser bag, which moves around as you practice your kicking and punching combinations. You have to move with this bag as if you were fighting. You've got to keep your guard up. Because the bag is so light, you've got to move with the rebound; otherwise, you may get knocked in the face.

The Slip Bag

The double-end bag, or slip bag, is a leather ball held in place by an elastic string that is attached to the ceiling and the floor. This bag ricochets back and forth as you strike, leaving you no time to think. This is called reflex training.

The Speed Bag

Speed bags work pretty much the same way, teaching hand-eye coordination. By hitting these bags, you'll build speed, timing, and rhythm; it's like jumping rope for your hands.

Building Your Own Gym

Okay, you have some extra room in your garage. You're thinking that maybe you should start your own gym. Good idea! After all, practice makes the perfect kickboxer, and I'm sure the extra workout will further reduce the waistline. But what will it take?

Yes, you'll need a pair of bag gloves and handwraps. You'll also need a mirror, a jump rope, and a 70-pound heavy bag. And that's about it. The heavy bag can easily be attached to the crossbeams in the garage by a chain, and it can be taken down and stored away when you're not using it so you can park your car. If you're hanging the bag yourself, make sure there is plenty of room for you to move around the bag and let the bag swivel back and forth as you strike it. The nice thing about the heavy bag is it will still be your friend after you beat up on it.

However, like a good car salesman, we want to let you know about the add-ons that can create the best home gym—and certainly the coolest garage on the block. First, invest in a double-end bag; it is easy to set up and is great for practicing your hand work. If you have a little extra money, buy a speed bag as well. Again, you'll be able to develop your speed skills.

Kickboxing Buzz

A heavy bag costs $100 to $120; bag gloves $20 to $40; handwraps $5 to $12; wrestling shoes $25 to $100; jump rope $8 to $30; 3-pound dumbbells, mirror, and slip bag are optional.

If you stick to the basics, your gym will be just fine. But let's say you're short of garage space. You can purchase a free-standing gym or a free-standing punching bag. The free-standing bag is a self-supporting heavy bag that can be set up in a spare room or anywhere you have some space. And then there's "Bob." He looks and feels like a real person, but he's a free-standing dummy bag.

If you don't have an empty room, you can always move the sofa. If you decide to go with a freestanding gym, you'll need a little more room to hold a heavy bag and a few other training devices. Free-standing equipment comes in all sizes, and with a range of price tags. As long as you have the money, you can get as deluxe as you want. You'll be able to find "Bob"—and all sorts of other types of bags and gyms—in any kickboxing catalog.

Shopping for Kicks

Here's an at-a-glance list for your kickboxing shopping needs.

Kickboxing Shopping List

Gear	Cost	Aerobics Kicker	Fun Kicker	Serious Kicker
Handwraps	$5–12		X	X
Bag Gloves	$20–60		X	X
Sparring Gloves	$45–150		X	
Mouthpiece	$2–100			X
Groin Protector	$15–40			X
Breast Protector	$15–40			X
Shin Pads	$25–40			X
Foot Pads	$10–30			X
Headgear	$65–150		X	X

The Least You Need to Know

➤ Look for an instructor's kickboxing trophies, videotapes of competitions, and any kind of memorabilia that indicate a solid kickboxing career before you join a gym.

➤ Learn to wrap your hands.

➤ Cardio-kickboxers can retire their spandex. They only need a loose pair of shorts to throw some powerful kicks.

➤ Equipment needs vary depending on how far you want to go with kickboxing. However, headgear, mouthpiece, groin protector, shin and foot pads, boxing gloves, and handwraps are standard safety equipment.

➤ Get to know the equipment at your gym: heavy bags, Thai pads, focus pads, and kicking shields.

➤ You, too, can create your own gym.

Part 2

Your Secret Arsenal

There's a reason why kickboxing is so fashionable—and it's probably the same reason it is so much fun. People tremble when they hear you say, "I'm a kickboxer."

In this part, you'll learn how to strike, block, and dance. That's right, kickboxers dance by putting together kicks and punches. Even though kickboxing is the latest fitness workout, its kicks stretch back to the ancient roots of Thailand's Muay Thai, Japan's karate, and Korea's tae kwon do. The punches are borrowed from the ring. That's right—nobody will mess with you; you're now The Terminator.

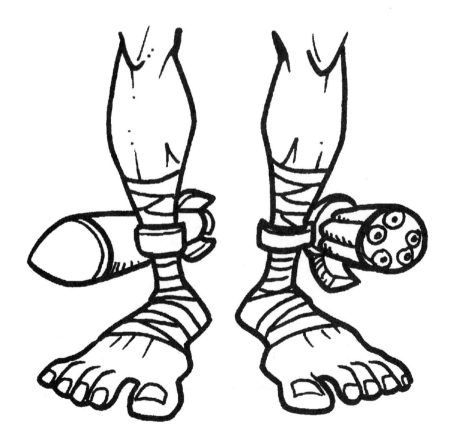

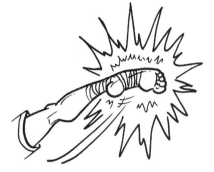

Chapter 4

Holy Kick-Butt: The Deadly Kicks

In This Chapter

➤ The fighter's stance

➤ Kicks: your long-range weapons

➤ The muscles you are working

➤ The kicks of kickboxing

➤ Knee strikes: your short-range weapons

Need some flex in your kick? How about some spin? You're about to learn the "sensational six." As a modern kickboxer, you'll fine-tune these kicks: front and rear leg front kick, side kick, roundhouse, round kick, and turn kick. Remember, even though kickboxing is touted as a modern sport, these kicks stretch back to the ancient roots of Thailand's Muay Thai, Japan's karate, and Korea's tae kwon do. All have trademark kicks which were "borrowed," so to speak, to make up the dynamic kicks of kickboxing.

Why kicks? Kicks are essential for two reasons. First, kicks are long-range weapons; if you can fire a variety of good kicks, you can keep your attacker from getting too close. Thus, kicks provide another way for you to protect yourself in a self-defense situation. Second, your thigh muscles, some of the biggest in your body, can generate a lot of power. A powerful kick has more impact than a punch. Your legs are stronger than your arms. For example, a 100-pound woman can generate as much power with her kicks as a 200-pound man can put into a punch. Most of the time, a larger would-be attacker will get right in your face, intimidate you with his size. A good shift kick to the midsection can stop him in his tracks; kicks close the body-size gap between men and women.

Strike a Pose: Stances

A good kickboxer keeps his opponent on his toes, wondering where the next move will land. A neutral position gives no clue as to strategy, giving you an advantage over your opponent.

A neutral kickboxing stance also balances your weight—50 percent on each leg—putting you in a solid position to either throw or block kicks and punches. Your base of support lies between your feet. Think about it: You can't be pushed over if your feet are slightly more than shoulder width apart. To find a good stance, envision a clock in your head; now, place your right foot forward, on high noon, and your back foot at 5 o'clock, pointing toward 1 o'clock. Remember that if your feet are too far apart or too close together, you can easily be pushed off balance. The following figures show the Do's and Don'ts of a fighter's stance.

The image on the left shows the perfect fighter's stance; the fighter on the right has his feet too far apart.

Now consider your hands. To protect your body, your hands should be in a vertical position, with your elbows at your rib cage as if you were holding daggers in your hands. Moving forward, this stance will be referred to as the fighter's stance; commit it to memory.

Kicks are thrown from either the back or front leg. For that reason, kickboxers stand with either the left foot or the right foot out front. For example, if you're a right-handed person, you'll stand with your left foot forward. It's just the opposite for lefties. However, don't be surprised if your coach makes you fire kicks from both angles to build strength and improve technique.

Depending on how you shift your weight, these poses stabilize you for each kick. For example, for more power in your kicks, fire from your rear leg. For speed, kick with your front leg. Rear leg kicks are often called offensive kicks. On the other hand, front leg kicks are used defensively. Or, to put it another way, use your front leg to fend off a would-be attacker, and then assault him with a powerful rear kick.

Building Leaner Legs and a Better Butt

Kicking mainly uses the muscles in your legs and butt. Good news, right? Well, that's also the reason why you tire so quickly—you're moving big muscles. This hard work *does* reap big benefits, though. When you tell your muscles to kick, you're calling for more muscle fiber. In return, you're burning more calories. The bad news is that you can expect to feel the results before you see them—in other words, you might be a little sore.

Most kicks begin with your hip flexors, the area of muscle that picks up your knee. The muscle that runs down the thigh, called the quadriceps, assists in executing the kick.

If you flip over to the backside of the leg, the hamstring group becomes 100-percent active. Then there are the smaller muscles that are sometimes overlooked, but important: *gluteus medius* and *minimus*. Ladies, you're very familiar with these muscles—they make up the outer butt muscles and attach to the biggest working butt muscle, the *gluteus maximus*. Turning your kick out slightly calls for the butt muscles in addition to the other leg muscles that run up and down your leg, known as the hip adductors and abductors.

Practically all the muscles in your legs are engaged during a kick—even the support leg is using calf muscles, *gastrocnemius* and *soleus*, to stabilize your body for the kicking leg. Finally, you need your abdominals and back muscles, sometimes called core muscles, to help stabilize the body as well.

Kick-Tales

A bit of history: Kickboxing's lightning-fast kicks come from Korea's tae kwon do; the powerful kicks derive from Japan's karate; and the leg sweeps and knee strikes are taken from Thailand's Muay Thai.

Getting a Good Kick Start

This is your new mantra: fold, execute, snap back, set down; fold, execute, snap back to fold, set down. Say it again and again to perfect your kick. The following figures show the sequence of kick events.

Fold leg, execute kick, return to fold, and set leg down in fighter's stance.

Understand that when you kick, your base of support balances on one foot. That's the reason you snap the leg and quickly return it to the floor. Otherwise, if you let your leg dangle in the air, your opponent just might grab it or kick your base leg from beneath you; neither scenario is good.

Your eyes should remain on your opponent at all times. As a beginner, you might tend to take your eyes off the target as you kick. In doing so, you've given your opponent the perfect opportunity to kick you. Even worse, you can completely miss your target. Focus on your target; only then will you land a blow that may get his attention.

Think about your working muscles as you kick. Throw your entire body into the kick, not just your leg. You'll be amazed by the force behind your kicks, if you use your abdominal and leg muscles to generate enough oomph.

Hoping to inflict some pain on your opponent? Well, not quite, but you don't want to hurt yourself, either. So get to know the striking positions of your foot. The first one is with the ball of the foot; pull your toes back as you land the kick. Otherwise, you risk smashing them. The second striking position is with the heel of the foot; as with the ball of the foot, you need to lift your heel higher than your toes. Finally, strike with the top portion of your foot or shin. For this strike, you need to point your toes. The following figures show the various striking positions of your foot.

Kickboxing Buzz

Snapping a kick in a whipping motion dramatically increases the speed of a blow. Now, put your weight behind the "snap." That's how you will generate the kick's knockout power.

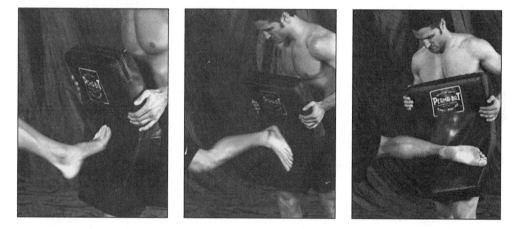

The three striking surfaces of the foot are the ball of the foot (left), the heel of the foot (center), and the shin (right).

On top of all these tips, don't forget to keep your arms up! After all, your arms protect your body from the other guy's secret weapons.

Introducing the Sensational Six

You've got the power; just reach within. The formula to explosive kicks can be defined like this:

Good technique + Speed = Power

Warning Warriors

Lacking flexibility may cause you to fall back on your rear, if you throw your kick too high. Be careful—bouncing off your backside can be painful. Furthermore, you'll give your opponent a leading edge.

Kickboxing Buzz

For the perfect fighter's stance, stand with your left shoulder and hand at a slight angle—hands up and chin down. Make sure your weight is balanced on both legs: One foot stands on high noon, the other stands on 5 o'clock and points toward 1 o'clock. Now, think lean and mean.

Knowing the proper technique and having a strong sense of balance help you deliver devastating results. For example, when the knee is raised in a high position, you can use it as an aiming sight for targets; after kicking, bring that leg right back so you're ready to step into the next move. Don't hop into the next move—regroup, slow down, and focus on your technique.

Of all the fighting techniques, kicks are the hardest to learn. No, you won't be flying through the air executing a flying side kick—those fancy kicks really don't work. If you want a big payoff, learn the following six kicks: front kick, rear leg front kick, side kick, front leg round kick, rear leg round kick (roundhouse), and turn back kick. Step by step, you'll learn how to throw these kicks.

We'll start you off with the easiest kicks, and then advance to the more difficult ones. Read through the entire process of each of the kicks first. Then go back to the front kick and slowly practice: Fold, execute, return to fold, and put the foot back into the fighter's stance.

Fighters have many rules. One that you should commit to memory is the front leg or arm is used for speed, whereas the back leg or arm generates power. Good fighters rely on both speed and power in the ring. You, too, will learn to strike from both sides. Let's start with the kick. Keep in mind that you're learning to execute these kicks from a right-handed perspective, so put your left foot forward.

Front Kicks

You'll get a whole lot of respect if you can execute a front kick; it's the easiest to learn. The term *front kick* can be a little confusing; it's actually two different kicks. You can execute the front kick from either the front or rear leg. To keep it straight, trainers often use the terms "offensive" or "defensive" front. In an offensive front, the kick comes from the rear leg; power is generated from the thrusting motion of the hip. However, you can quickly react with a defensive front by snapping the front leg in and out for speed. That's one reason why these kicks work well in a self-defense situation, you can defend yourself with either leg.

Defensive Front

Even if you have the flexibility, don't fire a strike to the head. For one, you'll lose the power that was meant for this kick. Also, your opponent will be able to grab your foot and flip you on your butt. Instead, aim for the knees, thighs, groin, or midsection. Note that you should throw this kick to the knee or groin only if you're ever in a self-defense situation. Strike your target with the ball of your foot.

Offensive Front

The rear leg delivers the power! For the rear leg front kick, that power comes from the body by thrusting your hip forward. Because you have your entire body behind the kick, you might be able to reach for the solar plexus—the chest area. With the exception of where they should land, the front and the rear leg front kicks are basically the same.

Here's how to execute a rear leg front kick:

1. Assume the perfect fighter's stance.

2. Bring up your right leg in a tightly bent position. This position is called the "fold." Raise the knee in a high position and use it as your aiming sight for targets.

3. Snap the lower leg out to the target, thrusting the hips forward so that you have enough power as the kick is being executed. Remember your striking position. Make sure that the toes are pulled back and that you strike with the ball of the foot.

4. After you hit the target, bring leg quickly back to the fold.

5. Set down your leg and return to the fighter's stance.

The following figures illustrate the rear leg front kick.

Kickboxing Buzz

In the ring, fighters can sneakily fire a trio of defensive kicks to create openings for the powerful offensive front; others, might take the one-legged defensive kick approach to tire their opponent. After the barrage of speedy kicks, he'll never know what hit him next—a powerful offensive front.

Kickboxing Buzz

Sometimes new kickboxers have a difficult time bending the toes back to kick with the balls of their feet. To help strengthen the muscles around the toes, walk around on the balls of your feet for a few minutes a day.

Doing it right: five steps to a powerful rear leg front kick.

Side Kick

Throwing a side kick takes a lot of patience because the body mechanics are more involved; at the same time, however, this kick generates a wicked sting. You can stop a rushing opponent in his tracks. Or how about launching this kick to throw your opponent off balance? The target areas generally vary from the midsection to the legs, but if you have the flexibility, why not aim for the head? Here's a tip, ladies: Many of you often have this kind of hip range. With the side kick, always use the heel of your foot to strike your target.

Here's how to execute a side kick:

1. Assume the perfect fighter's stance.

2. As you start to fold the leg, turn the support foot so that the heel points toward the target, turning all the way around.

3. Bring the folded knee up and across your body, somewhere near the opposite side of your chest (or as much as your flexibility allows). The foot is flexed so that the bottom of the heel faces the target.

4. As the leg snaps out, allow the hip to roll over or turn into the kick. Even though your body is slightly turned away from your opponent at this point, don't take your eyes off the target. The kick thrusts out in a straight line. The striking area is the heel of the foot. Make sure that the heel is slightly higher than your toes to help land the kick.

5. After the side kick strikes the target, snap it back to the fold as quickly as possible.

6. Set the foot down to return to the fighter's stance.

The following figures illustrate the side kick.

Kickboxing Buzz

With kicks, you can hit anywhere on the body. However, some targets are better than others, depending on the kick. For example, front kicks are more damaging to the stomach or thigh area. In general, you can strike low to the calf or as high as the head. Anywhere in between, such as the stomach, is a middle target. Any kick to the groin area is used only in a self-defense situation.

Follow these steps to fire a smoking side kick.

53

The Front Leg Round Kick

The round kick can reap the biggest payoff. You can strike a wide range of targets such as the calf, thighs, groin, stomach, chest, and head. Your only limit is your flexibility. Revered for its lighting fast "concussion" effect, this kick has speed and power. Use the front part of your foot or shin area to strike your target.

Here's how to execute a front leg round kick:

1. Assume the fighter's stance.
2. As you fold the front knee, turn the body completely sideways or pivot back as you point the knee toward the target.
3. The knee is horizontal. Snap the kick out quickly, hitting the target with the lower part of the shin.
4. Snap the leg back to the fold.
5. Set the leg down to return to the fighter's stance.

The following figures illustrate the front leg round kick.

Warning Warriors

Sometimes, when this kick hits a solid target such as a person or heavy bag, you'll be thrown off balance. What's important is that you regroup and return to your fighting position as quickly as possible.

Five steps to a snappy round kick, the most-used kick in your arsenal.

Kick-Tales

Bill "Superfoot" Wallace, kickboxing superstar, is known in the ring for his fast left leg, and thus for the speed of his left round kick. That's how he got the name "Superfoot." He retired as an undefeated world kickboxing champion.

The Rear Leg Round Kick, or Roundhouse

The rear leg round kick, also known as roundhouse, is more powerful than the front leg round kick because your whole body weight is thrust into this kick. You'll travel in a circular motion as you strike with the back leg. Your body size doesn't matter when casting this kick—if you learn to accomplish the snap correctly, along with putting your body weight into the kick, you're guaranteed a knockout.

Here's how to execute a roundhouse:

1. Assume the fighter's stance.

2. Raise the rear leg in a tight fold, with the knee high.

3. Bring the whole right side of your body forward. When the right side is completely turned, the folded right leg comes up to a horizontal position.

4. Snap the back leg out, striking with the lower part of the shin.

5. After the kick is recoiled to the fold, set it down and resume proper fighting position with the new side (your right side) forward. Learning to kick from both sides is important.

The following figures illustrate the roundhouse.

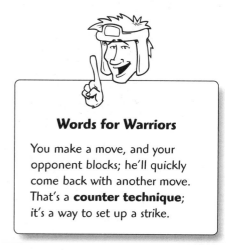

Words for Warriors

You make a move, and your opponent blocks; he'll quickly come back with another move. That's a **counter technique**; it's a way to set up a strike.

Right on: Your roundhouse can't miss with these sure-fire steps.

The Ultimate Turn Back Kick

The turn back kick, also referred to as the turn kick, is not common; it is used only as a fancy power move. Referred to as an "opportunity" kick, it can be used only in certain situations, such as a *counter technique*. (When your opponent makes a strike that puts him in a position to land a follow-up kick.) Because you're turning away from your target as you fire this kick, you lose sight of your opponent for a moment. You are in danger if you miss with this kick—your opponent has a chance to take you down. So it's best not to miss. Shoot for the stomach, ribs, midsection, or the solar plexus, and strike with the heel of your foot for maximum impact.

Here's how to execute a turn back kick:

1. Assume the fighter's stance.
2. Pivot on the balls of your feet, bringing the heels forward. At the same time, turn your head and swivel your right shoulder back. Keep an eye on your opponent over your shoulder.

3. Bring up the right leg up in a tight fold, with the foot flexed, ready to strike with the heel of the foot.

4. Turn your body completely backward; roll over your right shoulder. Snap out the right leg and heel.

5. After the kick lands, bring your leg back into the fold. Set down your leg. Now your right side is forward.

The following figures illustrate the turn kick.

Follow these steps to execute the turn kick.

Here's an overview of the "sensational six" and their striking positions. At first, you might want to strike softly, until you've committed to memory where the strike should land. You don't want to learn the hard way; it's very painful striking with the wrong part of the foot.

Kicks and Strikes	
Front kicks	Strike with ball of the foot
Rear kicks	Strike with ball of the foot
Side kicks	Strike with heel of the foot
Turn kicks	Strike with heel of the foot
Round kicks	Strike with the shin
Roundhouse	Strike with the shin

Warning Warriors

Don't forget to keep your hands up, even as you practice your kicks. Practice makes perfect. You don't want to drop your hands—your opponent will patiently wait for such an opening. You won't know what hit you.

Warning Warriors

When practicing your knee strikes, never forget that the knee strike is a strong, brutal technique. You can cause some severe damage, so be careful. Knee strikes hurt!

Close Quarters: Knee Strikes

If your legs fail as a weapon, try firing a knee strike. As far as powerful weapons go, knee strikes are effective regardless of your size. You can strike to any target: legs, groin, stomach, or head. Again, strike to the groin only in a self-defense situation. As far as technique, there's not much to this strike, which makes it very easy to learn.

You can generate more power if you hold on to your opponent. The most common type of grab is a double-handed grip: Bring your elbows together and make a vise-like hold around the neck, as shown in the following figure.

By grabbing the neck, you can throw off your opponent's balance and stabilize your own. In a defensive situation, you'll want to deliver a blow by pulling your attacker into your knee. By holding on to his neck, you're controlling the situation; it's too hard to deliver an effective knee strike if you're off balance.

In this section, you'll learn two different knee strikes. Both will be thrown off the rear leg. The first knee strike comes from a straight-on angle, and the second fires from the side. The striking surface of the knee is the main difference: The striking surface of the side knee strike is the meaty part of the side of the knee; the striking surface of the straight knee strike is the bone above the kneecap. The rear straight knee strike can be delivered with or without grabbing the neck. To execute the side knee strike, you'll have to grab the neck first for balance.

A double-handed grip.

The Side Knee Strike

Follow these steps to execute a side knee strike:

1. Grab the neck of your opponent; your weight should be evenly balanced on both legs.
2. Shift your weight to the front leg and lift the rear leg in a vertical position, with your knee at the side of your body.
3. Pull the hands toward the right side of your body. At the same time, swing the knee—keeping it vertical—into the target. The striking surface is the meaty part of the inside of the knee.

The following figures illustrate the side knee strike.

For maximum destruction, perfect the side knee strike with these three steps.

The Straight Rear Knee Strike

Take the following steps to execute a straight rear knee strike:

1. Grab the neck of your opponent.
2. Shift your weight to your front leg and pull the neck of your opponent down. At the same time, shoot the rear knee straight up and deliver a strike with the bone just above the kneecap.

The following figures illustrate the straight rear knee strike.

Just two steps to a power-ful rear knee strike.

You can kick to any part of the body. However, your goal is to show that you mean business. Firing a kick that has little impact or worse, doesn't land, tells your opponent that you're not ready to rumble. To win in the ring, you need to know how to inflict a serious hurt on your opponent.

Memorize the following table. The Good column tells you the best targets. When throwing a kick, aim for these targets for knockout results. The Bad column is your secondary set of targets in which, in a sticky situation, might not be such a bad idea. The Ugly column, by contrast, lists areas you should shy away from—the rewards are slim and unpredictable.

Kicks and Targets

Kicks	The Good	The Bad	The Ugly
Front	Stomach, groin, thigh	Chest	Head
Rear	Stomach, groin, thigh	Chest	Head
Side	Stomach	Chest, groin	Face, thigh
Round	Side head, kidney, thigh	Stomach	Chest, calf, groin
Roundhouse	Side head, kidney, groin	Chest, stomach	Groin
Turn	Stomach	Chest, groin	Face, thigh
Straight knee	Stomach, groin, groin	Side head	Face, chest
Side knee	Kidney, stomach	Side head	Thigh, face

The Least You Need to Know

➤ Assume the kickboxer's stance: feet slightly more than shoulder width apart. One foot stands on high noon, the back on 5 o'clock, pointing toward 1 o'clock.

➤ The muscles that work as you kick include leg, abdominal, and back muscles.

➤ The front kick is the easiest kick, fired from both legs.

➤ The side kick takes more time to master because you have to learn to stabilize your hip.

➤ The turn kick, also called the opportunity kick, can knock out your opponent if executed properly.

➤ Knee strikes are your close-range weapons. Use them when your opponent gets too close.

Chapter 5

Perfecting Your Punch: Splat!

In This Chapter

➤ Make a fist

➤ Using the jab

➤ Power punches mean business

➤ Kickboxing has its own punch

You may be a great kicker, but if you have a wimpy set of punches, you're doomed. For example, what do you do if your opponent gets too close? Strike with a punch, of course.

Kickboxing borrows most of its punches from classic boxing, but it also has a set of its own. These punches are used mainly in offensive and defensive need-for-speed situations. Because smaller muscle groups move your arms, your hands are faster and more accurate than your legs. Learn the punches in this chapter well, and you'll be able to throw a zinger of a blow in no time.

Punching Perfection

To go anywhere in kickboxing, you must learn how to punch. In fact, you'll have to refine your boxing technique because most good kicks are first set up by punches. Even though kicks are more powerful, you'll probably fire more punches in the ring. Remember, smaller muscle groups don't require as much energy, so punching doesn't tire you out as quickly. This strategy comes in handy, especially during the latter rounds of a fight or workout. As a beginner, you'll want to punch more just for that reason.

Kick-Tales

The first recorded prize fighter was an Englishman by the name of James Figg. He opened the first pugilistic academy in London. He couldn't read or write—but he sure could punch.

The perfect punch starts out with the perfect fist. When making a fist, be sure to roll your fingers in your palm. Ladies, you may have a little difficulty if you have long nails, so try to lay your fingernails flat in the palm of your hands. Your thumb rests on the outside of the index and middle fingers. When punching, use the first two punch knuckles, or the largest two knuckles. Try not to punch with the smaller knuckles—you might break them, especially if you're hitting to the head.

Here's how to make the perfect fist:

1. Open your hand.
2. Start to bend your fingers into a ball.
3. Keep rolling into a tight ball so that the surface knuckles are flat.
4. Tuck the thumb across the palm of the hand so it rests against the fingers.
5. Strike with the two largest knuckles.

Warning Warriors

Watch out! Fingernail marks in the palms of your hand and white knuckles are signs that you're gripping too tightly. Let loose (and consider cutting your nails)!

Strong and Sleek Arms

The punch rolls it all into one: sleek arms, strong back, ripped abs, and lean legs. Let's first talk about the dynamics of the punch. And then, you'll see how that punch gives the entire body a workout.

Power begins with your toes. The ball of the foot pivots as you begin to throw the punch, which then drives the legs—now we're talking power. Hip rotation follows the leg. The core muscles, abdominals, and back also work to help build intensity. In other words, your arm and shoulder muscles aren't the only hard-working muscles.

Of course, the major working muscles of the arm include the biceps and triceps. It's easy to train your biceps because they're sitting on the top portion of your arm—can't miss them—but what about the triceps? We often neglect them because we can't see them. You won't neglect them as you punch, though. You'll use them, along with a whole slew of other muscles including the shoulder muscles, deltoids, and rotator groups. Then there are the chest muscles, *pectoralis major* and *minor*, which assist as you execute a punch. Also, the punch requires that your biggest working upper body muscle, the *latissimus dorsi,* work in conjunction with the other back muscles, rhomboids, and trapezius to bring the punch back.

Punch Start

Are you a righty or lefty? Depending on your birthright, that's how you'll stand. A right-handed puncher fires power punches with the right hand, standing with the left side forward (this is sometimes referred to as the orthodox stance). A southpaw, however, throws power with the left hand, and stands with the right leg forward. Unlike boxers, kickboxers learn to throw punches from both sides. Because kicks and punches can be launched from either arm and leg, you'll need to develop both sides. Workout warriors, take note: You don't want one arm bigger than the other, so you want to work the body evenly. For learning purposes in this book, you'll always use an orthodox stance—sorry, lefties.

Attention, all beginners: Start throwing your punches at half speed, and then gradually work up to full speed as your technique improves. And don't forget to check yourself out in the mirror.

When practicing your punches, think about where they'll land. Punches land either to the head or to the body. Although the eyes, nose, cheeks, and temples make good targets, the ideal spots are the point of the chin and the lower jaw, which are also known as the *sweet spots*. When targeting the body, aim for the chest and stomach. The most damaging body shots are delivered to the upper part of the solar plexus, under the heart, and to the liver area.

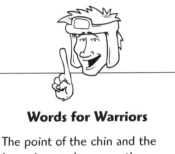

Words for Warriors

The point of the chin and the lower jaw are known as the **sweet spots.** A powerful punch on a sweet spot can result in an instant knockout.

Kickboxing Buzz

Have you ever stolen a cookie from a cobra? Probably not. But if you had, I bet that you would reach your arm out and back very quickly. When firing a jab, imagine that you're stealing a cookie from a cobra.

As you get closer to your opponent, kicking is no longer possible. Instead, use the *boxer's crouch*. Draw your shoulders together to make a tight ball—imagine a turtle pulling into its shell. Now your opponent has limited targets. But be aware that once you're in the boxer's crouch, you also have less room to throw kicks.

The Jab

If you want to come out on top, you need speed, speed, and more speed. Enter the jab, which is your fastest weapon, period. You can fire it in rapid succession—jab, jab, jab. Every fighter worships the jab, a dynamic punch that's usually used to set up power punches and kicks. You can throw it straight out to the face, jaw, nose, or eyes.

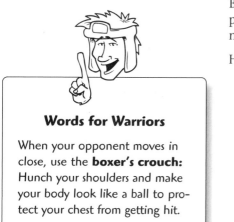

But be careful—despite the fact that the jab lacks power, it can inflict some serious hurt on your opponent.

Here's what you need to do to dish out a jab:

1. Assume the perfect fighter's stance.

2. Step forward with the left foot and extend your left arm. Form a fist with the lead hand and rotate the knuckles so that the palm of your hand faces down. Snap the fist out to the target. Warning! Don't fully extend the arm; leave a slight bend in the elbow so as not to hyperextend your arm.

3. Recoil your arm; return to the fighter's stance.

Words for Warriors

When your opponent moves in close, use the **boxer's crouch:** Hunch your shoulders and make your body look like a ball to protect your chest from getting hit.

The following figures illustrate the sequence of jab movements.

How about a jab that jolts? Follow these steps.

Power Punches

In the ring, power punches mean serious business. Most boxers use the cross, hook, upper cut, and overhand punches, as well as the power punch that kickboxing calls its own—the spinning back fist. With all these punches, the power comes from the body—that way, you inflict more damage on your opponent. The body shifts its weight from the rear leg to the front as the upper body twists into the punch. With a lot of practice, you'll learn to relax enough to generate enough speed to land the punch harder on your target.

Note that power punches are slower than the jab, and that slower punches give your opponent a chance to get out of harm's way. However, when you land a power punch, you might just score big with a knockout.

However, there are the fighters that never go down. Hammerheads stay standing no matter how hard the beating; power punches don't daze them. Your only hope is to fight a glass jaw; he's easily knocked out.

Many kickboxers refuse to step foot in a weight room because they fear that weight training will overdevelop their muscles. Big bulk can interfere with the ability to throw an effective power punch. Don't fret if your opponent is a big one, he might have a wimpy power punch. It's the small fighters that may flatten you. Here's a hot tip: Get ready for the fight of your life.

The Cross

Next is the meat-and-potato punch—the cross, which is sometimes called a straight right. The cross works hand in hand with the jab: You'll throw a jab with the lead arm, and then fire the cross with the other hand. Try to follow a straight line from your shoulder to your opponent's face, aiming for the chin. However, keep in mind that you might want to aim for the body to take your opponent by surprise—most jabs and crosses are thrown to the face, so it can be to your advantage to do the unexpected.

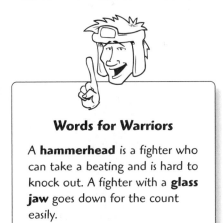

Kickboxing Buzz

The difference between a jab and a power punch is that a jab is fired with frequency in mind, using less energy and providing a higher connect percentage. The jab sets up the power punches. Power punches, on the other hand, need the weight of the body to generate force. Remember the kicks? Front leg kicks are similar to the jab—fired with speed and frequency in mind. Back legs kicks, like power punches, supply the power.

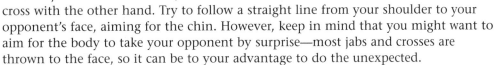

Words for Warriors

A **hammerhead** is a fighter who can take a beating and is hard to knock out. A fighter with a **glass jaw** goes down for the count easily.

Here's what you need to do to set up a cross:

1. Assume the fighter's stance.

2. Shift the right side of your upper body forward; the left side swivels back. Extend your right arm toward the target, pivoting on the ball of your rear foot. Drive your weight from the rear leg to the front leg. As the right shoulder rotates forward, snap the right fist out to the target in a horizontal motion. Warning! Don't overextend the elbow.

3. Recoil your arm, and resume the fighter's stance.

The following figures illustrate the cross punch.

Follow these steps to make a connection with the cross.

Kickboxing Buzz

Most fighters will go down after a hook—this punch is slyly powerful. Use it well, and aim for the chin or the side of the jaw for a knockout.

The Hook

The hook is a tough punch to master. Once you get the feel for this punch, though, it will become your most powerful weapon. Rumor has it that the hook causes more knockouts than any other punch. Hook to the chin for a knockout; to wear down your opponent, fire repeated hooks to the body. Execute the hook from your front and rear hand.

Because you'll probably feel awkward at first, let's break down the motion of the hook:

1. Assume the fighter's stance.

2. Bring right shoulder forward.

3. As you fire, bring the left arm to a 90-degree horizontal angle, so that your elbow faces away from your body. Make sure your arm stays up

equal to your shoulder. Hand positions may vary, depending on your training. Some coaches want you to keep the palm of the fist facing the ground, whereas others tell you to turn the knuckles toward the body. Both are correct—just find a hand position that's comfortable for you. Pivot on the front foot; your weight will shift to the front leg. Pull the right shoulder back as you punch. Aim for the chin. Strike with the palm toward your body.

4. Recoil arm to resume the fighter's stance.

The following figures illustrate the hook motions.

Hook 'em with these five steps.

Try the following prep drill to perfect your hook. Move your arm and twist your torso back and forth, keeping your arm at head level. Stop the motion when your fist goes just past your own nose. Now, pivot on your front foot to produce some power behind your hook. Don't swing your elbow back to get a head start—this mistake weakens your punch.

The Overhand Punch

The overhand punch (also called the overhand right or the go-to punch) is a variation of the cross punch. This punch works when no other punch does. Kickboxers, often skilled fighters, know how to block most things that are thrown or kicked at them, but the overhand can angle past most blocks. Bam! You score. Try the overhand punch to weaken your opponent's defense. Think about the cross; it's fired in a straight line to the face. The overhand punch, though, curves in a slight looping motion, rather than straight to the face as you fire. Aim for the side of the jaw or the temple to get the most Bam!

Here's what you need to do to land an overhand punch:

1. Assume the fighter's stance.

2. As you fire, the right shoulder twists forward and the left shoulder pulls back. Instead of firing the fist in a straight line, fire in a slight looping motion, the palm of the hand facing down.

3. The punch slides over and down to land on target. Recoil arm and resume the fighter's stance.

The following figures illustrate the overhand punch motions.

Your opponent won't overlook the overhand if you follow these steps.

The Uppercut

Bloody chins—and perhaps even a knockout—are often the result of an uppercut that lands on target. The uppercut, as its name implies, strikes upward—very sneaky, indeed. You'll use it at close range, and either hand will do. When is the best time to uppercut? Whenever you can!

Assume the fighter's stance, and then follow these steps to execute an uppercut:

1. Bend at the knees, keeping your hands by your cheeks. Put your left side forward.

2. Fire the right fist straight up, like a body builder's bicep pose, palm facing you. The fist connects with either the body or the sweet spot (the chin).

3. Lower your arm to resume the fighter's stance.

The following figures illustrate the uppercut.

If he's in your face, serve up the uppercut with these steps.

The Spinning Back Fist

If this one lands, only one word can describe the aftermath—splat! The spinning back fist is, by far, the most powerful and coolest punch to land—and it's a kickboxing creation. Your size doesn't matter. If you land it, you're guaranteed a knockout. Here is a word of caution, though: Use this punch only when you know for sure you'll land it. If not, you're left off balance, and you've just given your opponent the edge.

Kick-Tales

The spinning back fist was a signature technique of a Women's World Kickboxing Champion, Kathy Long. Let's hear it for the girls!

Here's what you need to do to throw a spinning back fist:

1. Assume the fighter's stance, and then turn backward, leading with your right shoulder. As your body spins, whip your right arm out in a horizontal position. The fist should be vertical.

2. Strike with the back part of your hand.

3. After the strike, you'll finish with the opposite side (your right side) forward. Recoil the arm to resume the fighter's stance.

The following figures illustrate the motions for the spinning back fist.

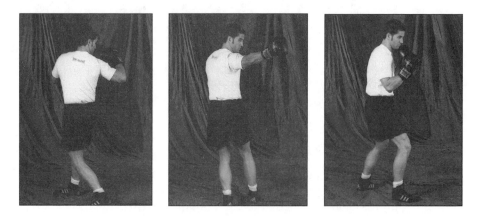

Here's the "Ultimate"; learn the spinning back fist in three steps.

Don't give your opponent a free shot; it's best to land on target. To be effective, memorize the targets in this table. In the ring and on the street, good technique never fails. Pick from The Good and The Bad columns. The least effective targets make up The Ugly column.

Punches and Targets

Punches	The Good	The Bad	The Ugly
Jab	Face	Chest	Side head
Cross	Face, chest, stomach	Side head, groin	
Hook	Side head, kidney	Face	Chest, stomach
Uppercut	Face, stomach	Chest	
Overhand	Face	Side, head	
Spinning	Side, head	Face	
Elbows	Face		

The Outlaw: Your Elbow

You never use an elbow strike in competition—it is illegal (except in Thailand). But you may use it in your kickboxing workout; and in a self-defense situation, it's your best choice. If kicks are your long-range weapons and punches are your medium-range weapons, your elbows (and knees) are your close-range weapons.

Your elbow makes a good weapon because the striking surface is the hard, bony part of the elbow. Also, because your elbow is unprotected, when you hit your target it's usually bone against bone. Your hands are protected by boxing gloves; when an elbow hits the eye, cheekbones, or the bridge of the nose, on the other hand, these delicate areas will immediately rip open and bleed. And because the elbow is thrown with a lot of power at close range, you can seriously disfigure your opponent. That's why elbow strikes are illegal in competition. Keep in mind that elbow strikes are just like punches—snapped in and out to the target to create a concussion effect.

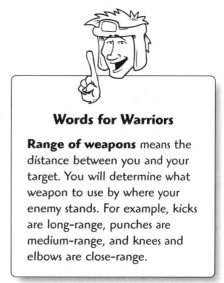

Words for Warriors

Range of weapons means the distance between you and your target. You will determine what weapon to use by where your enemy stands. For example, kicks are long-range, punches are medium-range, and knees and elbows are close-range.

Warning Warriors

In a self-defense situation, you don't want to hit with the back of your hand; the bones can easily break without the protection of a boxing glove. Instead, use the heel of your hand.

There are many different ways to throw an elbow, but the two most common techniques are the rear and front elbow strikes. Here's the motion for the front elbow strike:

1. Raise the left elbow into a horizontal position, with your hand close to your shoulder. (Note that the front elbow strike is thrown just like a hook. Don't make a fist, though, because a closed fist will tighten the forearm muscles and make the strike slower.)

2. Snap the left shoulder forward with the left elbow in the lead. As the elbow hits the target, retract the arm back to the home-base position.

The following figures illustrate the motions for the front elbow strike.

Fire the elbow strike with these two steps.

To throw a rear elbow strike, perform these motions:

1. Twist the upper body forward, with your right shoulder leading the way. As the right shoulder is coming forward, raise the right arm into the horizontal position. The right hand will be close to the right shoulder; do not clench the hand into a fist, leave it relaxed.

2. As the arm snaps forward, the elbow extends out and hits the target. After it lands on the target, snap your elbow back.

The following figures illustrate the motions for the rear elbow strike.

Don't let your opponent grab you from behind; fire a rear elbow strike in two steps.

The Least You Need to Know

➤ Use your first two knuckles to punch, and don't make a fist too tight; otherwise, your knuckles will turn white.

➤ You're working both the upper body and the lower body when you fire a punch.

➤ Left-hand throwers are called southpaws. They will stand with their right legs forward. Right-hand throwers will stand with their left feet forward, which is sometimes called an orthodox stance.

➤ There are six punches: jab, cross, hook, uppercut, overhand punch, and kick-boxing's own spinning back fist.

➤ Elbow strikes are close-range weapons that are illegal in competition except in Thailand.

Chapter 6

Hands Up, Chin Down

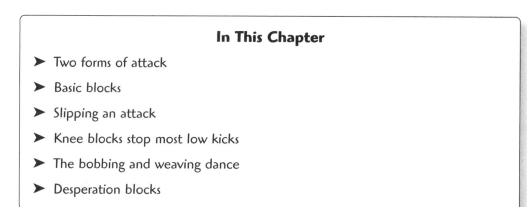

In This Chapter

➤ Two forms of attack

➤ Basic blocks

➤ Slipping an attack

➤ Knee blocks stop most low kicks

➤ The bobbing and weaving dance

➤ Desperation blocks

Do you want to get hit in the face? Okay, dumb question. After all, nobody wants to be used as a human punching bag. In this chapter, you'll learn how to be a moving target. And there's no bigger accomplishment than learning how to avoid being hit.

You'll learn how to block the other guy's weapons—punches, kicks, and knee and elbow strikes. For you young warriors who are eagerly waiting to get into the ring, learning defensive moves is naturally the next step. But what about everyone else? Even if you never step into the ring, learning how to block a punch will pay off.

If you can't be hit, you won't get hurt. Here's your chance to learn how to block—perhaps getting out of harm's way. What you'll also notice is that by adding some basic blocking moves, your legs, arms, and brain will work in unison. Up to this point, you've just learned how to kick, punch, and strike. These are offensive moves. Now, you'll learn defensive moves.

Put 'Em Up

Blocking means intercepting an attack. Sometimes, you can't get away from the other guy's weapons fast enough, so you'll have to learn how to take some punches. A block is just a way to cover up to avoid serious damage to your body.

Kick-Tales

"The lost art of defense" came about as the fight game, and especially kickboxing, turned into a more aggressive type of fight. An all-offensive sort of "do or die" philosophy emerged—strike, and strike hard enough to take your opponent down. That's our philosophy! We have always been a big believer in the saying "it is better to give than to receive," but to have the ability to block or—better yet—to make your opponent miss makes good fighting sense.

Do you remember the fighter's stance? Your hands are at home base, in a vertical position—like you're throwing daggers—and your elbows are tight against your ribs for protection. Keep your knuckles even with your chin. As you'll see, there's a very good reason for this stance; when a punch closes in, you can easily lift your hands to let your gloves—rather than your chin—absorb the impact. Tuck your chin toward your chest as you turn your face slightly away. Again, the gloved back portion of the hand takes on the punch.

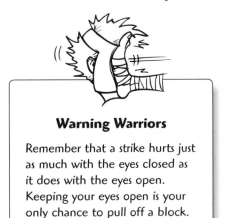

Warning Warriors

Remember that a strike hurts just as much with the eyes closed as it does with the eyes open. Keeping your eyes open is your only chance to pull off a block.

Blocking tools vary depending on your opponent's strikes. You'll use any part of the body that can take a beating: forearms, elbows, hands, and knees. As backup, you can also block with your shoulders or shins. After a while, you won't feel the blows; these areas become desensitized over time. Also, you may hurt your opponent as he strikes you because these areas become powerful weapons as you become a better kickboxer.

"Do I want to get kicked in the head or do I want to raise my arms and take it on the forearm?" You're probably thinking … "neither." But you have to choose, and you have to make that decision in a split second. Opt for the forearm instead of a kick to the head. Yes, it will hurt, but not as much as a blow to the head or—worse—getting knocked out cold. You're choosing the lesser of two evils. And while we're on the subject, blocking with your head, or even your stomach or thighs, is never a good idea.

As you have probably concluded, blocking may not be the best form of defense. When you only have a split second to decide, though, blocks may be your only option. You'll be a better blocker if you commit a few things to memory: Your left hand protects the left side of the body, and your right hand defends the right side of your body; your elbows and forearms will protect each side of your torso, so keep them snug against your body; and don't cross your hands, or you leave yourself vulnerable to an attack. Attacks come from two angles—slashes and stabs.

Slashes

Your opponent, if he's a smart fighter, will try to attack you from all levels and hit your most vulnerable areas. For example, he will probably launch an attack to the head or to the stomach. When a strike nears, it will land in either a *slashing* or *stabbing* motion.

Think about the sport of fencing. When Zorro slashes his indelible *Z* in the body of his enemy, he is making a slashing motion. A slash, then, is anything that resembles a side-to-side motion. A hook to the chin and a round kick to the stomach are good examples of a slashing strike. Other slashing moves, although rare unless you're an expert kickboxer, are the overhand punch, spinning back fist, and elbow strike.

Words for Warriors

A **slash** is anything that resembles a side-to-side motion, whereas a **stab** comes straight at you.

Stabs

Again, think about Zorro. He carves a *Z*, and then takes his sword and thrusts it into his enemy's body. That's an example of a stab. A stab attack will come straight at you and mostly target the upper body and head. A jab or cross to the face or a side kick to the chest are examples of stabs.

Super Blocks: Catching and Parrying

A good fighter's goal is to take his opponent out. He'll do just about anything—attack your body or, worse, launch a strike to your head, which is your most vulnerable target. That's why you have to learn how to defend yourself. You don't want someone else to use your head for target practice. We've already talked about a basic block. Let's look at two other ways to block: catching and parrying.

In the orthodox fighter's stance, your left side is forward. For catching and parrying, you'll block your opponent's left-hand punch with your right arm, and vice versa.

The Catch

To *catch* an attack, imagine that the punching fist is a fast-pitched baseball nearing your head. Focus on that ball at all times. When it approaches, *catch* it with your rear hand. At the same time, your upper body leans slightly back as you shift your body weight to your rear leg. You can catch any punch, regardless of whether it is a stab or slash.

Parry

A *parry* deflects the strike rather than catching it; you can use either hand to parry a strike. Parrying a strike makes better sense because you'll end up in a better position for a counter attack. You'll parry stabs, such as jabs and crosses.

Picture this: You're in the orthodox fighter's stance. A jab to the head comes from your opponent's left hand. You will use your right hand to parry the jab. First, open up your fist, inside your boxing glove. As the right hand swats the punch away from your face, quickly turn your right shoulder forward to add power. With your body weight behind the parry, deflecting the punch away from your face makes it easier. Here's the scary part: Don't reach out for the punch. You have to let the punch come to you and then sweep your glove across your face, only from ear to ear so you can quickly return to the fighter's stance.

Words for Warriors

A **catch** stops the motion of the attack, whereas the **parry** deflects the attack.

For the cross you'll parry the same way, but you're now switching blocking arms. Remember, a cross to the cheek will come from your opponent's right hand, so you'll twist your left shoulder forward and use your left hand to block. Use your forearms or elbows instead of the palms of your hands.

Block a Slash

Slashes, hooks, and round kicks are easier to block. To block a right-hand hook, for example, you'll use your left hand to deflect the punch. As the hook approaches, keep your hands in a vertical position and turn your body slightly forward. For balance, keep your shoulders square. You'll raise your left arm. If the hook sails in the direction of your head, rotate your shoulder and raise your hand so either your hand or forearm absorbs the punch. If, however, the left hook comes for your ribs, rotate your right shoulder forward and leave your hands in the vertical position. The hook should hit the upper arm.

Let's say that your opponent throws a rear leg round kick to your head. To block the left side of the head from a slashing attack, step forward with the left leg and raise the forearm to intercept the blow (see the following figure, left). As you step forward, slightly turn the left side forward, and keep your head down.

The difference between the right and left blocks is that with the left block you step into the kick and turn your right shoulder forward until your body is square. Then, you raise the right arm up to meet the kick (see the following figure, right).

Blocking a right round-house kick (left) and a left round kick (right).

Lifetime Warranty

Long-range weapons can inflict some painful results; for example, a side kick to your stomach could leave you hovering in your corner. That's why it's a good idea to learn how to block them, and block them well.

You already know that kicks are going to land in either a slash or stab motion, and that your arms block punches and some kicks. But if you want a 100-percent guaranteed block against low-level kicks, use your knee. To stop a kick dead in its tracks, place your knee in the path of the attack. Don't worry, you won't injure your knee; in fact, a bent knee makes a very hard weapon. Don't be surprised if you hurt your opponent, though. Use your knees to block both slashes and stabs. To block any attack, shift your weight to the rear leg and raise your front leg slightly. As the kick comes at you, raise and turn your knee into the kick, ideally allowing the strike to land on the top part of the knee. You'll use your knee to block low kicks and body shots.

To block slashes and stabs, shift your body weight back and raise the knee.

Stare That Punch Down

It's time to learn how to duck and slip those punches, which is also called bobbing and weaving. Most of your opponents are head hunters, meaning that they will aim for your head 80 percent of the time. The fight game is very similar to a game of chess: The better you get, the more you can figure out where that punch is going to end up and get away from harm. And that's your goal, to "slip an attack." How? Stare that punch down, focus on its landing, and then make it miss.

Duck an Attack

Making your opponent miss is truly an art; it's easier to duck. Slashing attacks are often ducked. You may be thinking, "Come on, I can duck." You probably can; how-

ever, if you don't learn how to duck correctly, you'll end up in a vulnerable position. For example, your opponent's knee or elbow might make contact with your face. Ducking, and especially ducking kicks, can leave you open for an attack unless you know how to do it.

You want to remember two things. First, keep your hands up by your head when ducking. This way, if you misjudge the strike, your hands can block it (see the following figure). Second, if your first instinct is to bend forward at the waist, resist it. Bending down can throw you off balance, leaving you in position for a counter strike; worse, you may end up with a knee in your face. Instead, bend at the knees while keeping your chest up. Squat down as far as needed to avoid the strike.

Warning Warriors

Learning how to slip and duck is scary because you've got to let the punch come to you. Don't worry, though. Ultimately, you're going to learn to slip that punch.

When your opponent throws a punch, squat down, keeping your back relatively straight. Now you can quickly pop back up to the fighting position to throw counter shots.

Slip an Attack

If you turn your body at a slight angle, you can avoid most strikes—slip an attack. However, this technique takes a lot of time to learn. The fighter who masters the art of slipping will wear down his opponent faster in the ring, thus winning the fight. And of course, if you can slip a punch, you can escape harm. The three slips are broken down by angles: back, left, and right slips.

Kickboxing Buzz

Sure, blocking a strike is easy, but it's not always your best form of defense. Rather, make a "miss." You shouldn't want to get hit at all.

All you do for the back slip is take a step back with the rear foot and shift the weight to the back leg (see the following figure). Turn the upper body so that your back slightly faces your opponent. Raise your left shoulder to add some extra protection for the chin. After the punch retracts, follow it by shifting your weight to both your legs. Get back into the fighting position to launch a counterattack.

As your opponent throws a punch, take a step back and turn your shoulders. You can back slip any punch just by stepping out of range.

You'll use the right slip for jabs, crosses, and overhand punches. As your opponent throws a jab, step forward with the left leg into the punch (see the following figure). At the same time, bring your left shoulder completely forward so your left side faces forward. Shift your weight to the front leg and dip your left shoulder down to avoid the punch. After the punch is thrown, step back into the fighter's stance to launch a counterattack.

For the right slip, you'll have to step into the punch. If you don't, your opponent has an opportunity to throw another punch.

For the left slip, you step slightly to the left and forward so you have a little extra room to clear the punch (see the following figure). Naturally, your weight shifts to the left leg as your right shoulder twists and dips forward. The punch will go over the right shoulder. After the punch is thrown, step back into the fighter's stance to launch a counterattack. Try to launch a counterattack after you have blocked or slipped a strike—that's when your opponent will be most vulnerable. Even if you miss the counterattack, your opponent will back off from his pursuit, giving you an opportunity to regroup.

For the left slip, step slightly to the left and forward so you have a little extra room to clear the punch.

The Full Contact Dance

To duck or slip strikes, you'll shift your weight from one leg to another. This motion connects the duck, the slip, and the block. In other words, you'll move from technique to technique by weaving or rolling to avoid those punches that near your head.

This shifting of weight helps put a groove into your defensive technique. The following figure shows the full contact dance.

The full contact dance: Slipping the left jab; weaving into the next slip; slipping the right cross; ducking the left hook; weaving back into a fighter's stance; blocking the right roundhouse to the head.

Drills: Bob, Weave, and Counter

There area few different ways to practice the bob and weave. You've got two choices here: You can practice with a partner or you can practice the art of slipping by yourself. Either way, you'll do the drills for 2 minutes, and then take a 45-second rest. Shoot for five rounds. Even though these are just drills, remind yourself that you're eye to eye with your opponent—keep your head up and squat down using your knees rather than bending over at the waist.

With a Partner

The following figure illustrates our first drill: a series of punches and slips.

From top left: Slip the left jab; counter with the right uppercut; slip the right cross. Bottom, l-r: Counter with the left hook; duck the left hook; counter with the right cross.

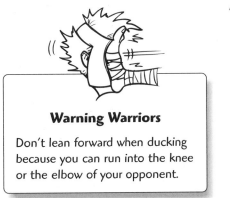

Warning Warriors

Don't lean forward when ducking because you can run into the knee or the elbow of your opponent.

Tie a Rope

For the second drill, stretch a rope across the center of the ring. You'll dip, come up, and step forward as you walk along the rope. As you duck under the rope, step forward and to the left (or right) with the left (or right) leg. Be sure to squat using the knees. Travel back and forth to train the brain and body to feel this movement. For variety, add a jab or an uppercut as you come up. Dipping and rising will add the driving power to your punches.

Desperation Blocks

Desperate times call for desperate measures. Let's say that you misjudged a strike, closed your eyes while a punch neared your face, or lost your balance after ducking a strike. Use the following desperate blocks—they're your last resort when nothing else works.

The Knee-to-Elbow Block

If you're not sure where the kick will hit, use the knee-to-elbow block (see the following figure). The good news is that this block protects a lot of area, from as low as the legs to as high as the head. However, it's extremely difficult to move and throw a counterattack from this position. This puts you at a disadvantage. Without movement after a block, you're vulnerable to other attacks.

As the kick closes in, raise the left knee up to the left elbow. Your left hand moves up to the top of your head, making a straight line.

Double Arm Block to the Head

Use this block only as your very last resort. For example, if your opponent throws punch after punch to your head, use the double arm block. It's also a good choice if you're confused as to what defensive block to use. What makes this block successful is that as the punch lands on the arms, you can move to one side or the other to get out of range of other strikes—you've just bought yourself some time. You have to be careful, though. This block automatically leaves you open for an attack, and it will temporarily blind you from seeing your opponent's next move (see the following figure).

Kickboxing Buzz

As deadly as knee and elbow strikes are, they are equally good to block the other guy's blows. Protect yourself by using your elbows and your knees. They'll likely inflict some severe damage to your opponent.

Drop your chin and raise both arms, keeping them vertical. The arms should be about 3 or 4 inches apart, and your hands should be touching your forehead.

The Reinforced Block

If your opponent has a powerful roundhouse kick, use this block. You'll have to cross your hands, but only for this block.

By crossing your hands, one on top of the other, you can reinforce the block (see the following figure). Be careful! Because your arms are crossed, you're leaving the right side of your body open for an attack. That's why you should move right back into the fighter's stance after executing this block.

Raise the left arm to intercept the kick, and place the right arm beside the left to reinforce the block.

The Clinch

Although the clinch, or bear hug, is technically not a block, it is a desperate defensive move, good to learn in case you're ever in a bind. With the clinch, you'll grab hold and pull your opponent close to you (see the following figure). You'll want to tie up his hands by grabbing him. By keeping him close, you're getting out of kicking range, which enables you to execute close-range weapons (such as a knee strike). In the clinch, you risk getting hit, so be careful. But because you are so close, he can't hit you hard, and you can push him off balance.

With the clinch, you'll grab hold and pull your opponent close to you. Try to tie up his hands by grabbing him.

The Least You Need to Know

➤ Slashes and stabs are two types of attack.

➤ If you do not learn how to block, you will probably get hurt.

➤ Knee blocks stop most kicks.

➤ Slipping and ducking help you avoid a strike, making your opponent miss you altogether.

➤ The bobbing and weaving dance connects one technique to another.

➤ You can count on desperation blocks to get you out of a jam.

Chapter 7

"Float Like A Butterfly, Sting Like a Bee"

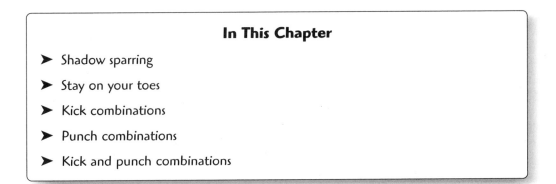

In This Chapter

➤ Shadow sparring

➤ Stay on your toes

➤ Kick combinations

➤ Punch combinations

➤ Kick and punch combinations

Many martial arts imitate the fighting styles of animals: The long-legged crane is graceful, the tiger is powerful, and the leopard symbolizes speed. Yet you never hear about the elephant, and for good reason. Although graceful in its own way, this massive animal will likely be heavy on his toes—like dead weight. That's not the way to a victory in the ring; you have to stay light on your feet.

Movement will be one of your strongest points both in the ring and out, especially if you want a good workout. The master fighter, Muhammad Ali, kept light on his toes as he waited for the perfect opportunity to strike. This led his coach, Bundi, to coin the phrase, "Float like a butterfly, sting like a bee."

You're probably not at a point where you're moving from kick to punch to strike with such grace, but you're about to learn. The next step is shadow sparring. You, too, will master the fight dance. With this skill, you can create your own unique style of kickboxing.

The Fighter's Dance: Shadow Sparring

Shadow sparring is an imaginary fight between you and an invisible opponent. Although he is invisible, you'll put together a series of kicks, punches, and strikes to outmaneuver him. Shadow sparring, then, strings together everything you have learned up to this point: kicks, punches, strikes, and blocks.

There are four good reasons to learn to shadow spar:

1. Shadow sparring will help you develop your own flow and rhythm between combinations.

2. Shadow sparring warms up the body for a workout or fight. You start sparring slowly, and then you increase the intensity.

3. Shadow sparring prepares you mentally for the ring or the street. For example, as you practice combination after combination, these combos become second nature to you. In the ring, you might automatically recall a combo and fire it off. You'll have an advantage over your opponent if you can effectively throw a series of combinations. On the street, these combos just may save your life some day.

4. These combos are a great workout, especially if you're not planning to step into the ring.

Words for Warriors

Shadow sparring, sometimes referred to as **shadow boxing,** means putting together technique after technique: kicks, punches, strikes, and blocks. Shadow sparring is the blueprint to your kickboxing; it can be used both offensively and defensively.

Getting started is not easy, but we're going to help you. The hard part is stringing together combinations—and we have done that for you. As your kickboxing improves, you can create your own moves to invent your own flow and style of kickboxing. Remember, all you're doing is what you have already learned:

Jab and cross

Jab, cross, and front kick

Jab, cross, front kick, and slip

Notice the pattern in between each technique—that's shadow sparring. It's that easy.

Yes, you'll probably feel silly sparring in front of a mirror, but that's how you'll improve as a kickboxer. Maybe this scenario will help: As a child, did you have an imaginary friend? Well, imagine that now he is your enemy. Shadow spar with him in the mirror. If you really can't get into sparring by yourself, have your trainer or a friend stand in front of you.

Make sure you shadow spar for two to three minutes at a time—the actual length of a kickboxing round. And, depending on your conditioning level, you'll want to spar for three to five rounds. Remember, sparring is a warmup and workout. The pace should start easy, and then pick up to simulate a real fighting tempo. You'll be slightly winded when you finish.

The nice thing about shadow sparring is that you can do it anywhere; for example, if you can't find a gym on the road, why not shadow spar?

Kick-Tales

Japanese martial artists put together a series of blocks, punches, and kicks to use against an imaginary opponent. This formal exercise was designed to refine their fighting form. *Kata*, the Japanese word for "form," is still practiced in traditional martial arts. Shadow sparring is an updated form of kata.

Footwork: Stay on Your Toes

Now that you know the basics—kicks, punches, strikes, and blocks—you'll learn how to put them together. As you advance in this sport, you'll always return to the basics, so it's important to establish a good foundation to build on. Shadow sparring helps, but following are a few more lessons in movement to help you successfully build combinations. Good movement is key: If you have good movement, your opponent can chase you, but he may never catch you.

Get used to staying on the balls of your feet. If you lean back into your heels, you'll lose your balance. Watch a boxer: He dances on his toes, never on his heels.

You'll also have to learn how to pivot correctly. All punches and kicks use the pivot for mobility and power. In addition, pivoting helps you move from technique to technique. To pivot, rotate on the ball of the lead foot, and squat slightly as the rear foot turns behind you. Your stance, orthodox or southpaw, doesn't matter—pivoting works the same both ways (see the following figures).

Use the pivot for mobility: Square off (left), and then pivot on the ball of your lead leg (right).

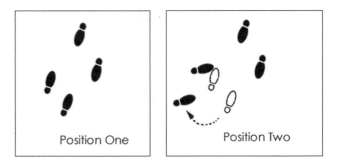

Position One   Position Two

Shuffling is another way to move. You'll use shuffling to get close to your opponent, as well as to escape from him. Shuffling is nothing more than a *step-drag*. In your fighter's stance, turn your front by pushing off the rear foot. Both feet should glide forward on the floor, sort of like a one and two step. You can also shuffle back and side to side.

To get close to your opponent, or to escape from him, shuffle forward (left) and then drag the foot from behind (right).

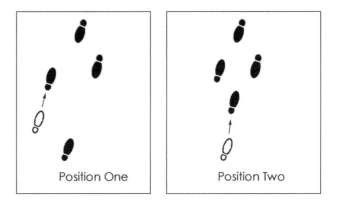

Position One   Position Two

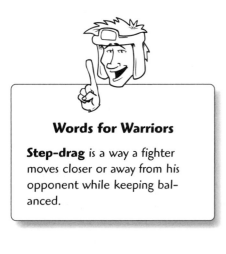

Words for Warriors

Step-drag is a way a fighter moves closer or away from his opponent while keeping balanced.

Before you try these combinations, take a look at how your body moves. Practice shuffling, pivoting, and balancing on your toes. Start with a single kick, such as a left leg front kick. Kick several times in a row and watch how your body snaps back into the fighter's stance. Remember to keep your arms up and your eyes on your opponent at all times.

You may even try some walking drills to focus on perfecting one technique at a time. For example, throw a right side kick, moving with it, and then throw another right side kick. You can travel the length of a room or gym, and then turn and use the opposite leg to go back. The same concept applies to punches. Fire a series of jabs into the air, followed by crosses. After you feel comfortable with each technique, you can string them together. Add some movement and a little shadow sparring, and soon you, too, will move like Muhammad Ali.

Put Your Best Foot Forward

Kicks can inflict some serious damage if executed correctly. To put you in the proper mindset, pretend that your hands are tied, preferably near your ribs—you definitely don't want to give your imaginary opponent an open target! Your legs are now your only weapon. Use these combos to practice kick after kick. Again, you'll sharpen your kicking skills and develop your own flow.

We list several combos in this section, but there's no reason you cannot develop your own. Experiment! If you develop a combination that works for you, keep it. The key to successful training is creativity.

If you're a beginner, don't rush learning good technique; practice makes perfect, you know. Remember the formula for good kicks:

> Good Technique + Speed = Power

Start by kicking low. Your target is the lower half of the body: calf, knee, and thigh. Repeat each kick until you feel comfortable enough to advance to the more difficult kicks. Hold off on the combinations until you feel steady with your balance. Don't forget the process: Fire a kick, do a little dance, and get back into your fighter's stance.

The combinations discussed in the following sections are the real thing, so commit the motions to memory (and memorize their nicknames):

> Front leg front kick (front kick)
>
> Rear leg front kick (offensive front)
>
> Front leg round kick (round kick)
>
> Rear leg round kick (roundhouse)
>
> Side kick (side kick)
>
> Turning back kick (turn kick)

Sequence of Attacks

You're in the offensive mode; now develop your attack sequences. Kicks can be thrown high or low. An example of a high target is the head, and low targets range from the calf to the abdomen. You can work your way up the body or down, and you can drive a punch or kick to the left or right side of the body. You can also strike to the abdomen and then hit a really low target, such as the calf. You've got two goals: to find weaknesses in the other guy's defense, and to keep him busy by blocking the blast of attacks. Wear him down, and create an opportunity for a knockout. That's why combos are used—to keep everyone guessing where the next strike will land.

Varying your targets is just as important while you're working out as while you're fighting. Besides kicking high and low, you'll want to throw kicks from both legs—which will help you burn many calories.

Kickboxing Buzz

No one wants to get hit. Your opponent will bob, weave, catch, or parry so you can't land a strike. To increase your chances of connecting with your opponent, throw a variety of kicks and punches at all levels and angles. Your goal is to keep him guessing where the next strike will land. In the process, maybe you'll catch him off guard and knock him out.

Kick Combo #1: Offensive Front Kick-Round Kick

The offensive front kick is a low-level kick. Fire it to the chest to knock the wind out of your opponent. Then, back that kick up with a round kick, either to the head or thigh.

Here's what you need to practice:

1. Assume the fighter's stance.
2. Turn the body square and throw the offensive front kick. Remember, offensive kicks fire from the back leg.
3. Retract the leg back to the starting position.
4. Turn the body sideways and launch the round kick.
5. Set the foot down at the completion of the kick. Make sure that your hands are up at home base.

The following sequence of figures illustrates the offensive front leg round kick.

Offensive front kick is thrown to the midsection. Get back into the fighting position, and then launch a round kick.

Kick Combo #2: Front Kick-Roundhouse

Most beginning combos will start with the front kick because it's a fast-moving kick and easy to learn. Use it to strike the stomach or thigh to stop or shake up your opponent. After that, fire the more powerful roundhouse. You can strike anywhere with this kick: body, head, or legs.

Here's a step-by-step breakdown of this combo:

1. Assume the fighter's stance.

2. Lift the knee and execute a front kick.

3. Retract the leg back and set it down in the fighting position.

4. Draw up the rear leg into a fold and follow the right shoulder with the rest of the right side of the body.

5. Bring the right leg up to a horizontal position and fire the roundhouse.

6. Bring the kick back to the fold, and then set the foot down.

Kick Combo #3: Side Kick-Turn Kick

The side kick can leave your opponent off balance if it is thrown with good technique. You'll land with your back facing him, so you can fire a turn kick while he's unsteady. Aim for the chest or stomach.

Here's a step-by-step breakdown of this combo:

1. Assume the fighter's stance.

2. Start with a side kick. Fold the lead leg into the fold for the side kick and fire it at the target.

3. After you land and recoil the kick, you'll end up with your back to the target, which is a perfect opportunity for a turn kick.

4. Continue the turning motion and shoot the turn kick.

5. After you hit the target, set the foot down and get back into the fighting position, with the opposite side forward.

Kickboxing Buzz

Most beginner kicking combinations start with the front leg kick; it can be thrown quickly and doesn't require much balance. The front kick is the safest kick to execute.

Kick Combo #4: Front Kick-Round Kick

Throw the kicks in this combination with the same leg. With the front kick, aim for the stomach or thigh. The round kick usually lands to the side of the head. You're now ready to drive a punch, if you haven't taken your opponent down.

Here's a step-by-step breakdown of this combo:

1. Assume the perfect fighter's stance.
2. Use the lead leg to throw the front kick.
3. Your body will end up in square shoulder stance. As soon as your foot touches the ground, shift your left side forward.
4. Throw the round kick.
5. Set the foot down and resume the fighter's stance.

Kick Combo #5: Low Roundhouse-High Roundhouse

This combo is the power KO (knockout)! Start with a roundhouse to the thigh—a stunning kick, especially as it lands. Shift your body forward and throw a right leg roundhouse low to the thigh (see the following figures). Remember that your opposite side is forward after executing the roundhouse. Don't stop there: Follow that kick with a left leg roundhouse to the head for the knockout.

Launch a powerful roundhouse to the thigh to stun your opponent. After setting the right foot down, throw a left roundhouse to the head.

Kick Combo #6: Roundhouse-Side Kick

Experienced kickboxers can detect a roundhouse almost immediately as it's fired. More than likely, most fighters will deliver a countermove. That's when you launch a side kick to the stomach or chest—they'll never see it coming.

Here's a step-by-step breakdown of the roundhouse-side kick combo:

1. Assume the fighter's stance.

2. Launch a roundhouse to a high target.

3. After the kick is executed and the foot is set down, your opposite side is forward in the fighter's stance, so roll the hip over and fire a side kick. Both these kicks are thrown with the same leg.

The Old One-Two

Want to throw some great punches? Put these combos into action—you'll perfect your punching skills, get a great workout, learn to protect yourself, and burn mega-calories in the meantime. It's pretty easy to block a jab, but when you throw a jab, cross, and hook in rapid-fire succession, you're taken seriously. Always think about your opponent. One punch probably will not faze him, but several blows may daze him.

As was mentioned before, just because we've listed a few combos in this section doesn't mean that you can't make up your own. We all have our favorite punches. Put a few combos of your own together to give you an advantage over your opponent.

To learn these combos, start by putting two punches together. Then add a third, and then a fourth punch to increase the difficulty. No matter what gym you choose to train in, you'll see these combos time and time again, even in the cardio classes. In the end, there aren't any shortcuts, just practice, practice, practice. Like kicks, punches have nicknames; with punches, though, it's a numbering system. Each punch has a specific number, 1 through 6. This numbering system makes it easier for a trainer to call the combos:

Kickboxing Buzz

Want a recipe for speed and power? Try firing a jab, and then follow up with a right cross.

>   Jab = 1
>
>   Cross = 2
>
>   Hook = 3
>
>   Uppercut = 4
>
>   Overhand = 5
>
>   Spinning back fist = 6

1-2 Combo: Jab-Cross

Most combinations will start with a jab-cross; it's the building block for most other combinations.

Quickly strike out your lead arm (left), and then cross with the other hand.

1-2-3 Combo: Jab-Cross-Hook

By adding the hook, you have another chance to hit your opponent, especially if he blocked the 1 and 2 shots. Try the hook if your opponent blocks the straight punches of 1-2 combo. Launch the hook after the cross recoils.

1-2-3-4 Combo: Jab-Cross-Hook-Uppercut

The 1-2-3-4 combo is a perfect mix of speed, power, and a variety of angles of attack. Run with the uppercut when your opponent blocks the jab, slips the cross, and ducks the hook.

1-4 Combo: Jab-Uppercut

Use this combo if your opponent constantly ducks your punches.

You throw a jab, which your opponent ducks (left); launch an uppercut to the ducked head (right).

1-4-3 Combo: Jab-Uppercut-Hook

If your opponent blocks the uppercut, then you have no choice but to fire another headshot. So add the hook.

If your opponent blocks the uppercut, his head will probably be forced up, leaving it open for another head punch. Now, blast him with a hook.

1-4-3-2 Combo: Jab-Uppercut-Hook-Cross

All these power-packed punches should finish off your opponent.

After the first three techniques are thrown, the cross follows with a lot of power.

When throwing all these power shots, keep in mind that all of them may not be thrown at full power. Use the first three punches for speed.

1-5 Combo: Jab-Overhand

This is another simple but very sneaky combo. Your opponent will be expecting a cross after your fire a jab. Instead, throw an overhand to daze him.

Throw a jab to the head (left). Then comes the sneaky part: Your opponent will be expecting another 1-2, but you'll throw an overhand right instead of the cross (right).

1-5-3 Combo: Jab-Overhand-Body Hook

This combo not only changes the angles of attack, but the levels of attack as well.

When you fire a jab-overhead punch, your opponent will bring his hands up high to protect himself against the punches (left). Bend deep at the knees, placing your head at your opponent's chest level. Then deliver a hook to the unprotected body (right).

1-5-3-2 Combo: Jab-Overhand-Body Hook-Cross

A cross will secure the knockout after the hook to the body weakens your opponent.

A powerful set of moves to "off" your opponent. This is the same as 1-5-3 combo, but after the body hook, you'll straighten up your legs slightly and launch a cross at your opponent's face.

1-6 Combo: Jab-Spinning Back Fist

It's powerful and it gets the job done—the jab-spinning back fist.

Throw a jab; it will get blocked (left). Spin through with the spinning back fist. If you land it, you'll most likely be looking at an unconscious opponent (right).

1-6-2 Combo: Jab-Spinning Back Fist-Cross

The spinning back fist may leave you unsteady, but the pay off will be worth the trouble.

When your opponent either ducks or backs up to avoid the spinning back fist, follow through with an opposite side cross.

Dynamic Duos

We would all probably agree that ballerinas are graceful. So are kickboxers. Okay, maybe not in the tutu-plié sense, but we dance. For us, grace and beauty come in the form of combining kicks and punches.

Blending kicks and punches is tough. That's why you should start with a few combos, perfect them, and then master the more difficult ones. Try to throw these combos without thinking about them. Get the idea? You'll want to move from side to side and back and forth, mix punches and kicks, use power and speed, and kick low and high. Clearly, you'll have an advantage, either against a kickboxer in the ring or a thug on the street, if you can develop a flow while you kick-punch-kick. The more combinations you have memorized, the harder your technique is to block.

The list of kicking and punching combinations is endless. The following list will help you get started. Notice that you'll start with just two techniques. Practice them for a while; then, continue on to the three- and four-move combinations. Start in the fighter's stance, with your left foot forward.

Combo 1: Jab-Roundhouse

This combo is a basic set-up to most power moves. So start with the steps below:

1. Assume the fighter's stance.
2. Step forward with lead leg and throw the jab.
3. As the jab recoils, bring the rear shoulder and leg forward to launch a round-house.
4. Place the kicking leg down in the new lead position; the opposite leg is now forward. Resume the fighter's stance.

After you set the kicking leg down in the lead, perform the following jab-cross motions for more punch:

1. Throw a right hand jab.
2. Follow up with a left cross.

Combo 2: Jab-Round Kick

This combo if often called a probing or setup combo because both techniques move lighting fast.

1. Assume the fighter's stance.
2. Take a short step forward and throw the jab. You need to take a short step in order to set up for the front leg round kick.
3. As the jab recoils, fire a front leg round kick to the target.
4. Recoil the kick and place the leg down in fighter's stance.

As the kick recoils, consider adding another jab, and a cross:

1. Start forward with a jab, and then throw a cross.
2. Return your hand to the fighting position.

Combo 3: Jab-Cross-Rear Knee Strike

As you fire a jab and cross, your opponent will draw his hands up to block. That gives you the perfect chance to fire a rear knee strike to an unprotected midsection.

1. Assume the fighter's stance.

2. Step forward and throw the jab and cross.

3. Grab your opponent and fire a rear knee strike. Set the leg down to fighter's stance.

After knocking the wind out of your opponent, throw a round kick to knock him out cold.

Combo 4: Jab-Side Kick

The jab draws your opponent's arm up high to block it. Now is a good time to fire a side kick to his unprotected ribs.

1. Assume the fighter's stance.

2. Step forward and throw a jab.

3. As the jab recoils, turn the body sideways and fire a side kick out and back to fighter's stance.

You can round off this combo with a turn kick. As the side kick leg sets down, pivot backward and launch the turn back kick. Set the kicking leg down with the new side forward. Resume fighter's stance.

Kickboxing Buzz

Use the 1-2-round kick combo. Besides being our favorite, it takes your opponent by surprise. More than likely, your opponent will back away from the 1-2, not realizing that they put their body in perfect range for the front leg round kick.

Combo 5: Front Kick-Jab-Cross

This combo is the most basic of all combos. But, start here with these steps to build your combo arsenal.

1. Assume the fighter's stance.

2. Execute a front kick.

3. Set the kicking leg down and fire a jab, followed by a cross.

For good measure, consider closing with a hook and roundhouse:

1. Add a hook to follow the cross.

2. As the hook recoils, bring the rear leg forward to drive the roundhouse.

3. Set the kicking leg down in front to a fighter's stance. Your opposite side is now forward.

Combo 11: Round Kick–Jab–Cross–Rear Leg Front Kick

Your opponent will quickly tire from blocking all these speed and power shots. Change up the angle of attack, and you might pop him one that he can't block.

1. Assume the fighter's stance.

2. Fire the front round kick.

3. As you set the leg down, throw a jab, followed by a cross.

4. After the cross recoils, execute a rear leg front kick; then resume the fighter's stance.

The Least You Need to Know

➤ Shadow sparring involves stringing together techniques.

➤ You should shadow spar for 2 to 3 minutes per round. Depending on your conditioning, strive for three to five rounds.

➤ Kicking combinations give you an awesome workout. By changing the levels of attack, you get your body moving and grooving.

➤ Drive your punches to the left or right side of the body to tire your opponent.

➤ Mix power shots with speed punches to surprise your opponent.

Part 3
It's Time to Sweat

Has pushing the pedals on the Stairmaster become a bore? Running more of a chore? Weights—no more! It's time to put some sweat-drenching bliss back into your workout.

We've written this part with two goals in mind: to give you a heart-pounding workout at home and to prepare you for your workouts in the gym. We'll show you how to be your own coach and tell you why kickboxing is a total body workout. You'll master throwing a punch and executing a deadly kick, as well as learn how to slough off the unwanted pounds and avoid kickboxing injuries.

Chapter 8

Be Your Own Coach

In This Chapter

➤ Your target heart rate

➤ Setting goals for your workout

➤ Working the bags

➤ Finding a sparring partner

➤ Watching out for common kickboxing injuries

Do you really need a trainer? That depends on you. Having a personal trainer will help you improve your techniques faster, and will probably motivate you to work out. But maybe you don't have the time, or maybe you have a crazy schedule and can't get to the gym. So why not train yourself?

You've got the basics, now all you need is self-motivation. We want you to be able to train yourself. You need to know how to take your heart rate, and you need an understanding of some of the common injuries. We're going to tell you how to set goals for yourself and work the bags. If you find a partner, you'll be able to train at home with focus mitts and kicking shields. If you have a coach, he'll be so impressed to learn that you're working without him!

Survival of the Fittest

How are you going to reach your fitness goals by kickboxing? We think that you will be more committed to accomplishing your goals if you know what to do. So, before we get started with the exercises, please take the four following simple assessment tests. If testing yourself is not appealing, another option is to be tested by a personal trainer; most health clubs offer this service for free. The results of these tests provide you with a starting point.

Test 1: Sizing Up Your Body

Invest in a cheap tape measure and measure the circumference of your arms, waist, and legs. Jot down the numbers:

Left arm: _____

Right arm: _____

Waist: _____

Left leg: _____

Right leg: _____

Test 2: See What's Shaking

Now, jump up and down and observe what wiggles. Your goal is to tighten anything that moves, so write down what shakes:

_____ .

_____

_____

Test 3: Work Up Some Sweat

Walk one mile as quickly as possible, but without running. Listen to how your body feels. If, for example, you're breathing heavy and dripping with sweat, consider exercising at a beginner level. On the other hand, if you're hardly breathing, you can add more intensity to your workout. Write down your time:

_____

Muscular endurance involves using your muscles repeatedly over a set period of time. Do as many sit-ups as you can in one minute; this part of the test measures muscular endurance of the abdominal muscle group. Good, strong abdominals can diminish lower-back problems. Following is an elbow-to-knee method for doing sit-ups:

1. Lie on your back, and bend your knees; your heels should be flat on the floor.

2. Touch your elbows to your knees.

3. Return to a lying position.

Test 4: Testing Your Flex

This test is helpful in determining your hip and back flexibility. A good full range of motions can help you with your kicks and prevent lower back pain. Just touch your toes and hold. Keep your knees as straight as possible. Record two things: How far can you reach? How many seconds can you remain in that position? Give yourself three trials.

Your goal is to improve from these tests, so the results of these tests can help you establish fitness goals for yourself. Kickboxing will help you improve in all four areas, after only a month or so of exercising. For example, let's say that your goal is to squeeze into a pair of pants, perhaps a pair that you haven't worn since college. These workouts will help. Five days of exercise, working at an intensity of 50 to 80 percent for 30 to 60 minutes each time is a standard exercise plan for weight loss.

Set a six-week review. Test yourself again. Can you fit into those pants? Did you make your goals, or do you need to change your program? You'll make your goals only by challenging yourself with every workout.

Count Down: Heart Rate

We have one word of caution: There are times when your body tells you how hard you should be working (for example, when you're tired). Use the perceived exertion scale to determine how hard to work. First time kickers use muscles that haven't been used before; they may tire quickly. For example, let's say that you're in great shape, a marathon runner. However, because you're using a different set of muscles, you feel like you're working at level 9. In actuality, you're probably working at level 6. The fact that you're in great shape doesn't mean that you should keep working. Rather, you should listen to your body. That's why perceived exertion is a good indicator of what your body is capable of doing. In other words, when you're tired, you may not be able to work as hard.

Use the intensity Borg scale, or perceived exertion scale to monitor your own intensity level while working out. Your goal is to work out between levels 7 and 8, which correspond to intensity levels of 70 percent and 80 percent of maximum heart rate, respectively. So, to put it another way, your goal is to sweat. If you're not sweating, increase the intensity. For those of you who are just starting, work at a lower intensity, for example level 5 or 6, but intermittently push yourself to level 7.

Perceived Exertion Scale

0	Bed rest
1	Watching television
2	Getting up to make popcorn
3	Slow walk
4	Walk
5	Brisk walk, breathing is slightly elevated

continues

continued

Perceived Exertion Scale	
6	Light exercise
7	Vigorous exercise
8	Very vigorous exercise
9	Intense exercise
10	All out exercise

Going Solo

You don't have anyone to work out with? Not a problem—work the bag. Bag work is a major part of your kickboxing workout, and you can easily do it anytime and anywhere. All you need is a bag—you can buy a free-standing bag for your living room—a pair of gloves, and enough oomph to hit it … hard.

Warning Warriors

You should visit your own medical doctor and get a complete check-up before starting any exercise program. Check your blood pressure, get a complete blood work up (including cholesterol report), and a complete stress test. You need to feel comfortable and relaxed about exercising, especially if you're just beginning.

There are tons of ways to work the bag, but the easiest is to do it in rounds. Yes, you'll be a fighter for an hour. Set your timer for two minutes, which is the length of a kickboxing round. Hit the bag continuously for two minutes. Take a minute's rest in between rounds. Within the hour, shoot for five rounds.

To add variety to your solo workout, you can alternate bag work with sit-ups, squats, lunges, and so on. The workouts will go something like this:

1. Hit the heavy bag for two minutes.

2. Do sit-ups for one minute. Or, run in place, and do lunges or squats. (Beginners might want to just walk around, and then go back to another punching round.)

3. Start to add kicking rounds as the session goes on.

4. Mix up your punches and kicks. Beginners might want to hold off mixing techniques until you feel comfortable with your technique. The idea is to mix it up so that you don't get bored.

At first, try to throw about five jabs, five crosses, five hooks, and so forth. Then add your kicks. Make sure that you come back to your fighter's stance every time. Regain your balance before firing another shot; then, recycle the same punches. In doing so, you will build your strength, endurance, balance, and eventually speed.

Vary your shots between speed and power: Tap the bag with some punches, and then add some wallop for the power shots. Don't forget to use your entire body. Call out your work for every round; for example, you might want to call round one "jab with speed work," round two "cross with power," and so on—you get the idea. Mix up the basics with counts of five; then, add more work as you advance.

Bag work is important for two reasons. First, it provides resistance. If you're just striking the air, you have no resistance. Like weight training, the bag causes you to work harder because of the resistance. Second, hitting the bag gives you the feeling that you're hitting a live target.

Put your favorite music on and dance—just like Ali—as you punch. It's not always about how hard you hit the bag. Instead, focus on staying light on your feet, and on using your entire body to work on speed, timing, and centering the body after every perfect punch. You'll use your legs and arms while moving, burning more calories than you would on a treadmill.

When you hit the bag, you always win. Had a bad day? Hit the bag to release the tensions of the day. It will give you a feeling of power and accomplishment, even when things are not going so great in other areas of your life.

Target Practice

The saying "Practice makes perfect" is never truer than in developing kickboxing training skills. But to succeed, you also need patience—you won't kick like Bruce Lee after a few sessions. It takes time to perfect your moves.

Warning Warriors

Beginners, you might want to start with three 2-minute rounds and work yourself up, round by round, as you become more comfortable with your technique, endurance, and strength. You won't believe how long two minutes can feel when you're working out.

Kickboxing Buzz

By returning to the fighting position after every shot, you're training your mind and body to automatically resume a protective position.

Let's review: You've learned several combinations. You probably have not mastered them yet, and that's okay. Now you'll use those combinations with equipment. You'll have to find a willing partner, someone who will hold a kicking shield as you kick and the focus mitts as you punch. Have anyone in mind? Don't worry, partners! There's plenty of padding to protect you. If you're practicing solo, try these combos on the bags. That's the beauty of this sport; you always have a partner—yourself.

What will you be striking? Sometimes you just strike, hoping that your weapon will land somewhere, but there *are* designated vulnerable targets that you want to aim for (see the following figure). Visualize these targets as you hit: Obviously, the nose is a sweet spot; so are the eyes and the chin. You also want to strike to the stomach and the top of the thighs. In a self-defense situation, shoot for the groin.

Mitt Poses

Mitt poses are different combinations, which your trainer will set up. He'll don a pair of focus mitts, sometimes called pancakes, to help you develop your boxing skills and get a killer workout. He'll call out combos while holding the pancakes at different angles, and you'll have to throw a series of punches and combinations.

Words for Warriors

Focus mitts are sometimes called **pancakes,** and your coach will hold them as you punch the mitts. You've got to listen up for the **numbers** because coaches won't call a punch by its name.

As a designated holder, you should know how to hold the mitts. Some trainers prefer to use a slapping motion to meet the punches; others move toward the punches as you aim for the mitts. Either way is correct. Experiment and find the system that is most comfortable for you.

Before using the punching combos, you want to review the six punches. Do you remember the numbers that represent these punches? If not, make a cheat sheet and memorize them. As you think of the different combos, call them out by their designated numbers. For example, call out a jab/cross combo as a 1-2. After all, that's what your trainer or partner will say: "Give me a 1-2." The following figures show some of the punches from a right-handed fighter's perspective.

Human body target practice: rating the target areas.

The jab can be thrown either to the left or right mitt, whatever the trainer calls—so be prepared. Make sure the mitt that you want to hit faces the kickboxer as the punch lands.

The cross will always be thrown to the right mitt. The mitt should face the kickboxer as the punch lands.

The hook hits the left mitt. Turn the mitt sideways, to almost a 90-degree angle from the mitt angle of the cross. You want the punch to land squarely on the mitt.

With the uppercut, aim for the right mitt if you're throwing an uppercut off the back leg. Turn the mitt down to meet the uppercut squarely.

For the overhand right, hold the mitt pose as you would with the cross; just tilt the mitt slightly upward.

Be careful! The spinning back fist is fast and powerful; you may want to double up the focus mitts for reinforcement against the blow. The blow itself will land on the left mitt. Hold the left mitt high and across the head, by the right side of the face. The right mitt will be placed behind the left one for reinforcement.

Kicking Shields

Your coach will hold a large rectangular shaped pad, known as a kicking shield, to help you practice your kicks. You'll have to move with your coach as he moves with the pad. He'll call kicks high and low, and at different angles, to help you improve your technique and build power.

Warning Warriors

Holding the mitts can be very hard on the elbows and tendons, especially if you're training more than one person a day. The secret to reducing this stress on the arms is to learn use the mitts correctly. When the punches come toward the pancakes, be sure to move the mitts slightly toward the punches and meet them.

Coaches, keep in mind that the power of a kickboxer's kicks improves along with his technique; you might become a little uncomfortable absorbing these blows, regardless of the thickness of the pad. Try to find a good fit—a kicking shield with enough padding.

The key to avoid getting beat up while holding the kicking shield is to flow *with* the energy of the kick, not *against* it. In other words, as the kick lands, move in the same direction. It's important to give some resistance, but don't absorb the full power of the kick.

Let's take a look at the front, side, and turning back kicks (see the following figure). These kicks are all lumped together because they land on the shield at the same angle: straight on. Hold the shield tight to the center of the body and lean forward on the front leg. As the kick hits the shield, let the force of the kick rock your weight to the back leg. This motion will help diffuse the force of the kick.

The front kick (left), side kick (center), and turn kick (right) land on the shield straight on.

Round Kicks

Remember that the round kick lands to the sides of the body, head, or legs. Or, to put it another way, the round kick is a slashing attack to the side of the body. You'll still hold the shield close to the body, but at a slight side angle. If the round kick nears the right of your body, step slightly to the left as the kick lands.

The left round kick is for the brave and dedicated coach only. Holding shields, in general, is a task for the tough ones, because getting kicked with a roundhouse really hurts. Hold the shield firmly against your hip with the long part of the shield covering the whole thigh, down to just below the knee. Turn the pad toward the angle of the attack.

Words for Warriors

The **kicking shield** is a rectangular pad that takes some abuse from your legs. A very skilled coach knows how to hold this pad correctly so you can effectively practices your kicks.

Coaches beware! Roundhouse kicks can hurt.

117

Behold: The Dreaded Leg Kick

The dreaded leg kick is another kick to watch out for. Be sure to lean the pad against the lead leg. As the leg kick comes toward the pad, shift your weight to the rear leg and lift your front leg into the pad. When the kick lands, it will hit the lifted leg and pad, and the energy of the kick will dissipate without the trainer having to take it fully on the leg. Proper positioning of the shield is very important in order for the trainer to give both the proper angle of attack for the kick and to protect from injury (see the following figure).

The dreaded leg kick is another kick coaches should not underestimate.

Thai Pads

With Thai pads you'll be able to practice both your kicks and punches; in addition, you can practice your elbow and knee strikes.

Thai pads, not to be confused with focus mitts, slip over the hands and forearms for better protection from wild shots. Because of the extra protection, you'll have more targets to strike. You'll be moving into the kick or punch, much as you did with focus mitts. But now you'll step with your entire body, rather than just your hands. By stepping with your entire body, you'll avoid injuring or straining the tendons in your forearm.

Warning Warriors

Don't practice the turning back kick on the Thai pads.

For a clue as to how to hold the Thai pads, think back to the two different attacks: slashes and stabs. For example, for the round kicks (which are slashes), you'll hold the Thai pads together in a vertical position at the level you want the kick to come. As the kick approaches, turn your body sideways. For the front and side kicks (stabs), on the other hand, you'll hold the Thai pads together in a horizontal position at stomach level. Keep the pads in front of the body.

Now we're going to is practice a few combos using coaching lingo. For example, a jab-front leg round kick-jab-cross combo is shortened to a 1-kick-1-2.

Combo #1: 1-Round Kick–1-2

Because of the different angles of attack, you'll work the pads at all angles. To get warmed up, start here:

1. Assume the fighter's stance. Catch the jab with the right pad.
2. Bring the pads together vertically and turn the body to the right to absorb the left round kick.
3. Catch the jab with the right pad.
4. Catch the cross with the right pad.

The following figure shows the motions in sequence.

Working the pads takes practice. This combo makes you use the pads at different angles.

Combo #2: 1-2-3-Roundhouse

This combo has both power and speed. Make sure you're ready to receive these blows.

1. Assume the fighter's stance.
2. Catch the jab with the right pad.

3. Catch the cross with the right pad.

4. Catch the hook with the left pad.

5. Step back with the left foot, turn the body to the left, and bring the pads together vertically to absorb the roundhouse.

Combo #3: Front Kick-Round Kick-1-2

Be careful! After the front kick is executed, you have to turn your body to the side to absorb the shock from the left round kick.

1. Assume the fighter's stance.

2. Cross the pads horizontally in front of your body to receive the front kick.

3. Turn the body to the right, holding the pads together vertically to absorb the left round kick.

4. Catch the jab with the right pad.

5. Catch the cross with the right pad.

Combo #4: 1-2-Straight Knee Strike-Round Kick

Don't forget to double pad-up for the knee strike. Then you'll get the pads back in position for the round kick.

1. Assume the fighter's stance.

2. Catch the jab with the right pad vertical.

3. Catch the cross with the right pad vertical.

4. Stack the pads in a crossing pattern, with the pads facing the floor. The doubled-up pads help to absorb the blow of the knee strike.

5. Bring the pads up together and hold them vertically to absorb the left round kick.

Battling Burnout

As your own coach, you need to know the signs of burnout. No matter what kind of exercise program you choose, at some point you'll experience minor setbacks; you can quickly burn out if you don't change your program. Kickboxing is no exception. After all, throwing kick after kick, punch after punch can get boring.

Vary your program. Try to find a fun partner to practice your kicks and punches. Or, a coach can make it fun for you by yelling out different combos, making you do more sit-ups, and laughing with you as you try to perfect your punches. You may want to try sparring, or check out a cardio-kickboxing class. And use the bags; hitting something that won't hit you back is the best part.

Set weekly goals for yourself. Treat yourself to a new outfit or a piece of cheesecake that you've been craving—but only if you reach your goals.

RICE It!

Hate injuries? Feeling that you're missing out on all the fun—not to mention getting out of shape—as you wait for your injury to heal? You're not alone. You need to stay focused on the big picture, though—don't let minor setbacks stop you from achieving your goal.

Beware of overtraining; kickboxing is a high-intensity workout. As a beginner, you may do too much, too soon, too often. Let a day go by after your workout so your body can rest. Otherwise, you may be tired—too tired to work out. That's a hint that you may be doing too much. You might want to take some time off or switch to a lower-intensity workout—especially if you're dreading your workouts. If you don't heed your body's warnings, you might set yourself up for more serious injuries such as sprains, tendonitis, and fractures.

Don't ignore your pain; you can recover sooner if you admit that you're hurt. Then allow enough time to recuperate. Get used to hot water soaks and massages for aching muscles, and ice bags for minor pains—these are popular remedies to the common kickboxing woes. And don't forget about RICE. No, not white rice, but the treatment RICE:

➤ **Rest**—*Rest* as soon as you feel the pain or notice the injury. You may aggravate a minor injury by ignoring the pain—especially if you are a beginner.

➤ **Ice**—*Ice* an injury as soon as possible. In fact, you'll never go wrong by putting ice on an injury. A pack of ice can decrease the swelling and reduce the pain. Intermittently apply ice for 72 hours, never keeping the ice bag on for longer than 20 minutes (so your circulation can return). It's probably not a good idea to put ice directly on your injury, so wrap a towel around the ice pack.

➤ **Compression**—*Compression* can also help to reduce the swelling by stopping the blood from flowing to the injury. Buy an elastic wrap, such as an Ace bandage, to wrap your injury. Be sure not to wrap too tightly. Leave it on for 30 minutes, and then loosen it for a few minutes before tightening again.

➤ **Elevation**—*Elevate* your injury whenever possible. Let's say that you feel a little pain in your wrist. Prop your hand up on a pillow, above your heart. Again, this will stop the blood from gathering around the injury. Also try to elevate your injury while sleeping.

Warning Warriors

If you're dreading your workout or feeling too tired to work out, you may be overtraining. Listen to your body. Take some time off or switch to a lower-intensity workout.

121

RICE is the most common way to treat an injury. If you have any doubts, go see your doctor. Acting quickly will get you back to working out sooner.

My Aching ...

As fitness warriors, you should be aware of some the more common injuries of kickboxing. Kickboxing is not typically a brutal sport, unless you're battling it out in the ring. However, you may occasionally suffer from a foot, hand, or wrist injury. If you're careful while you train, you can avoid getting hurt, but it happens to the best of us.

Warning Warriors

Striking positions for your kicks are the heel of the foot, the shin, and the ball of the foot. Don't forget; otherwise, you risk banging your toes while working out.

... Toes

Be careful when kicking—your toes are vulnerable to bending all kinds of ways. Knowing the striking positions of the foot will help protect your toes. Mat shoes can keep you from bruising or jamming the toe joints. You'll know immediately if your toes are bruised— you'll shriek with pain as you try to put on your shoes. Although torturous, bruised toes don't have to slow you down too much. After all, you can still throw punches. More serious foot injuries are fractures and breaks. If you even suspect that you have a fracture or break, go see your doctor.

... Knuckles

It's ironic that the most delicate part of your body is used to punch. No, that doesn't make much sense ... just blame it on boxing. In any case, you'll wear padded gloves to protect your hands. And, of course, a good hand-wrapping will cut down on hand injuries. Your knuckles may be sore, at first. Soak your hands in a bowl of ice water to reduce the pain. You may also want to invest in a small piece of foam rubber for extra padding. Place the foam rubber on the curve of your knuckles, and then wrap your hands as usual.

... Wrists

A good wrap job should cut down on wrist injuries. There are two types of injuries to look out for: joint sprains and strained tendons. Don't let this injury drag on without visiting your doctor. To help prevent future wrist problems, you should tape your wrist with sports tape. Note that you can still work out—a hand injury shouldn't throw off your kicking game.

As your own coach, ask yourself, if you are just sore or really injured. Know that when you train hard, your body will throb. Work out those aches and pains, but know when to quit, especially if you're injured. Rest. Take care of weary muscles. Get yourself fighting-ready before you return for your next workout!

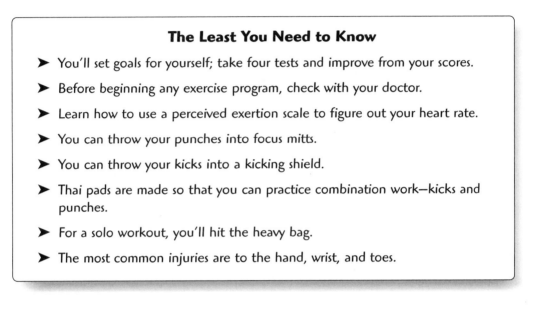

The Least You Need to Know

➤ You'll set goals for yourself; take four tests and improve from your scores.

➤ Before beginning any exercise program, check with your doctor.

➤ Learn how to use a perceived exertion scale to figure out your heart rate.

➤ You can throw your punches into focus mitts.

➤ You can throw your kicks into a kicking shield.

➤ Thai pads are made so that you can practice combination work—kicks and punches.

➤ For a solo workout, you'll hit the heavy bag.

➤ The most common injuries are to the hand, wrist, and toes.

Chapter 9

Head to Heel Like Steel

In This Chapter

➤ Weight training for the kickboxer

➤ Stretches for kickboxers

➤ Workout guidelines

➤ Ways in which kickboxers condition

➤ Balance work

Muscle burns fat! That's right—muscle burns more calories than fat, even in your downtime. Why? Because muscle requires more energy than fat. Kickboxing can give you more muscle, more speed, and more endurance while melting the fat away, transforming your common body into an one that resembles the body of a Greek god.

The exercises in this chapter will prepare you for your intense workouts—especially if you're a novice kickboxer. Workout warriors should kickbox two or three times a week. Also, think about adding some aerobic work to improve your cardiovascular endurance, or perhaps consider pumping iron to round out your weekly workouts. Regardless of whether you're going for total fitness or the world title, the goal is the same: to look like an Adonis while kicking butt.

Pushing Iron

Some kickboxers won't set foot in the weight room, whereas others swear that weight training improves their kickboxing. Regardless, pushing iron can balance your weekly workout routine. If you're a beginner, weights can help you get in shape for kickboxing, and perhaps even prevent injury.

When you begin to train, it's a good idea to pick a kickboxing gym that also has a weight room. This can save you time and money. If you don't find a gym with both, pick one that's close to your work or home. If your gym is convenient, you'll find fewer excuses for not working out.

Kickboxing Buzz

You'll condition your body in all levels of fitness: flexibility, muscle endurance, muscle strength, aerobic and anaerobic, coordination and balance, and speed of muscles.

Words for Warriors

What's the safest way to weight train? **Pyramiding.** Start with a light set of weights. Add more weight for your second set and so forth. Your muscles will thank you; they get a chance to warm up.

As you read about these exercises, notice that most of them can be done with dumbbells. This way, you can have a little variety in your training.

Beginning Your Training

Once you find a gym, you can begin your training. Keep in mind that you don't need to achieve maximum muscle size—no need to look like a body builder. Be careful, or you may sacrifice speed and mobility for a muscle-bound body. Instead, you want to build muscle stamina. Clearly, you've got to get those muscles ready to throw punches and kicks, over and over again.

You'll train all muscle groups in one weight training session, hence kickboxing's nickname: "The Full-Body Workout." In your training session, start with one or two sets, and then build up to three sets. The third set should be tough. Move fast in between your sets (60 to 90 seconds instead of the usual 90 to 120 seconds) to reap some aerobic and anaerobic benefits. Also, use a lighter set of weights for your first set, and then add more weight as the muscles warm up. This type of weight training is called *pyramiding*; it's the safest way to train.

Know Your Limits

How much should you lift? Unfortunately, choosing weights will require a trial-and-error type of attitude. There isn't one set weight for all muscle groups, and your strength will vary from one muscle group to another. Here's one way to choose your weight: Pick a weight, and then try to lift it two to four times. If, by the third rep, it is too heavy to lift, you've hit your working max. Use that information: To find your starting weight, take 80 percent of your working weight. You should have a spotter to help you, just in case the weight gets too heavy.

If you're just starting, lift a weight 10 times, with good form. That's one set. If you can easily lift that weight, you can safely move up in repetitions, or reps, to make a set of 12 or 15, depending on the exercise.

When should you lift? That depends on what kind of kickboxing you're going to do. For example, if you're planning to take one-on-one workouts twice a week, don't weight train the day after one of your workouts. Because weight training is also an intense workout, you'll want to do it only after a light-day workout. On the other hand, if you're cardio-kickboxing, you can weight train the next day. Weight training provides resistance. In your cardio class, although intense, you're only striking into the air; therefore, weight training can balance your weekly routine. Essentially, you need to alternate heavy and light day workouts so that you don't over train.

Be Careful!

There are hundreds of exercises to choose from; however, this isn't a weight-training book, so the exercises in this chapter will only help you get started.

You should be careful not to overtrain your muscles. For example, even though the weight work targets all muscle groups, kickboxers who are hitting the bags should omit the shoulder work—you'll get plenty of shoulder work when you throw punches, especially with the added resistance of the bags.

Don't hold your breath as you train. In fact, even in your kickboxing class, learning to breathe correctly will improve your moves. Typically, you want to exhale on the hard part, and inhale on the easy stuff, as you release. If you hold your breath, you risk feeling dizzy, and perhaps even passing out. This is part of the reason it's always a good idea to have someone train with you. (Other reasons include spotting and having fun!)

Work Your Muscles

The main punching muscles in your arms are your biceps, triceps, shoulder, and back muscles, so we'll focus on these. Of course, you also need strong leg muscles for your kicks, so we'll work the quads, hamstrings, and butt and calf muscles. Finally, you won't be able to punch or kick well if your core muscles—abdominals and back muscles—aren't strong, so we'll work these as well.

Kickboxing Buzz

If you consider yourself a cardio warrior, you should weight train your shoulders. This way, you're getting a resistance workout, too. Remember, though, that your goal is to put power in your punches, not to overdevelop or injure your muscles.

When working out, start with the large group of muscles and work down to the smaller ones. For example, you'll start with leg work, and then move on to your back, chest, shoulders, and arms. You should use full range of motion; in other words, slow down the exercises. This way, you'll put more tension on the working muscle by making it work harder, and you'll be able to control and create resistance through the up and down movements. Count 2 seconds as you lift up, and 4 seconds as you increase the resistance in the down move. Controlling your movements means never bouncing through them; without this control, you may injure yourself.

Upper Body Boost

Okay, motivated muscle head, you've got to get the upper body in shape for throwing a lot of punches—especially if you're a novice kickboxer.

The following exercises are standard. You'll start with your chest muscles or pectorals, but of course you also have to work the opposite set of muscles: the back muscles. Your largest muscle is your *latissimus dorsi*, which is a fancy term for the outer part of the back. Once you get to the back workout, you'll begin with all kinds of lat work. Kickboxers have great *lats;* training the whole back gives you overall strength and the stability required for throwing punches. After working the back, you'll go into your shoulder work or deltoids, and then you'll finish up with tricep and bicep work.

Barbell Flat Bench Press

To do thebarbell flat bench press, lie on your back with your shoulders about 5 or 6 inches away from the rack. For stability, place your feet on the ground. With an overhand grip, grab the bar; your hands should be a little more than shoulder-width apart. Lift the bar off the rack, making sure not to lock your elbows. Move the bar out so it's directly above your shoulders.

Bend your elbows and lower the bar to your chest; aim for the upper part of the chest. Then, push the bar up to the starting position. Don't arch your back as you push the bar up.

Flat bench press works all the chest muscles (pectorals), front of shoulders (anterior deltoids), *sides of torso* (serratus anterior), *and rear of arms* (triceps).

Barbell Incline Press

For the barbell incline press, sit down on the incline bench, straddling the seat. Set your feet firmly on the ground. With an overhand grip, place your hands slightly wider than your shoulders. Lift the bar off the rack and position it above your collarbone.

Keep your elbows back and slowly lower the bar down to your collarbone. Press the bar up to the starting position.

The incline bench press essentially works the chest muscles (pectorals), front of shoulders (*anterior deltoids*), sides of torso (*serratus anterior*), and rear of arms (triceps).

Warning Warriors

Lower your weight if you're bouncing the weight bar off your chest. Chances are that you're working with a weight that is too heavy, which could lead to all types of injuries. To protect yourself, don't arch your back; keep your spine neutral, always.

Dumbbell Press

For the dumbbell press, lie flat on a bench. Extend your arms up over your chest, moving the dumbbells in a triangular motion. They should almost come together, but not quite touch.

Lower your arms, leading with your elbows, toward your shoulders. The challenge is to keep the dumbbells even. Pause, and then press up to the starting point.

Dumbbell presses primarily work the chest muscles (pectorals) *and front of shoulders* (anterior deltoids).

Dumbbell Upright Row

For the dumbbell upright tow, stand with your feet hip-width apart. Make sure that your knees are not locked out and that your pelvis is in a neutral position. Hold the dumbbells in front of you, on your thighs. Your knuckles should face front.

Bend the elbows and lift the dumbbells to your collarbone. Pause, and then lower to the starting position.

129

Upright rows work the upper back (trapezius *and* rhomboids), *and front and middle of the shoulders* (anterior *and* medial deltoids).

Warning Warriors

If you're hitting the bags or sparring, working the shoulders with weights is not necessary. You get plenty of shoulder work just by punching. Cardio-kickboxers, however, should weight train their shoulders because their workout lacks resistance.

Dumbbell Reverse Fly

For the dumbbell reverse fly, sit on the edge of the bench with your knees bent. Lean forward so your chest touches your thighs. The dumbbells should rest in each hand, and your knuckles should face up. Place your arms in line with your shoulders. Keep your back and neck straight, and don't look up.

Lift your arms up to draw your shoulder blades together. Bring your arms up to your shoulders, with your knuckles still facing up. Pause, and then return to the starting position.

Dumbbell reverse fly works the upper back (trapezius *and* rhomboids), *and middle and rear of the shoulders* (medial *and* posterior deltoids).

Dumbbell Front Raise

For the dumbbell front raise exercise, stand with your feet hip-width apart. Make sure your knees are not locked out and your pelvis is in a neutral position. Hold the dumbbells in front of you, on your thighs; your knuckles should face front.

Lift your arms to the front in a count of four until they reach shoulder height. Pause, and then return to starting position.

Dumbbell front raise works the front of the shoulders (anterior deltoids).

One-Armed Dumbbell Rows

To perform one-armed dumbbell rows, kneel with your left knee on the bench and right foot on the floor. Your back is flat; your hips and shoulder are square. Place your left hand about 6 to 8 inches in front of your torso for support. The dumbbell is placed in your right hand. Hang your arm down in a straight line with your shoulder, with the knuckles facing front. You should feel a slight stretch. Look down at the bench so your neck stays aligned with your spine.

With your elbow leading the way, bring the dumbbell to your hip; rotate your knuckles out. Slowly lower the dumbbell to the starting position.

One-armed dumbbell rows work the middle back (latissimus dorsi *and* teres major) *and rear of the shoulder* (posterior deltoid).

131

Wide Grip Lat Pulldown

For the wide grip lat pulldown, sit down and place your legs under the leg restraint. Hold the lat machine bar with an overhand grip. The grip should be about shoulder-width apart to take the slack out of the cable. Keep the spine straight and the abdominals contracted.

Pull the lat bar down to the upper part of your chest, bending your elbows behind you. Pause. Then, slowly return to the starting position.

Lat pulldown primarily works the middle back (latissimus dorsi *and* teres major) *and rear of the shoulders* (posterior deltoids).

Close Grip Lat Pulldown

To execute the close grip lat pulldown, sit down and place your legs under the leg restraints. Hold the lat machine handle with a reverse grip, with your palms shoulder-width apart and facing you. Take the slack out of the cable.

Pull the bar down to the upper part of the chest, bending your elbows behind you. As you pull the bar down, slightly arch your back so that your chest sticks out slightly and your shoulder blades come together. Pause. Then, slowly return to your starting position.

Lat pulldown primarily works the middle back (latissimus dorsi *and* teres major) *and rear of the shoulders* (posterior deltoids).

Seated Row Machine

To use the seated row machine, sit down and grab the handles in a vertical position.

Pull the handles back, keeping your elbows out by your side. Let your elbows lead the way; keep your chest against the chest pad. Pause. Then, slowly return to the starting position.

Triceps Pushdown

For the triceps pushdown, stand facing the machine. Grab the handle with a narrow overhand grip; hold the bar at chest height, with your elbows bent. Keep your elbows close to the front of your body.

Warning Warriors

Don't forget to breathe on the hard part. Inhale on the easy work. *Never hold your breath!* If you have a red face, you may be holding your breath.

Extend your arms without locking the elbows. Keep your elbows glued to your rib cage as you lower the handle to the top of your upper thighs. Then, slowly return to the starting position.

Seated rows target the core back muscles (latissimus dorsi and teres majors).

Tricep pushdowns isolate the rear muscle in the upper arm (triceps).

Barbell Curl

Next is the barbell curl. While standing, grip the barbell with an underhand grip, keeping your arms hanging in line with your shoulders. Rest the barbell on the upper part of your thighs. Keep your legs shoulder-width apart and your toes straight ahead. Soften the knees.

Curl the barbell up toward your shoulders. Pause. Then, lower the barbell to the starting position.

Curls work the front of the upper arm (bicep).

Lower Body Blast

Split-second blows require strong legs. Power comes from speed. Focus on strengthening the muscles in your entire leg: quadriceps, hamstrings, calves, inner and outer thighs, and hip flexors. Most of these exercises will strengthen all parts of the leg, so you'll get a complete leg workout.

45-Degree Leg Press

For the the 45-degree leg press, place your feet on the sliding platform. Your feet should be about 12 inches apart and pointed straight ahead. Straighten your legs and release the brake of the sliding platform.

As you bend your knees to your chest, lower the weight as far as full range of motion will allow; you should resist the weight, using only your thighs and buttocks. Keep your back straight. Don't roll your shoulders forward. Pause, and then press the weight to the starting position without locking your the knees.

Warning Warriors

Attention all kickboxers: You won't be kickboxing five days a week, unless you're training for the big fight. Since kickboxing is such an intense workout, you should kickbox only two to three times a week. You should take a day off in between intense kickboxing workouts by doing a less intense workout.

The leg press works a few muscle groups: front of thighs (quadriceps), *rear of thighs* (hamstrings), *and the butt* (gluteus maximus).

Squats

Now for squats: Stand underneath the bar on a squat rack. Position the bar squarely on your upper back. Place your hands near the ends of the bar, and place your feet shoulder-width apart with your toes straight ahead. Straighten up and take a step or two back. Look straight out, head level, to keep focused.

Bend your knees, keeping your upper body upright. Maintain a normal curvature of the spine as the knees squat a little past a sitting position. Drive the weight up without bouncing. Straighten the legs to the starting position.

Squats do more for your butt than any other move. Squats target the butt (gluteus maximus), *the front of the thighs* (quadriceps), *and the rear of the thighs* (hamstrings).

Leg Extensions

For leg extensions, position yourself on the seat so the backs of your knees hang off the edge of the seat and the rollers rest in front of your ankles. Hold on to the handles on either side of the seat for upper body support.

Slowly straighten your legs and push the pad upward. At full extension, pause, and then slowly release to starting position.

Leg Curls

For legs curls, lie face down on the bench. Hook your heels under the pads of the machine. Hold the handles on either side to keep the upper body stable.

Flex your hamstrings and press your heels toward your butt, as full range of motion will allow. You don't want your hips to raise up as you curl. Pause, and then slowly lower to starting position.

Leg extensions target the front of the thighs (quadriceps).

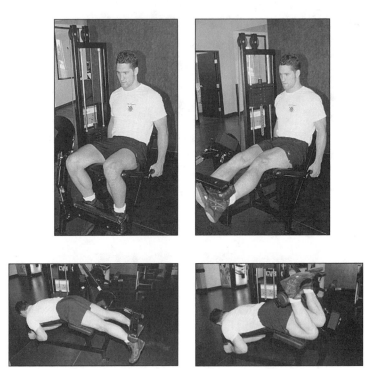

Leg curls hit the back of the legs (hamstrings).

Cardio Combat

Here's the secret ingredient that's been missing from your workouts: intensity. That's why kickboxing has literally replaced hundreds of aerobic classes and the boring cardio machines. You were getting bored and your body wasn't slimming down, right? Some of you might have even reached a plateau, meaning that your body hasn't changed in years. Now you've got to up the ante—that's why you need to kickbox. As much as we love kickboxing, though, we have to tell you that even with the cardio workouts, you should cross-train. You should add weight and flexibility work. Also keep in mind that kickboxing workouts are high-intensity workouts. In other words, you may want to cardio-kickbox three times a week, weight train twice a week, and do flexibility training another day.

As a kickboxer, you'll train in two modes—*aerobic* and *anaerobic*. Aerobic conditioning, as you may already know, calls for large muscle groups, such as those in the legs. You can usually go for a fairly long amount of time, depending on your endurance level. Most of the time, aerobic work will be rhythmic by nature: running, race walking, biking, aerobics classes, swimming, and all those cardio machines. And, of course, we can't forget cardio-kickboxing!

Such activities require large amounts of oxygen. The term *aerobic* simply means "with oxygen." Indeed, the higher the heart rate, the greater the amount of oxygen your body will need. With oxygen, you can work out longer, which is why this type of workout is called "endurance" training. Generally speaking, your heart rate shouldn't go over level 8 on the perceived exertion scale (which is discussed in Chapter 8, "Be Your Own Coach"; otherwise, you may go anaerobic. That's not necessarily a problem, except that your goal is to work out for longer periods of time, especially if you're shooting to reduce fat.

Anaerobic training, on the other hand, is explosive work such as sprints and jumps. Because the body works without oxygen, you can only go for short periods of time. Clearly, one is not better than the other; you need both types of training. Again, kickboxing wins because you condition in both modes.

Unless you're a fighter, you need to take a break from kickboxing. Beginners should start off kickboxing twice a week. Add some sort of aerobic work between your kickboxing workouts. There's no question about it; you need to let your body rest for one day before kickboxing again. But don't worry; even though you're not kickboxing, some type of cardio work can enhance your kickboxing and help you keep the fat off your body.

Workout warriors, go ahead and kickbox three times a week. But listen to your body. If you're tired all the time, maybe you're overtraining. Let your body rest between workouts. Or, cardio-kickbox once a week, and then train in kickboxing twice a week. You might also want to add some type of flexibility work to improve your kickboxing. Again, you probably don't want to add an intense weight training program the day after your kickboxing workout. Your workouts are for you. Stay challenged by doing it all, but don't hurt yourself.

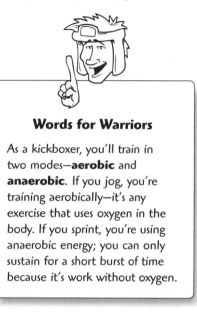

Words for Warriors

As a kickboxer, you'll train in two modes—**aerobic** and **anaerobic**. If you jog, you're training aerobically—it's any exercise that uses oxygen in the body. If you sprint, you're using anaerobic energy; you can only sustain for a short burst of time because it's work without oxygen.

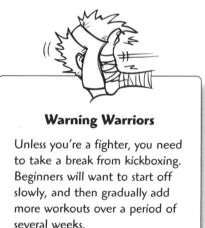

Warning Warriors

Unless you're a fighter, you need to take a break from kickboxing. Beginners will want to start off slowly, and then gradually add more workouts over a period of several weeks.

Stretch and Flex

Want to improve your kicks? You'll have to stretch. To increase flexibility, you've got to develop good range of motion in the hip joints. Why would you want to stretch? The more range of motion a joint has, the more speed it can generate when delivering a kick. Speed is the main ingredient in power. Therefore, as the range of motion in the joints increases, so do its speed and power.

Stretching before and after your workouts is a must. A good stretch after your workout is best because your muscles are warm, and they won't resist as much. You'll be doing *static stretching*, which is a slow and controlled stretch. In other words, no bouncing. Hold the stretch, and then gradually move deeper into the stretch to increase the range of motion. The goal is to feel a bit more than mild discomfort, but no sharp, burning pain. Hold the pose for 10 seconds, and then slowly relax. Repeat once, twice, or three times. Static stretching increases the flexibility of your kicks and can reduce muscle tension, prevent injury, and improve circulation.

You may want to consider a yoga or pilates class once or twice a week. In class, you'll work on improving your range of motion throughout your entire body.

The Russian split stretches your hamstrings and lower back. Let your partner spread your feet apart. Bend over and let your partner pull you as far as you can go; reach as far as you can between your legs and touch the ground.

For the Russian split solo, spread your feet apart. Bend over and reach as far as you can between your legs and touch the ground.

Words for Warriors

The **pilates method** was developed by Joseph H. Pilates in the early 1900s; it's a full body conditioning workout focusing on your core muscles. There are over 500 exercises that work to give you the best body and improve your posture and breathing.

The Russian split with a partner (left) and solo (right).

Max Muscle

Punch after kick, kick after punch—that's dynamic strength at its best. You've got to train your muscles to work over and over again. You really want muscle stamina, not brute strength. That's why most professional kickboxers will do hundreds of sit-ups, push-ups, and chin-ups—and so will you.

Balancing Act

Kickboxing takes a lot of balance. While kicking, you'll reduce your base of support to one foot. Beginners may feel a little too wobbly at first. But you can train yourself to find your balance, which is nothing more than keeping your center of gravity within your base of support. Think back to the day you learned how to ride a bike .... Maybe you still have the scars on your knees to remind you. Now, as you did then, you're going to train yourself to have a little balance.

With a little work, you can improve your balance. This will not only improve your kickboxing, but everything you do in life.

Stand on one leg. Close your eyes. Do you feel a little wobbly? Vision helps you to maintain your balance. That's one very good reason for you to keep your eyes on your target—so you don't fall over. Now stand on one leg, but keep your eyes open. Do you feel a little more stable? This type of balance is called static balance, meaning you're standing still.

Now, try a low kick. That's dynamic balance— you're moving. It's best to feel comfortable with both types of balance because you'll use them both in kickboxing. Eventually, as you kickbox, your balance will improve. But you may want to get a head start: Try standing on one leg, and then jump up. As you land, you're challenging your body to recall its center of gravity.

Are you ready to step into the ring? Hardly. But these exercises can enhance your kickboxing game. Remember kickboxing is an intense training workout. Along with kickboxing, you can train other ways, to meet your body goals. Experiment, and make working out a part of your life.

Kickboxing Buzz

Working the bag, a major part of your kickboxing workout, combines all levels of fitness: cardio work, power/strength, timing, balance, coordination, dynamic strength, and speed.

The Least You Need to Know

➤ As a kickboxer, you'll train in all areas of fitness: aerobic, anaerobic, dynamic strength, flexibility, coordination, and balance.

➤ Beginners should weight-train to prevent kickboxing injuries.

➤ If you want to cardio-kickbox only, weight-train the entire body.

➤ All kickboxers should cardio-condition.

➤ Don't kickbox more than three times per week.

Chapter 10

The Main Event: One-on-One Beginner Workouts

In This Chapter

➤ Your very first one-on-one workout

➤ Interval work

➤ Conditioning drills

Ever seen an overweight kickboxer? Probably not. There's a good reason for that: The workouts are intense and challenging. The one-on-one combines punches, kicks, jumping, and crunches into one powerful workout. In your workout, you'll be working up to a high-intensity level, and then recovering a lower intensity level, keeping your heart rate up the entire time. This way, fat doesn't have a chance to cling to your body.

Okay, so you're not a professional kickboxer, but you want a good all-body workout so you feel stronger and more powerful. You're not really interested in dance-like moves, and you don't have a bottomless pit of time. So why not train the one-on-one way? You'll start with the beginner work, and then move into intermediate. If you can find a partner, you can make contact with focus mitts and kicking shields; if you're solo, you can hit the bags. It's a great way to burn calories and tone your entire body.

Fat-Fight

In the ring, anything can happen. Fighters have to prepare their bodies for endurance, speed, strength, and abuse. Even though you're not popping into the ring, you can still train like a fighter!

Words for Warriors

Interval training is training that alternates between hard work and rest. You push yourself to your maximum—to the point of very heavy breathing—and then recover so you can talk, and then push yourself again, and then recover, and so on.

What does it take to toss a would-be-attacker to the ground, or to sprint away from harm? Energy—and lots of it. Because these movements require short bursts of power, they're anaerobic. (We touched upon this in Chapter 9, "Head to Heel Like Steel.") Anaerobic training means conditioning to a heart-pounding pant. While you aerobic train, on the other hand, you should be able to talk. In the one-on-one workout, you'll do both—this type of workout is based on *interval training*. You'll work to your max, and then recover, only to push yourself again. You'll train for about one hour, without stopping.

One reason interval work creates the lean and mean is that it demands so much more quick energy during the workout. This can help you to burn more fat in the "afterburn," which means that your body will continue to burn calories even after you're finished training.

Just Getting Through It: Beginners

Here's your first one-on-one. You're about to face off with us. We're going to challenge you physically, and probably mentally. Don't go through this workout thinking that you can't—you can. Just stick to the program. Unless you've been involved in other martial arts, you're starting as a beginner. Why? Because we're the coaches, and we said so! There's a silent rule in kickboxing: "Trust the coach—she knows what she's doing."

It doesn't matter if you're a marathon runner or an aerobics champion; in kickboxing, you'll use muscles that you swore you never had. It's a completely different workout than any other training. It's true, though, that if you're in good shape, the work will be easier. Regardless, follow this workout step by step and picture by picture. The format will be the same for all the one-on-ones.

You'll build from each workout; notice the progression chart at the end of the chapter. Don't jump ahead until you've mastered the moves from each workout. If you jump ahead, besides short circuiting your brain and body with too much information, you risk sacrificing good form; more importantly, you might injure yourself. You can always pick up speed as you become familiar with the workout and moves. That said, it's time to start—let's sweat.

Find a stopwatch. Set it for 2 minutes. That's your working interval. After you push yourself for a solid 2 minutes, you can take a 45-second to 1-minute rest. You have two options: You can either walk around or you can completely rest, depending on your current fitness level. If you are already conditioned, you can walk or run in place. Beginners, on the other hand, should use this time to get a drink of water. You need to be able to talk during your rest break. However, don't bend over at the waist to catch your breath. Instead, keep your head above your heart to bring your heart rate down.

As with all the workouts, you'll begin with a warmup. Notice that some of these warmups call for light weights such as dumbbells. At first, you may come up short because holding a set of 3-pound dumbbells takes a good deal of shoulder strength. Don't fret. If you get tired, drop the weights. Your goal, eventually, is to finish the 2 minutes with the weights in hand.

Put your hands together as if you're praying. It's time to flush out the stress from your brain and focus on your kickboxing. Then begin your one-on-one workout routine.

The main event at a glance:

1. Jump rope (5 minutes)
2. Rest for 45 seconds to 1 minute
3. Left foot side to side (2 minutes)
4. Rest for 45 seconds to 1 minute
5. Right foot side to side (2 minutes)
6. Rest for 45 seconds to 1 minute
7. Standing mountain climbers (2 minutes)
8. Rest for 45 seconds to 1 minute
9. Stretch
10. Ab work (20 reps)

Then technique learning and review at a glance:

1. Punch the focus mitts (two 2-minute rounds)
2. Rest for 1 minute
3. Kick the kicking shield (one 2-minute round)
4. Rest for 1 minute
5. Punch and kick the Thai pads (two 2-minute rounds)
6. Rest for 1 minute
7. Push-ups (20 reps)
8. Sit-ups (20 reps)
9. Lunges (10 reps per leg)
10. Stretch

Warm-Up Call

Do you ever have that stiff feeling when you get out of bed? That's because your muscles are not quite awake yet; they're stiff, and grateful for every slow step you take. The same holds true for your workout: In order to avoid unnecessary pain or injury, you must gradually get your muscles used to your kickboxing workout regimen. Gradually easing into this workout tells your muscles that they are about to do some hard work; the advance warning makes the work a little easier. In other words, warming up can help prevent injury to your muscles. You'll start with sport-specific exercises; let's warm up the muscles you work while kickboxing.

Learning the Ropes

You'll start by jumping rope to improve your coordination and rhythm; this exercise also provides cardio-conditioning. In the fight game, you hear a lot about timing. Fighters instinctively know when to fire the perfect strike or block a kick. That's timing, and you can build it by jumping rope. Your body movements will follow the thoughts in your brain.

To jump rope, grab the handles and hold them close to your waist, with your elbows close to your sides. As you swing the rope, jump once per rotation. Use your wrists, rather than your whole arm, to turn the rope. Keep your jumps low, no more than an inch off the ground. Concentrate on keeping your back straight and shoulders up. Remember, you're training like a fighter: Stay light, land on the balls of your feet, and keep your knees soft. Once you get the hang of it, try the boxer's shuffle—shift your weight from one foot to the other. Or, try crossing the rope: Keep your hands low as you cross them in front of your body, and hop through the loop. Jump rope for 5 minutes. Or, if it's your first time, jump rope for 2 minutes and rest for 1 minute.

Side-to-Side Work

After jumping rope, you'll do side-to-side work to help warm up your shoulders, back, and abs. If done correctly, you'll also feel the burn in your legs. Side to side rehearses the moves that you'll do later in your workout—this exercise copies the body position used in executing punches and blocks.

Start with your left foot forward (see the following figure). Bend your knee, and make sure you're on the ball of your foot. Your rear leg is also bent, with your heel off the ground. Hold your arms in a horizontal position, with the knuckles facing each other. Hold a 3-pound dumbbell weight in each hand.

You'll twist at the waist while lunging for 2 minutes. Notice that as you rotate the right shoulder back, the left elbow comes forward; your legs remain anchored in a lunge position. Your arms should stay equal with your shoulders as you twist back and forth. In other words, the only thing moving is your waist.

Rest for 1 minute and then switch legs for another 2 minutes.

Lunge with your left leg forward, and then twist at the waist.

Standing Mountain Climbers

For this exercise you'll look like a toy marching soldier, but it's an effective warmup for your mind. This exercise is important because you've been taught your entire life to move in opposition—notice how your body moves when you walk, opposite hand and foot. In the fight business, however, you need to move with the same hand and foot, and with power. You'll use this warmup to train your brain to think like a fighter.

In the starting position, hold the weights at chin level, with your hands in the fighting position. To do this exercise, you'll simultaneously lift the same arm and knee. As you lift your arm, your hand will turn so that your knuckles face forward. After the lift, return the hand to the fighting position and place the foot down. As soon as you return to the starting position, lift the other arm and knee. After doing this for 2 minutes, rest for 1 minute.

Limber Up: Stretching

Have you broken a sweat? Good! That's your cue to do a few light stretches to prepare your body for kickboxing. These exercises specifically stretch the muscles you're about to work:

1. Start by rotating your neck. Stand with your feet shoulder-width apart, and your arms at your side. Then shift your head 10 times from shoulder to shoulder, ear to ear. Don't roll the neck back.

2. Continue with large arm circles. Stand with your feet shoulder-width apart, and your arms at your side, and circle your arms back for 10 reps. Then reverse the circle for 10 reps. Start slow and pick up speed as you go.

Warning Warriors

These stretches are not meant to increase your flexibility. You'll do that after your workout. Instead, move fairly quickly through these stretches. Don't skip the warmup and stretch cold. Remember, your muscles are stiff. They need some movement before the stretch.

3. Now, prepare to swing your arms. Cross your arms in front of your body, as if hugging yourself and then reach back; your shoulder blades should come together. Do 10 reps.

4. Rotate your hips. Place your hands on your hips, and your feet shoulder-width apart. Thrust your hips forward and circle to the left. Do 10 reps, and then circle to the right.

5. To circle your knees, place your hands on midthigh. Let the bottom half of your legs make a circle, clockwise and reverse. Do 10 reps.

6. Circle your ankles. Rotate your left ankle in a circle, both clockwise and reverse. Do 10 reps, and then switch legs.

After these stretches, you'll do 20 sit-ups. (That's how you'll complete every warm-up interval.)

Kickboxing Buzz

A lot of students tend to drop the right hand when throwing a jab. Others drop the left hand when throwing a cross. These are bad habits. Instead, keep your hands up, in the guard position.

Learning and Review: A Little Jab and Cross

You'll weave, jab, and cross as an imaginary opponent closes in on you. However, you want to work slowly through your punches. When you throw them into the air, pretend that someone is on the receiving end—don't just throw them aimlessly. Also, don't forget to snap your jab fast and quickly return to the fighter's stance.

Throw five jabs with your left foot forward; in this stance, the left arm is jabbing. Then, work the right arm with the cross. Try to follow a straight line from your shoulder to your opponent's face; aim for the cheek. Finish with five crosses.

After you've worked both punches, practice the old 1-2. Work the jab-cross five times, and then switch legs, placing your right foot forward. Your jabbing arm will now be the right arm, and you'll use the left for the cross. The cross works hand in hand with the jab; for example, you'll throw a jab with the lead arm, and then fire the cross with the other hand. When you finish, walk around for 45 seconds to 1 minute.

Strike Out: Knee Strike and Round Kick

Strike a pose: Place your left foot forward. Start with the rear leg knee strike. Imagine grabbing your trainer's neck. Now, pull him into your knee—that's how you'll generate more power. Throw your knee strike into the air 10 times, and then switch legs.

A round kick, often called the front round kick, takes a little extra time to throw correctly. Think about your target areas: calf, thighs, stomach, chest, and head. As you kick, point your toes so your shin lands on target. At first, aim for the knee area, until you feel good about throwing this kick; you don't want to teeter as you pick up your leg. Don't forget to snap it out and back in for speed to create power. Do 10 kicks, and then switch legs.

Mix and Match

Now it's time to put your hands and feet together. You'll mix and match the punches and the kicks you've just learned. Somewhere between getting hit and hitting your opponent is distance—the area between two fighters. By putting your punches and kicks together, you're training your mind to react within distance. For example, you may be too far away to land a punch or too close to fire a kick; you'll have to shuffle to move you closer to or farther away from your opponent. It's hard to think about the next move, but combos can program your brain to react automatically under pressure. By learning some combos, you'll have a better feel for when to strike high or low, right or left, and close- or long-range. Combos prepare you for whatever may happen in the ring.

Put your hands up, and place your left foot forward. You'll throw five sets of each of these combos (don't forget to switch legs):

➤ Combo #1: Jab-Round Kick

➤ Combo #2: Jab-Round Kick-Jab-Cross

➤ Combo #3: Jab-Cross-Round Kick

➤ Combo #4: Jab-Cross-Knee Strike

➤ Combo #5: Jab-Cross-Knee Strike-Round Kick

➤ Combo #6: Knee Strike-Round Kick-Jab-Cross

Kickboxing Buzz

As you move with your training partner, be careful not to cross your legs because this can cause you to lose your center of bal-ance. It's a bad habit that your opponent would love to take advantage of. Stay in your fighter's stance as you shuffle.

Hit the Pads

It's time to up the ante: Add resistance to your workout by striking the pads. Have you found a training partner to hold the pads? If not, the heavy bag will do. This interval is easy: Simply hit the pads with jabs, crosses, knee strikes, and front round kicks. Stay light on your toes. As your trainer moves with the pads, so should you. Or, if you're hitting the heavy bag, move with it. Start with your left foot forward, and exhale every time you strike.

With resistance, you'll tire out a little faster. Try to go for a straight 2 minutes. Then you can take a rest for 45 seconds to 1 minute. With the focus mitts, do two rounds of rapid punches: five jabs, five crosses, and five 1-2 combos. Keep repeating those sets until the time runs out. Rest, and then repeat the round with the right foot forward.

When you work the kicking shield, use sets of five again. Five is the magic number: five round kicks and five knee strikes. For this interval you'll only do one round, so switch legs in the middle of the round.

You'll add the combos when you use the Thai pads. Try to get through all the combos; spontaneity will keep you on your toes. Your coach should repeatedly call the combos out to you. Again, you'll do two 2-minute rounds. Take a 45-second to 1-minute rest between each interval. Keep moving, though.

Conditioning Drills

Repeat after me: "We love conditioning drills!" Say it over and over. Conditioning is very important because you must train your muscles to throw punches and kicks in rapid succession; training your muscles in this way gives them what is referred to as *dynamic strength*. You'll hate all the push-ups and sit-ups, but that's how you'll train your muscles to work over and over again. You're going for muscle stamina, not brute strength.

You need to complete two sets of push-ups along with your ab and leg work; this is detailed in the following sections.

Push-Ups

Here's your first drill: push-ups. Before you turn your nose up—everyone does—know that push-ups work more muscle groups in the least amount of time. Besides, there isn't a kickboxer alive who doesn't do push-ups. Your goal is to complete 20 military push-ups. However, if you can't, fall to your knees to finish the set. As a last resort, you can finish with the mini push-up.

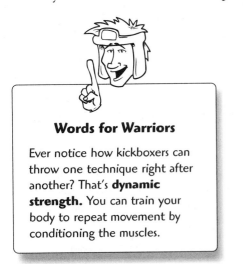

Words for Warriors

Ever notice how kickboxers can throw one technique right after another? That's **dynamic strength.** You can train your body to repeat movement by conditioning the muscles.

1. Start with military push-ups. Do as many as you can, and then fall to your knees to finish 20 reps. If you have never done a military push-up, start out on all fours, and then lift yourself up, keeping your body parallel to the ground. Your arms should be a little wider than shoulder-width apart. Support the lower part of your body by balancing on your toes. Suck in your abs and make sure that your back is straight. Make a straight line from your head to your heels. Next, lower yourself slowly, keeping your head up and looking forward. Lower yourself down until you are 1 or 2 inches above the ground.

2. Continue with knee push-ups. Kneel on all fours; lift yourself up, keeping your body parallel to the ground. Remain on your knees. Your arms should be a little wider than shoulder-width apart. Suck in your abs and make sure that your back is straight. Lower yourself to the floor.

3. Finish, only if needed, with mini push-ups. Lie flat on the ground, with your hands shoulder-width apart. Push yourself up, leaving your hips on the ground.

Amazing Abs

Shake, rattle, and roll—in kickboxing you'll use your body to twist, bend, and move. But you've got to have a good set of *core muscles:* the abdominal, lower back, and other major muscles that attach to the pelvis, working together to support and stabilize the spine while you punch and kick. Weak abdominals can throw you off balance when you strike, possibly injuring you. Ab work, and lots of it, should be the focus of every workout.

Start with the full range sit-ups. If you can't finish 20, go right into your crunches. It helps if you have someone stand on your toes for support. If you have never done a sit-up—or if it's been a very long time—substitute the sit-ups for crunches (crunch and punch). Add the frog-kicks only after seven or more workouts—these abdominal exercises are reserved for the advanced beginner.

Words for Warriors

Core muscles make up your midsection. They are your abdominal and back muscles, plus the other, smaller muscles that attach to the pelvis. They all work in harmony to stabilize the spine and help maintain good posture and alignment when you throw a punch.

Yes, you did a set of 20 in the warm-up interval. Sorry, that set doesn't count, you'll do another set of 20. We want you to begin with the full sit-up. If you can't finish, then do crunches.

Here's the drill:

1. Start with sit-ups. Lie on your back, with your feet a comfortable distance from your butt. Bend your knees. Position your hands in the fighter's pose; pull your belly button in toward your spine and sit up.

2. Next is a sit-up and punch combo. Lie on your back, with your feet at a comfortable distance from your butt. Bend your knees. Position your hands in the fighter's pose; pull your belly button toward your spine. When you sit up, twist and strike your arm out as if you're punching. Make sure your arm reaches to the opposite side of your knee.

3. Continue with an abdominal curl. Lie on your back, and bend your knees so your feet are a comfortable distance from your butt. Place your arms behind your head to support your head. Don't interlock your fingers; place only your fingertips together. Your elbows should be visible in your peripheral vision. Contract your stomach muscles as if you were going to pull your belly button in toward your spine. Lift your torso until your shoulder blades clear the floor, exhaling as you lift.

4. Finish with some frog kicks. Sit on the floor with your knees close to your chest and your hands behind your back. Kick your legs out in front; your back will recline slowly. Focus on pulling your navel toward your spine, so that your back is a little rounded.

Lean Legs

What makes a good kick? Strong legs. What drives a punch? Powerful legs. Good kickboxing, then, is all about your legs.

For this workout, do 10 lunges with each leg. Gradually, work yourself up to a solid 2 minutes, then rest.

To do the lunging exercise, start with your feet shoulder-width apart; step out with your left leg, leading with the heel (see the following figure). Bend both knees so that the front knee is in line with the heel and the rear knee faces the floor, with the rear heel lifted. As you rise, push off with the front heel.

Want good kickboxing legs? Then lunge them with these steps.

Finish Line: Stretching

How high can you throw your kicks? Clearly, that will depend on your flexibility. It's a good idea to take the time to stretch. The best time is after your workout. Because your muscles are warm, they'll be more responsive to lengthening. Hold your stretch for 30 seconds, and don't bounce—static stretches only.

Tune in to your body as you relax: Use your body weight to increase the stretch; inhale deep breaths as you stretch, and then exhale as you release the tension; try to maintain alignment. In other words, it's not how far you stretch, but how good your form is. Notice the way the muscle fiber runs. No shaking—that's overstretching.

Sometimes, you may be more flexible in your shoulders than your legs—flexibility is not the same throughout the body. Here's the scoop on your flexing exercises:

1. Start with a standing V (spread your legs to make a small V). Your knees should stay soft. Turn your upper body to the left and reach for your foot. Hold for 30 seconds. Then, turn to the right and repeat the stretch.

2. Follow up with a groin stretch (see the following figure, left). While standing, lean into a left side lunge. Keep the right toe pointing toward the ceiling. If you have knee problems, don't take this stretch to a full side lunge. Notice that the knee is in line with the heel. Don't let the knee bend past your toes. Hold this position for the stretch.

3. Continue with a Chinese stretch. With your feet spread apart, bend over and reach as far as you can between your legs. Touch the ground, keeping a slight bend in your knees. Turn your torso to the right so that your chest is over your knee. Then, turn to the left.

4. Do a butterfly stretch. From a seated position, put the bottoms of your feet together and pull your heels up as close to your butt as possible. Then, slowly press your knees down to the floor.

5. Close with a back stretch (see the following figure, right). Extend your left leg. Cross your right leg over the left. Now, twist your upper body in toward your knee. Then, twist away from the knee for about 30 seconds or so. Switch legs.

Dynamite! You've made it through the "Main Event." We have guided you through the very first workout—you're now on your own. With every few workouts you should add more technique. Be creative, and have fun. Before you graduate to the intermediate level (give yourself 9 to 12 training sessions), you must be able to throw the basic strikes and complete five rounds of resistance work using focus mitts, kicking shields, and Thai pads. Or you can use the heavy bag, if you're going solo. And don't forget the conditioning drills: 100 sit-ups and 60 push-ups. If you're training twice a week, you may be able to move a little faster after about 4 to 6 weeks. Refer to the following progression table for guidance.

The groin stretch (left) and the back stretch (right).

Workout by Workout Number

Workout #	Techniques	Combos
1–3	Jab, cross, knee strike	1, 2-1, round kick
		1, round kick, 1, 2
		1, 2, round kick, 1, 2, knee strike
		1, 2, knee strike, round kick
		Knee strike, round kick, 1, 2
4–6	Hook, offensive front kick	1, 2, 3–1, 2, offensive front
7–9	Front kick, roundhouse	Front kick, 1, 2–1, roundhouse
		1, roundhouse, 1, 2
		Front kick, 1, 2, 3, roundhouse

The Least You Need to Know

➤ You'll jump rope before every workout.

➤ In the beginner one-on-one workout, you'll do all the basic punches and kicks: jab, cross, hook, front kick, and knee strike.

➤ The steps are the same for all one-on-ones.

➤ Give yourself 12 workouts before you move on to the intermediate one-on-one.

➤ Distance is the area between two fighters.

➤ Exhale on every strike.

➤ You have to stretch before and after your workout.

Chapter 11

The Next Edge: Intermediate and Advanced Workouts

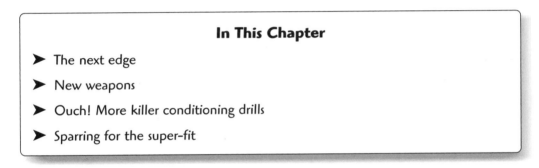

In This Chapter

➤ The next edge

➤ New weapons

➤ Ouch! More killer conditioning drills

➤ Sparring for the super-fit

Let's turn up the burn. By now, you should have committed to memory the jabs, crosses, and hooks. Furthermore, you should have no trouble throwing a front kick and roundhouse. Do you feel strong? Have you witnessed your body change? These are good signs that you're ready to move on to the next edge.

So, where do you go? How about sparring? Before you run for the hills, know that sparring can be a lot of fun. That's right—you're not going to exchange war marks, stitches, or fat lips. You won't even bruise; there is such a thing as touchcontact sparring.

Or, you can don gear and pretend that you're going for the world title. The type of sparring you do depends on you; if you want to fight, you'll have to strike it out with a partner. But if you're the super-fit type, craving a new challenge, sparring will give you a great workout.

A "Smoking" Intermediate Workout

The "smoking" intermediate workout is essentially the same as the workout for beginners that was discussed in Chapter 10, "The Main Event: One-on-One Beginner Workouts."

Following is the "smoking" intermediate workout at a glance:

1. Jump rope (5 minutes)
2. Rest for 45 seconds to 1 minute
3. Left foot side to side (2 minutes)
4. Rest for 45 seconds to 1 minute
5. Right foot side to side (2 minutes)
6. Rest for 45 seconds to 1 minute
7. Standing mountain climbers (2 minutes)
8. Rest for 45 seconds to 1 minute
9. Stretch
10. Ab work (20 reps)

With the intermediate workout, however, in the "learning and review" interval you'll add the more advanced turn and side kicks, as well as the overhand punch, uppercut, and spinning back fist. Workout warriors, you may just want to stick with the moves in the beginner's workout because they are the most frequently used. However, if you're stepping it up a notch, you should add the moves in the following list:

1. Shadow sparring (two 2-minute rounds)
2. Punch the focus mitts (three 2-minute rounds)
3. Kick the kicking shield (one 2-minute round)
4. Punch and kick the Thai pads (two 2-minute rounds)
5. Heavy bag (two 2-minute rounds)
6. 15-second punch drill (one round)
7. Front kick drill (one round)
8. Push-ups
9. Sit-ups
10. Lunges with kicks (1 minute)
11. Stretch

Learning and Review: Synergy

Review the combos from the "Main Event" in Chapter 10. Add your new punches and kicks slowly. For guidance, look at the progression chart. As your workouts continue, you'll add side and turn kicks, uppercuts, overhand punches, and spinning back fists. For examples, turn to the progression chart. Notice that on your twelfth workout, you'll add a side kick.

That's easy enough, right? Now, repeat the old techniques and add a side kick while practicing in the learning and review interval. Remember the magic number: five. Follow the same routine as before (for example, five jabs, five crosses, and so forth).

Warning Warriors

It's not a good idea to keep your mouth open or stick your tongue out when striking—you might bite your lip or tongue. If you get punched, you could get "jacked-up," which means that your jaw locks open.

After that, go to the mirror; it's time to shadow spar. Yes, you'll have to watch yourself box an imaginary opponent. You may have a hard time getting started. If you have a trainer, ask him to call out a few combos. Or you can be creative and make up your own combos. You'll do two 2-minute rounds with a 45-second to 1-minute rest in between.

The Pain of the Game: Drills

You're adding three new conditioning drills to your workout. Keep in mind that you'll learn an array of new conditioning drills as the workout goes on. You can pick and choose. Ladies, don't work only your legs; men, don't do just push-ups. Mix up your conditioning drills.

You'll alternate between a 2-minute bag drill and a 2-minute front kick drill. Then, go right into your conditioning drills (one set only). Start with a push-up set: Do a set of 20; rest; do a set of 15; rest; do a set of 10; rest; close with a set of five. Follow with 60 sit-ups: Make it a combination of sit-ups, sit-ups and punches, and frogs. Then, finish this workout with a 1-minute leg drill—kicking lunges.

15-Second Punching Drill

Find a heavy bag. This drill is fairly simple, but it can leave you breathless. You'll jab and cross the punching bag, rapidly and don't stop, for 15 seconds; rest for 15 seconds; then repeat the old 1-2. Hit the bag four times. That's it, one round—fifteen seconds on, fifteen seconds off.

Front Kick Drill

Either find a partner to hold a kick shield, or kick the underbelly of a heavy bag. Strike the bottom of the bag as fast as possible. You'll kick for a solid 2 minutes. The kick is similar to a front kick motion, but instead of striking with the ball of the foot, you'll strike the bag with the top portion of the foot to help toughen up the shin and foot area. Think speed!

Walking and Kicking Lunges

Next are the familiar lunges. Start with the basic lunge: Place your feet shoulder-width apart, and then step out with your left leg, leading with the heel. Bend both knees so that the front knee is in line with the heel and the rear knee faces the floor, with the heel lifted. As you rise up, step forward with the right leg and execute a front kick. Recoil it back and set it down into a right leg lunge. Lunge for 1 minute. Now, you're done.

Intermediate Workout by Workout Number

Workout Number	Technique	Combos
12–15	Side kick	1, side kick
16–17	Overhand punch	1, 5–1, 5, 3
18–19	Uppercut	1, 2, 3, 4–4, 3, 2
20	Turn kick	1, turn kick–1, side kick, turn kick
21–22	Spinning back fist	1, 6–1, 2, 3, 6

The Next Edge: Advanced Workout

By now, you should have honed your kicks and punches. Likewise, you should be able finish 10 to 12 rounds: focus mitts, kicking shields, Thai pads, and bag work, in addition to all the conditioning drills up to this point. Only then are you ready for this workout. The estimated transformation time is 4 to 6 months. That's right—unless you put the time in, you're not ready for this workout:

1. Jump rope (5 minutes)
2. Left foot side to side (1 minute)
3. Left arm extension side to side (1 minute)
4. Left standing mountain climbers (1 minute)
5. Rest for 45 seconds

6. Right foot side to side (1 minute)

7. Right arm extension side to side (1 minute)

8. Right standing mountain climbers (1 minute)

9. Rest for 45 seconds

10. Ab work (40, 20, 20, 20)

11. Rest for 1 minute

12. Stretch

Here's the learning and review interval drill:

1. Shadow sparring (three 2-minute rounds)

2. Punch the focus mitts (three 2-minute rounds)

3. Kick the kicking shield (three 2-minute round)

4. Punch and kick the Thai pads (three 2-minute rounds)

5. Heavy bag (three 2-minute rounds)

6. Diamond push-ups (20 reps)

7. Medicine ball push-ups (10 reps)

8. Hindu squats (20 reps)

9. Interval sprints (one 2-minute round)

10. Abs (20 reps)

11. Stretch

Don't sweat it; changes are few at the advanced level. The major change is a new set of conditioning drills. We also added two new techniques: roundhouse to the thigh and elbow strike. You can also learn how to spar with a partner. Notice that you can even do a spar workout. By this time, you should be familiar with the routine, so you can mix it up for some variety. For example, you may like the "smoking" intermediate workout, but bored with the conditioning drills.

You can add a few of the advanced conditioning drills; it doesn't matter. Stir things up; remember, it's not about brute strength, but challenging yourself.

Warning Warriors

You should advance to the "next edge" only if you can complete 12 rounds of resistance work and a ton of conditioning drills. You must know your punches and kicks.

Ease Into It

Start by jumping rope for five minutes. Then, it's time to train like the big boys and girls: This means longer rounds and shorter rest periods. Mix up side-to-side drills and standing mountain climbers. Your new warm-up routine is 1 minute side to side, 1 minute arm extension side to side, and then 1 minute standing mountain climbers. Do these warmups one after another, without rest. Then you can rest for 45 seconds.

For your side-to-side arm extensions, start in same position as you do for the side to side drill. The arms are not in a horizontal position; rather, they are held in a fighting position (see the following figure). Twist your right shoulder forward, followed by your left. As you alternate, extend your arms as if you were throwing a punch.

Side-to-side arm extensions add variety to the advanced workout.

Same Old Stuff: Stretching

Nothing has changed here. This is a good time to add a few stretches of your own. You should be in tune with your body. Take more time to stretch weak areas or inflexible muscles that can improve your game.

Crank Up the Crunches

We have one new killer ab exercise to add: the bicycle crunch. With the bicycle crunch, you will do 40 reps. Take a few minutes to recover, and then do 20 sit-ups, 20 sit-up and punch combos, and 20 frogs. Then you can rest. There is no need to burn yourself out; this is just the warmup.

When you are rested and ready, continue with the bicycle crunch. Lie on the ground with your hands behind your head. Bring your left knee up toward your chest; touch your right elbow to your left knee. Bring your right knee up as you straighten your left leg out, meeting the right knee with the left elbow (see the following figure).

The bicycle crunch tightens up your abs.

Learning and Review: Thunder Under 'Em

Your kicks should receive a good amount of respect, they can be extremely powerful. For that reason, we have reserved the deadliest kick for last: the leg kick which is a roundhouse kick thrown to the thigh. In addition, you'll add a deadly elbow strike to your arsenal. Both weapons, if thrown correctly, can disfigure or cripple a person.

The roundhouse kick can literally sever the thighbone or knock you down if it is thrown with full power. Likewise, the elbow strike can be a deadly weapon (which is why it is illegal in sport kickboxing, except in Muay Thai). You'll learn it for self-defense purposes; in fact, you'll use it only in a self-defense situation—it may save your life someday.

Remember the magic number: practice each of the strikes five times. Then switch legs. Now is a good time to practice the old techniques.

Warning Warriors

The elbow strike is for close-range combat. Keep in mind that when you practice, an elbow strike can cause permanent damage to you or your training partner. Use caution. Turnabout *is* fair play, especially if you elbow your coach.

Pro-Mirror

By now, you know "how" and "why" you should shadow spar. There is no need to feel silly boxing to the mirror; every fighter does it. In this interval, you'll box for three rounds. In the first round, you'll work on boxing techniques. Then, in the second round, add your kicks. Finish up in the third round with combo work.

After each set, you'll have a *working rest*. In other words, it's payback time—during the working rest, you'll work your abs for 45 seconds.

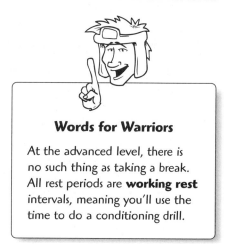

Words for Warriors

At the advanced level, there is no such thing as taking a break. All rest periods are **working rest** intervals, meaning you'll use the time to do a conditioning drill.

Maximize Your Method: Mix It Up

It's important to remember that when you work out, you've got options. You can throw all these techniques to the mitts, shields, Thai pads, and the heavy bag to continue to sharpen what you've learned up to this point; or, if you need a challenge, you can add your new moves. Check out the following combinations for a little guidance. Remember, you'll do 2 minutes on, and then take a 1-minute rest. (Because you're doing resistance work, you can take a 1-minute rest break.)

Technique	Combination
Elbow strikes	1, rear elbow–1, rear elbow, front elbow
Rear/front	1, 2, front elbow–2, front elbow, rear elbow
Roundhouse	1, leg kick–front kick, leg kick
	Round kick, 1, 2, leg kick
	1, 2, 3, leg kick

Crank Up the Conditioning

Here's a tip: All coaches are sadistic—they will make you do all sorts of evil conditioning drills to finish off your training. Kickboxers, welcome to Hell on Earth.

This section contains several new drills; however, you'll do only two sets of push-ups, two sets of abs, and two sets of legs. You can use any of the drills up to this point. Eventually, you want to work your way up to three sets of each; go ahead and try it. Note that some days you'll whip through the workout with no problem; others, you'll be lucky to finish.

Alternate the drills in this section. Start with push-ups, continue with abs, and finish with legs. Recycle that set one more time. For example, say your first set consists of 10 medicine ball push-ups, 10 medicine ball sit-ups, and 20 Hindu squats. In your second set, do 20 diamond push-ups, 20 decline medicine ball sit-ups, and then run interval sprints to finish. Don't rest between your sets; try to keep the momentum going throughout both sets of drills. Your goal is to work to failure, which means your muscles hesitate as you do another rep.

The Diamond Push-Up

The diamond push-up is similar to the military push-up, but it's more difficult (see the following figure). Get on all fours. Place your hands on the floor with the thumbs and forefingers of each hand touching, so that they form a diamond. For balance, place your feet shoulder-width apart. Next, lower yourself down slowly to about 2 or 3 inches from the ground; then, push yourself back up to the starting position.

The diamond push-up is a variation of the military push-up—and a challenge.

Shoot for 20 reps, or just do as many as you can. You can always go back and do the push-ups from the intermediate workout: one set of 20, one set of 15, one set of 10, and one set of five. However, unlike the intermediate workout, you won't be resting between sets. For example, if you've completed your first set of 20 pushups, you'll go directly into an ab set, and so forth.

Medicine Ball Push-Up

You'll do two kinds of medicine ball push-ups; we'll start with the easier of the two. Once you've built up some muscle, you can advance to the other variation. Medicine ball push-ups not only result in a fine pair of arms, they also help you learn how to stabilize your body—a skill that will come in handy in the fight game. Start with 10 reps, and gradually work up to more.

Kickboxing Buzz

Women, especially, have a hard time with the diamond push-up. That's exactly why you should add a few to your push-up routine. For all your hard work, you'll be rewarded with a set of great triceps—no more floppy skin hanging down on the backs of your arms.

Here's the scoop on the beginning medicine ball push-ups:

1. Start by placing both hands on the medicine ball, with your arms extended. Place your legs on the floor, shoulder-width apart.

2. Lower yourself slowly until your chest touches the medicine ball, and then push yourself back to the starting position. Repeat this exercise 10 times.

For the advanced medicine ball push-ups, assume the same starting position as with the easier push-ups:

1. Start by placing both hands on the medicine ball, with your arms extended. Place your legs on the floor, shoulder-width apart.

2. Lower yourself down slowly until your chest touches your hands, and then return to starting position.

3. Drop your hands to the sides of the medicine ball, and lower yourself until your chest touches the medicine ball.

4. Now, spring yourself up so that your hands rest on the medicine ball.

Alter Your Abs

Caution: The ab work you're about to witness is not for the weak torso. Make sure you have the strength to pull them off; otherwise, you can seriously hurt yourself. For resistance, you'll add the weight of the medicine ball. You'll do 20 reps.

Again, if you don't like this selection of ab work, go back to the intermediate work: 20 sit-ups, 20 sit-ups and punches, 20 frogs, and 20 cycles. Remember, there is no resting between these sets!

If you're up for it, do 20 reps. You can pick the ab exercise. Good luck!

1. **Medicine ball sit-ups**—Lie flat on your back, with your legs raised straight up in the air. (Have your partner or coach, if you have one, support your feet, or use a wall for support.) Your arms are over your head, holding the medicine ball. With your arms straight, bring the medicine ball up to your feet, and then return to starting position.

2. **Decline medicine ball sit-ups**—Sit down on a decline bench and hold the medicine ball over your head. Curl up, keeping the ball on your chest. As you curl up, throw the medicine ball to your coach. He'll throw it back so you can lower your back to the bench again.

3. **Push down leg lifts**—Lie on your back. Your coach will stand at the top of your head. Grab the coach's ankles for balance; the coach will hold your feet. Your coach will push your legs down. Lower them with control; keep your legs straight, and don't let them hit the ground. Then bring them back to the coach's hands.

4. **Medicine ball drop sit-ups**—This exercise is to toughen up the full contact warrior's stomach for strikes. Lie on the ground with your knees bent. The coach will straddle your knees. The coach will drop the medicine ball on your stomach. Let the ball hit your stomach, and then catch it before it rolls off. Sit up and hand the medicine ball back to the coach.

Warning Warriors

Don't forget to drink lots of water—about 16 ounces before and after the workout. And take only small sips while working out.

Legs: Termination

You'll finish your advanced workout with leg exercises. You've got options here, as well. Your goal is 40 Hindu squats, but to make it easy on yourself, you can start off with 20. If you don't like the squats, you can go back and do the lunges with the kicks (from the intermediate workout). You'll finish this one-on-one with sprints—and probably with a little trash-talk about your coach.

Use the following steps for the Hindu squats (see the following figure):

1. Start with your feet shoulder-width apart; your hands should be in front of your body. Center your weight on the balls of your feet.

2. Bend at the knees, and lower yourself down so that your butt almost touches your calves. At the same time, reach behind your heels. Your arms will provide a little support as you lift your heels off the ground and pause in the squatting position. As you push up from the squat, push off the ground with your heels. Your arms should end up in the front of your body.

Hindu squats are a natural cure for weak legs.

To finish with the interval sprint drill, mark off about 18 yards and place markers at every 6 yards. Start at one end and sprint to the first marker, and then back to the starting line; sprint to the second marker, and then back to the starting line; turn around and sprint to the third marker, and then back to the starting line. Depending on how mean your coach is, you'll run this drill for 1 or 2 minutes. In doing this drill, you'll find out if you can stop on a dime.

Getting Ready to Spar

Hitting someone sounds like a lot of fun ... but only if he can't hit back, right? It's not a lot of fun if you end up with a sore butt. However, that rarely happens when you're sparring in a safe environment. At times, sparring can be dangerous, which is why you should make sure that your coach has real experience in the ring. If not, he has no business preparing you for the ring. Maybe he is a good fitness coach, sincere in his efforts to train you, but when it comes to the ring nothing replaces experience.

Sparring is a valuable experience; it shows you which techniques work and which ones don't. You need that kind of feedback before you face off with an opponent.

Make sure that your gloves and headgear, as well as the rest of your gear, are in good working order. Take a practice round with your equipment to make sure it fits correctly. Also, the surface of the ring in which you'll spar should be clear of debris and slip-proof.

Men need the following safety equipment for sparring:

➤ 16- to 18-ounce boxing gloves

➤ Sparring headgear

➤ Mouthpiece

➤ Shin pads

➤ Foot pads

➤ Groin protector

➤ Petroleum jelly

Women should have the following safety equipment:

➤ 14- to 16-ounce boxing gloves

➤ Sparring headgear

➤ Mouthpiece

➤ Shin pads

➤ Foot pads

➤ Women's groin protector (optional)

➤ Breast protector (optional, but mandatory in competition)

➤ Petroleum jelly

Kickboxing Buzz

Use petroleum jelly to prevent cuts. If you put it on the bony areas around your eyes and cheeks, it can help cut down on the open wounds that result from powerful strikes.

Spar Time

Consider sparring only if you can complete 12 rounds of work using mitts, shields, pads, and bag. Start with three rounds of sparring. Three rounds may seem like a piece of cake, but don't be too sure of yourself yet—it takes a lot out of you, especially as you increase your sparring level:

➤ Advanced warmup

➤ Stretching

➤ Ab routine

➤ Three 2-minute rounds of shadow sparring

➤ One 2-minute round of focus mitts

➤ One 2-minute round of kicking shield

➤ One 2-minute round of heavy bag work

➤ Three 2-minute rounds of sparring

➤ Two 2-minute rounds of focus mitts

➤ One 2-minute round of kicking shield

➤ Two 2-minute rounds of Thai pads or heavy bag

➤ Diamond push-ups (10 reps)

➤ Medicine ball push-ups (10 reps)

➤ Abs (20 reps)

➤ Hindu squats (20 reps)

➤ One 2-minute interval sprint

➤ Stretch

Kickboxing Buzz

If you're stepping into the ring, you'll spar for as many sets as the fight. For example, some kick-boxing bouts lasts five rounds. So, you'll spar for five rounds.

The Midas Touch: Touch Sparring

You'll start by *touch sparring*. Find a partner who can control the amount of power in his punches and kicks. Keep in mind that we're talking about touch sparring, *touch* being the operative word. If your partner lacks restraint, it's probably not a good idea to spar with him. In touch sparring, you'll lightly touch your partner as you rehearse your techniques (see the following figure, left). Don't worry—you'll still get a good feeling as to what a punch looks like as it closes in on your face. The good news, though, is that there is no sting.

As far as striking is concerned, you need to feel it. No amount of bag work can prepare you for what a real-life strike to the shin feels like. The head is off limits, though.

As you spar, you'll finally get to use some of your blocking skills: parrying and catching. With spar-ring, you're linking together all the techniques that you've learned—it's just like an actual fight. You might want use this opportunity to try some of those fancy combos.

The Light Touch: Light Contact

Next up: *light sparring*. With this type of sparring you get to strike with a little power. When the strike lands, it's with a light thump; the blow is

Words for Warriors

Know the different levels of sparring. **Touch sparring** is just that—touching your opponent; **light sparring** involves hitting with less power as you strike; **body contact** sparring entails full-blown strikes, but only to the body; and in **full contact** sparring, you can hit anywhere on the body—with power.

just hard enough to let your partner know that you mean business (see the following figure, right). Unless you're a fairly experienced kickboxer, you shouldn't make head contact. The tempo of the spar should be fairly quick to give you the feel and thrill of a real fight.

Touch sparring (left) and light contact sparring (right).

Body Shots: Body Contact

Next, gear up for *body contact*. (You are gradually working toward making full contact.) First, start by firing full-powered strikes below the chin and above the waist. There's no need to worry about getting your head knocked off because the head is off-limits in body contact sparring. In this type of sparring, you'll really feel the impact behind a powerhouse shot. This works both ways, though; you, too, get to land a few strikes, with a target that is more challenging than the heavy bag.

Warning Warriors

Under the guidance of a good coach, sparring can be very safe. He'll tell you when you're ready to add strikes and blocks.

Start by punching to the body. Afterward, throw a few combinations. And don't forget about your blocks. Finally, after you feel really comfortable, add your kicks.

Total Body Shots: Full Contact

Sounds ominous, doesn't it? Despite the name *full contact*, you're not looking for an all-out fight-fest or the chance to pummel your partner to death. Think about it: Sparring wouldn't be much fun if you got knocked out every time you trained. Not only does a knockout hurt, your brain can't survive such abuse.

First, find an old pro, someone skilled in sparring. Let that fighter control the match. You need to throw all your techniques. Your partner, though, will be anticipating your next move—remember, he's smarter than you. Most coaches will pair up fighters of different skill levels so that no one really gets hurt. If both fighters are beginners, the sparring session can turn into a brawling mess with no real gain—just pain.

You don't have to jump into the ring to benefit from full contact sparring; it can teach you some valuable lessons outside of the ring. For example, with this type of experience, most women can walk through life less fearful of an attack. Knowing what a punch feels like and being able to protect yourself is empowering. Regardless of your reason for training, know that your coach will not let you get hurt, especially if you're not training for the big fight. Most coaches emphasize safety. The key is to start slow and work your way up. Listen to your coach. And don't forget: hands up, chin down.

Warning Warriors

Don't think about stepping into the ring without sparring; it's a necessary step to master because ringside knockouts are a very real possibility. Controlled sparring matches can protect you in the long run, both in a self-defense situatuion and in the ring.

The Least You Need to Know

➤ Advance to the "smoking" intermediate workout only if you can recite the basics on command and finish five rounds of resistance work, 100 sit-ups, and 60 push-ups.

➤ In the "smoking" intermediate workout, you'll practice side and turn kicks, uppercuts, overhand punches, and the spinning back fist.

➤ The "next edge" can be a workout for the fitness warrior or for the kickboxer who wants to train for the ring.

➤ Shadow sparring should be taken seriously.

➤ If you have a good coach, you won't get hurt when sparring.

➤ Make sure your safety equipment fits well.

➤ You can spar at four different levels: touch, light, body, and full contact.

Chapter 12

Cardio-Combustion: Body of Perfection

In This Chapter

➤ Cardio-kickboxing: putting the spark back in aerobics

➤ Make your own music tape

➤ Different levels of cardio workout

Not so long ago, you ruled your aerobics class ... perhaps you even reigned over the entire gym. But that got boring, so you're thinking kickboxing might put the spark back into your workouts. Well, unwrap the wraps; stash the gloves; and find some good music to get you sweating—don't worry if you've never taken an aerobics class.

Cardio-combustion puts your kicks and punches in sequence—there is no stopping. Cardio-kickboxing is a hybrid sport: a mix of aerobics, kickboxing, and dance. Get ready for a "kick butt" workout; it's time to dance.

Cardio-Smart

Everybody is doing it—and in record numbers. That's why you should know a few things about safety before you begin.

We've been taking aerobics since its inception, and teaching for more than 10 years, so we've seen a trend or two. It started with high-impact aerobics, where students packed in like sardines to work out. Then came the rumors—"High-impact causes this or that injury." Suddenly, working out had a rap sheet a mile long, and students quickly fled the aerobics scene.

Fighting it out is good for you! You must make sure, though, that this great workout is also safe. Safety clearly depends on your instructions. To get the safest possible workout, know this: Recognize what you can and can't do. We all have limits; don't make any move that hurts; slow down if you're tired; and work on perfecting your form.

Lock Nothing

In cardio-kickboxing, you'll be striking into the air. Earlier, we said that the bags and pads provide resistance as you strike; in cardio-combustion, on the other hand, you'll create your own resistance. Aimlessly striking in the air may cause injuries to your shoulders, elbows, or lower back. Try to imagine that you're hitting a bag; the bag stops your arm from fully extending and your elbows from locking out by fighting you back. The same thing is true with your kicks—don't lock out your knees.

Warning Warriors

Don't lock out your knees or elbows as you throw kicks and punches. Create your own resistance. Think about your striking areas: the heel of the foot, the shin, or the ball of the foot.

Think back to the striking areas. For example, with a front kick, you want to strike with the heel of your foot. Also review where your strike will land. There's no need to execute a front kick to someone's head. If you're fighting it out, your front kick is more effective if it is thrown to the gut—any higher, and you'll lose power.

Ever had a back problem? It's no fun! Don't try to keep up if you're sacrificing good form. Again, watch your kick as you execute it, and make it land on target. Don't casually throw your legs in the air. If you lose form, stop and march it out until you feel strong enough to do it right. Throwing kicks over your head will give you a sore butt—and that's about it. You can get just as good a workout by throwing your kicks low.

Body Abuse

Are you one of those people who thinks, "Wow! I'll lose five pounds a week if I work out every day?" Take note: The most common reason for injuries is overuse. If you're just starting, cardio-kickboxing can be tough. Throwing kicks takes a lot of energy; this is considered a high-intensity workout. If you can't get out of bed the morning after a workout, you've probably pushed yourself too hard. Or if you keep getting hamstring or leg sprains, scale back—these are signs of overuse. Cardio-combustion should be limited to two to three times a week.

Here are some safety tips that will help prevent injuries:

➤ Don't do a full kick; instead, bring the knee up to the fold until you can control your kicks.

170

➤ Limit cardio workouts to two or three times per week.

➤ Strength train to get in resistance training.

➤ Don't slouch forward.

➤ Focus on your abs, shoulders, and back while weight training.

➤ Stay flexible by stretching.

➤ Don't kick too high.

➤ Warm up with light kickboxing moves.

➤ Slow down if you can't maintain correct form and control.

➤ Don't lock out any joint.

Warning Warriors

Some reported common injuries that can occur while cardio-kickboxing are torn knee ligaments, ruptured neck disks, and rotator cuff damage. These problems might stem from doing too many moves, too fast, and with inadequate training and warmup.

Aerobics 101

Don't worry, you're not expected to learn every detail of aerobics; we're just going to cover the basics. Here are a few things to keep in mind: Don't work out barefoot, and make sure your tennis shoes are in good shape and provide a lot of shock absorption. Also, pay attention to your form; as with other forms of kickboxing, you might want to stand in front of a mirror.

Dance to the Beat

It's a good idea to make your own tape. After all, it's the beat of the music that gets us moving and grooving. Most aerobic music is set to a certain amount of beats per minute; the intensity increases as the music speeds up. In other words, for a heart-pounding workout, speed up the music. Beginners might want to slow down the music; if the music is too fast, you might lose control over your moves by trying to keep up.

Pick 10 of your favorite songs—music that makes you want to stand up and dance. To figure out if the beats per minute will work, time each song for 30 seconds, and clap to each beat. Write down that number, or memorize it. Next, multiply that number by two. The number you end up with will approximate the number of beats per minute. Do this for each song. Your tape should come close to 130 to 140 beats per minute. If all that sounds like too much trouble, you can ask an aerobics instructor to get you a tape (or at least recommend one).

In Transit

If you've ever taken an aerobics class, you've probably noticed that some moves are repeated over and over again. Those moves link together patterns, and they keep your

171

In aerobics, we link combinations together by **transitional moves.** This movement keeps the routine flowing so that you can keep your heart rate.

heart rate up as you flow into the next move. These moves are often called *transitional moves*. For your workout, you'll have to learn five different moves: step touch, jump rope, bob and weave, jumping jack, and knee lift. Depending on your workout level—beginning, intermediate, or advanced—you'll use one of these before moving into the next set. For example, say you've done four sets of jabs. If you're at the beginning level, you might want to follow up with a march or step touch. At the intermediate level, knee lifts (with or without jumping) might be a good transitional move. At the advanced level, you might want to do a few sets of jumping jacks or act like you're jumping rope.

Transitional Moves

All sets will be done in counts of eight: eight jabs, eight crosses, eight 1-2 combos. A move that calls for speedy-fast or double time requires 16 really fast sets. Watch your form, though—you may lose it when moving super-fast.

Beginning Level	Intermediate Level	Advanced Level
March	Bob and weave	Jump rope
Step touch	Knee lifts without bounce	Jumping jacks Knee lifts with bounce

For the step touch, lower your arms to your hips (see the following figure, left). Take a step to the right with your left foot, gently touching it to your right foot. Then, take a step to the left with your right foot, gently touching it to your left foot. Repeat ...

To bob and weave, stand up with your arms in fighting position. Then step right, but keep your left foot out so that your legs are wider than shoulder-width apart; bend at the knees to a squat position. Don't slouch forward. Then, bob and weave with two step touches. Your right foot steps out, and your left foot follows. Right again, and then left. Arms stay in the fighting position. Alternate legs.

For the knee lifts with bounce, lift your left knee (see the following figure, center), swinging your arms up at the same time. Place your foot down. Alternate legs. You don't have to bounce.

When doing jumping jacks, your legs should land a little more than shoulder-width apart (see the following figure, right). Your arms will follow. Don't lock out your knees.

When jumping rope, stand tall, and swing your arms around as you jump.

The step touch (left), knee lift with bounce (center), and jumping jacks (right).

Fight to Be Fit

The workout will proceed as follows: You'll warm up the body for 5 to 8 minutes. Then you will do 35 minutes of cardio-kickboxing, 10 minutes of conditioning drills (ab work), and 5 to 8 minutes of cool down. Remember, you're working out in a non-stop 45-minute mode. Just follow the choreography described in the following sub-sections.

Start marching! Get your hands up and remember the number eight: Every move will be done in reps of eight. You'll do four sets of each. For example, after doing four sets of eight jabs, you will use a transitional move to slide into your next set of moves.

At first, you'll set up each move by going slow. Beginners, that may be enough of a workout; use the perceived exertion scale in Chapter 8, "Be Your Own Coach," to determine how you feel. While working out, remember the following two important points: Keep your abdominals tight, and focus on an imaginary opponent to create a little resistance.

Combustion: Warmup

In your warmup, you'll execute moves that mimic those used in a fight.

1. Start with a right step touch. Then, step touch into a right bob and weave. From the bob and weave, go back into the right step touch.

2. Next, step touch with jabs. From the step touch, bob and weave right with two step touches; throw a left jab (see the following figure, left). Then move left and throw a right jab.

3. Next you'll execute a knee lift. Start with your right knee; then, alternate and lift your left knee. Then go back into step touch with jabs.

4. Next, place your legs shoulder-width apart and move into a squat (see the following figure, center).

5. From the squat, keep facing front and move into a right lunge. Then, shift your body weight to the left lunge, and then back to the right, and so forth. Make sure you keep your knees over your heels as you shift back and forth (see the following figure, right).

Heat it up with a step touch and jab, squat, and front lunge.

Combustion Stretching

The following stretches are static, meaning that you don't move. Hold each stretch for about 10 seconds.

Start out with the runner's stretch, or front lunge, with your right leg forward (see the following figure, top left). Keep your left leg straight so you feel your hip stretch; your weight should be on the ball of your foot. Now, shift your body weight to the back leg and bend your left knee. At the same time, straighten your front leg to facilitate a hamstring stretch (see the following figure, top center). Then move back into a front lunge. Next, place your legs shoulder-width apart and assume a soft squat position (see the following figure, top right). Shift your body weight to the left, and then turn into a left runner's stretch. Rest your hands on the tops of your thighs, holding the stretch for 10 seconds. Then move into a left hamstring stretch.

Follow up with a spine stretch. Hands rest on your thighs. As you inhale, draw your belly button into your spine for a count of four. Then arch your back as you exhale for a count of four. Visualize a cat stretching its back. Sometimes, this stretch is called a cat stretch (see the following figure, bottom left). Drop your right shoulder (see the following figure, bottom right), followed by the left. Return your hands to your thighs and inhale up as if you're a cat to the fighter's stance.

Kick off your workout with these moves.

Protect Your Face

Keep marching, and keep your hands up to protect your face. In this workout, you'll do four punches—jab, cross, hook, and uppercut—and you'll work the speed bag. So let's turn the heat up by reviewing hand mechanics:

➤ As you jab, extend your fist and rotate your knuckles so that they face upward and are parallel to the ground.

➤ As you throw a cross, extend your arm forward and pivot on the ball of your rear foot. Shift your weight from your toe to your leg, to your torso, and then to your arm. With your palm facing down, extend your fist in a horizontal move. Remember to rotate your shoulder as you throw the cross.

➤ As you throw a hook, your arm turns in a 90-degree horizontal angle so that your elbow faces away from your body and the palm of your fist faces the ground. As you fire this punch, pivot on your front foot—your weight should shift to your front leg. Pull your left shoulder back as you punch, and aim for the chin.

➤ In throwing an uppercut, remember to bring your left shoulder back as soon as you rotate your right shoulder. Fire your fist straight up, so that its position resembles a body builder's bicep pose. Your palm should face you. As for your target, the fist should connect with either the body or the sweet spot (the chin).

Warning Warriors

The elbow should follow the fist. *Don't fully extend the arm!* Leave a slight bend in the elbow so as not to overextend your arm.

Sequence #1: Jab and Jack

At first, just walk through these moves; maybe do two sets of eight to get the feel of the sequence. Beginners, you can walk through all four sets. Note that you can get on your toes as you do these if you want to add a little bounce.

Your first move is the jab. Remember to rotate your knuckles so that they face the ceiling as you strike. Don't forget to add the recoil after you walk through the first or second set. After you complete four sets, pick a transitional move to switch which leg you have forward; it doesn't matter which leg you begin with. For example, fire eight jabs with the left leg forward, do eight jumping jacks, then fire eight more jabs with the right leg forward. Remember when you throw the left jab, your left leg takes a step forward. After you've worked both sides, do a set of uppercuts. The uppercut is a little tricky because you've got to use your entire body to get enough power. In other words, the power comes from the legs. So, bend at the knees to drive the punch straight up. Now pick another transitional move to take you into the opposite foot forward. After you complete your jabs and uppercuts, do a set of knee lifts to move into the sequence #2.

Sequence #2: Transform Your Body with Power Moves

After the transitional move, you will put your leg movements and punches together. Unlike the first sequence, there is no bouncing through these moves. Instead, focus on your form. Start with your feet shoulder-width apart, and your arms in fighting stance.

Your first move is a cross with a lunge (see the following figure, left). As you execute the cross, turn on the balls of your feet and move into a lunge. Remember, keep your knee aligned above your heel. Snap your arm back into the fighting position; as you do so, swivel your feet back so that they face front. Your feet should be shoulder-width apart.

Follow up with a hook with a lunge (see the following figure, center). As you fire the hook, turn on the balls of your feet and move into a lunge. Bring the hook back into a fighting position; again, place your feet shoulder-width apart.

Finish with side knee lifts. Angle your foot slightly to the side. As you do so, soften the stance of your support knee and bring your elbow to meet the raised knee. Pull your side abdominal muscles together as you lift your knee (see the following figure, right).

Do a cross with a lunge (left), followed by a hook with a lunge (center), and finish with side knee lifts (right).

Sequence #3: Jab, Jab, Cross, and Knee Lift

Get on your toes! This is a fun combo that allows you to be creative: Use the preceding photo sequences to put together combos. For example, here's one that will get your heart rate up: jab, jab, cross, and two knee lifts. Notice that this combo adds up to a count of eight. Complete four sets, and then use the jump rope exercise as your transitional move. Then do the opposite side.

Sequence #4: Shuffle, Shuffle, and Cross

As always, put 'em up! Then start to shuffle. Don't cross your legs as you shuffle. Drag the back leg to the front three times while jabbing. On the forth count, go into a lunge and fire a cross.

Kickboxing Buzz

Blow it all out as you strike. Inhale through your nose and exhale through your mouth. Don't hold your breath.

Kick That Butt Away

We'll walk through each kick, always beginning with the knee in a tightly bent position (called the fold):

➤ With the front kick, bring up your leg in the fold, holding the knee high and using it as your aiming sight for targets. Snap the lower leg out to the target, thrusting your hips forward to get enough power as the kick is being executed. Strike your target with the ball of your foot. After you hit the target, bring the leg quickly back to the fold.

➤ Don't rush the side kick. As you start to fold the leg, your support foot will turn, moving the heel so that it points toward the target. Bring the folded knee up, somewhere near the opposite side of your chest (or as much as flexibility allows). Flex your foot so that the bottom heel faces the target. As the leg snaps out, allow the hip to roll over or turn into the kick. At this point, your body is slightly turned away from your opponent, but don't take your eyes off the target. Thrust the kick out in a straight line. Use the heel of your foot to strike your target. Make sure that the heel is slightly higher than your toes; this will help you land the kick. After the side kick strikes your target, snap it back to the fold as quickly as possible.

Kickboxing Buzz

With kicks, you can hit anywhere on the body. Some targets are better than others, though, depending on the kick. For example, front kicks are more damaging to the stomach or thigh area. In general, you can strike as low as the calf or as high as the head. Anywhere in between, such as the stomach, is considered a middle target. Any kick to the groin area is used only in a self-defense situation.

➤ With the back kick, you will lean forward as you pick up the knee in the fold. Leading with your heel, send the kick backward. If you are kicking with your right leg, look over your right shoulder; look over your left shoulder when kicking with your left leg. Pull in your belly as you kick back. After landing the kick, place your kicking foot on the floor and return to fighter's stance. Your opposite side should now be forward.

Sequence #5: Front Kick, Squat, Front Kick

Execute this sequence with squats between each kick. Take the time to work through the sequence slowly and correct your form. Don't worry, you'll feel the burn. In this sequence, you'll throw four sets of front kicks. After the transitional move, repeat the sequence without the squats: right front kick and left front kick.

Sequence #6: Side Kick and Squat

Next is the side kick sequence. Open your legs a little wider than you would for a squat. Point your toes out slightly; make sure that your knees are above your heels. Now, step together (see the following figure, left). Notice that your butt is slightly turned to the side. Pick your right knee up (see the following figure, center); shoot your right leg out (see the following figure, right); bring the knee back to the fold; and then place your foot down. Return to a squat. Don't forget to work the other leg. After a transitional move, repeat the side kicks without the squats.

Step together (left), raise your knee up into the fold (center), and execute the side kick (right).

Sequence #7: Front Kick, Squat, Back Kick

For this sequence, we'll add the back kick. First, execute a left front kick (see the following figure, left); follow up with a squat (see the following figure, center); finally, execute a right back kick (see the following figure, right). Don't forget to work both legs forward.

For your transitional move, add the speed bag. With the speed bag work, you want to keep your hands moving rapidly in a circle as if you're hitting the bag. For the speed bag transitional move, assume a lunge position. As you hit the imaginary bag, remain in the lunge. Try not to move so you feel the burn.

Left front kick (left), squat (center), and right back kick (right).

Sequence #8: All Kicks

With this sequence, you can be creative. You can make up any leg combo using the moves depicted in the preceding photo sequences. For instance, here's an idea for a combo: March for three counts, and then kick on the fourth count. For example, march in place for three counts, and then fire a left front kick. March another three counts, and then fire a right side kick. Then, take out the marches so you're continuously kicking. The good news is that you don't have to finish this combo with a transitional move. Rather, step touch to a cool down. After that, go into the bob and weave.

Cool It Down

Now it's time for the cool down. Remember to keep your head up—it must remain higher than your heart until you stop panting. Hold the following stretches for 30 seconds, inhaling and exhaling through them.

First, do a set of pile squats. Open your legs a little wider than you would for a squat. Point your toes out slightly, and keep your knees above your heels. And squat down for two counts and then return to a pile position. Your goal is eight pile squats.

Follow up with a side-to-side stretch. Hold your arms out to the sides and lock your bottom half; move only your torso from left to right (see the following figure, left). Let your rib cage lead the way. Next, reach over your head with your left arm. Don't twist. Reach high over your head with your fingertips as if you're smelling your armpit, and then reach to the right to stretch your side (see the following figure, center). Next, turn to the side, moving into a slight lunge. Pull your belly in, and place your hands on the meat of your thighs. Lower yourself into a right runner's stretch (see the following figure, right). Remember to keep your knee above your heel. Also, keep the back leg as straight as possible so that you can feel the quad and hip flexor stretch.

Use these stretches to cool down.

Anchor your hips. Now move your rib cage from side to side. Next, we move into a hamstring stretch. Standing with your legs shoulder-width apart, bring your nose toward your toe, and your chest to your knee. You can bend the back leg as a modification.

Move back into the runner's stretch, still lunging with your right leg. Turn that lunge into a front lunge and keep your left toe and heel on the floor for the inner thigh stretch. Shift your body back to the center; place your hands on the meat of your thighs. Do all on the right leg until you come all the way up to a standing position. Then repeat everything on the opposite foot.

Finish off with a spine stretch: Inhale up, as if your spine is making a C curve, to a standing position. Now repeat the same stretches with the opposite leg.

Attention, Super Fit

There will come a time when you want to step up your workouts; this is a natural progression as you get in better shape. Following are a few things you can do to increase the intensity:

➤ Increase the music tempo, but not too fast—you want to retain good form.

➤ Add 15 more minutes of workout. For example, add more kicks and reps.

You can also add *plyometric* work: lots of power moves, hops, and jumps. These moves will raise your heart rate, so do only one set of eight. Keep in mind, these moves are high-intensity, meant to be used as a power booster. That's right, you'll burn more calories for all that hard work.

Words for Warriors

To put a lot of power in your workout, try **plyo-moves.** These moves range from jumps to hops. A set of **plyometrics** can send your heart rate soaring.

181

If you want to up the ante, start out by squatting three times. Hop on the count, and go as high as you can. Then, do another set.

For the plyo-jack, stand tall. Hop in for two counts (see the following figure, left), and then hop out for two more counts (see the following figure, right).

Explosive jacks: Squat low and then jump out into a jack.

The Least You Need to Know

➤ The most common injuries result from overuse of muscles and bad instructions or form.

➤ Don't abuse your body by cardio-kickboxing six times a week.

➤ Beginners should start with the knee in the fold.

➤ All moves will be done in reps of eight. You'll do four sets of each move.

➤ The music shouldn't be too fast.

Part 4
King of the Ring

After hundreds of lessons, numerous sparring partners, and many days of aches and pains, you're ready to take your workout to the next level. Beat workout burnout by training like a professional fighter.

Dreaming of signing autographs? Find out if you've what it takes to go the distance in the ring. This part provides a breakdown of a progressive, 8-week fight plan that will prepare you both physically and mentally for your next fight. Or, if you've got that competitive spirit, you can just train like a fighter—we won't throw you into the ring.

Chapter 13

The Lightweight:
Weeks 1 and 2

In This Chapter

➤ Eight weeks to the big event

➤ Train like a fighter

➤ A progressive training schedule that's set in stone

➤ Eating five times a day

➤ Identify weaknesses in your offensive and defensive moves

You're in good shape: You kickbox, you have a trainer, you even do yoga. Yet something is missing. You've been flatlining for months. You go through your workouts as if you're sitting in the dentist chair, waiting for a root canal.

To say that you've lost your spark—well, that's putting it mildly. Despite your best work, you still can't get rid of those seven or so extra pounds; it's as if a thin veneer of fat hides the hard body you've always dreamed of.

Sound familiar? You've probably hit a fitness plateau, a state of affairs that your everyday workouts can't reverse—no pep in your sprint, no zing in your punch, and no zap in your kick. Well, why not train like an athlete?

The Making of a Champion

We all admire the courage, dedication, and discipline of elite competitive athletes. Are you wondering what it takes? Physically, it involves strength, speed, agility, flexibility, endurance, accuracy, timing, and precision of techniques; mentally, it takes tenacity, spirit, strategy, attitude, and determination.

The 8-week training schedule that begins in this chapter and continues in Chapters 14–16 is multifaceted: You'll have eight weeks to get in shape for an actual fight, or you can use these eight weeks to simply train like a fighter. In other words, you don't have to climb through the ropes to be a champion, but after completing this training regimen you'll have the makings of a pro. Whether you're a young warrior or a wannabe, you're about to master the art of self-discipline.

The first two weeks of training (covered in this chapter) will be a lot of work, but this is a realistic representation of the price an elite athlete pays to be prepared for the ring. Not only will you sacrifice many hours for training, you'll also have to be committed to your overall health—how you sleep, eat, and take care of yourself is just as important as the workout training.

Rounds 1 and 2

In weeks 1 and 2, you'll be getting your ducks in a row, so to speak. These weeks will prepare you for the much tougher training that lies ahead. So right now you've got to get the little stuff out of the way. Start by going to the store to purchase a daily schedule book; this journal will be your lifeline to oversee your training. Let's call it a fight log.

For the next eight weeks, your alarm will buzz each morning at 6:00 A.M. sharp. In addition to becoming an early riser, you'll eat your meals at the same time every day, and you'll train like clockwork. Get the idea? It's a set-in-stone schedule. Your log will help you keep track of your training.

Nothing but H₂0

During your training you'll drink water, and lots of it. Otherwise, you may get a headache or feel irritable, exhausted, mentally drained, and worn out. These are all signs of dehydration, which is a very real possibility with this type of training. Furthermore, these symptoms will put a halt to your training.

So while you're shopping for your fight log, you need to buy gallons of water. Or, if you don't have time to shop, think about having water delivered to your home. Whatever the case, water will be your main drink while you train. Instead of the 8 ounces per hour required by an everyday diet, you'll drink 16 ounces per hour. You must make a conscious effort to drink water; bring your own bottle with you everywhere you go.

Water is the easiest, cheapest, and safest method of staying healthy. There is an easy test to determine if you're getting enough water: Look at your urine; it should be pale-clear yellow in color. Your urine will be a deeper yellow when you first wake up, which is normal because you have not been drinking. But as the day goes on, shoot for a pale yellow. While you're increasing your water, you should start to cut down on liquids that dehydrate you, such as coffee, tea, and soft drinks. Don't worry, you don't have to eliminate java altogether; just start watching how much caffeine you drink.

Gear Check-Up

Make sure your equipment is in good shape. Toss your smelly old hand wraps, and do the squeeze test on your gloves to make sure the padding hasn't worn away. You might want to go to the dentist for a fitted mouthpiece if the off-the-shelf ones won't do. You must have your own equipment if you want to train at this level. If you don't yet have the necessary equipment, now is a good time to try out some new gear. Make sure it's comfortable; you don't want your gear to restrict your kicks or punches.

A Feast for a King

Start thinking about your diet. Go to the store and stock up on grab-and-go type foods. Think small—during training, you'll eat five small meals a day to keep up your energy. Don't think calories; instead, think about the calories you'll burn. That's right: Like exercising, eating stimulates your metabolism. When you eat, you're making your body burn calories. This process is called thermogenesis; it uses energy to digest your food and absorb the nutrients from the foods you eat. That's one reason why you shouldn't skip meals—the caloric burn involved in eating is small, but it adds up. You want to keep the body burning calories all day long by eating small meals.

As you train, your muscles use up stored carbohydrates. This drying up of carbs can cause you to "hit the wall," a term athletes use to describe that dreaded moment when they can't take another step; it's a ball-and-chain feeling your legs get when the glycogen in your body runs out. Many athletes complain of light-headedness and weakness. You've got to eat a steady diet of carbs to fend off fatigue. Foods such as bananas, apples, figs, potatoes, rice, multigrain breads, and grapes are best for *grazing*.

Energize

Eat foods that give you energy. Have you ever had a smoothie? Smoothies are not only delicious, they make great snacks. If you use fresh fruit and soy milk or fruit juice, you'll get a mouth full of precious nutrients. Or try carrot juice, another energy drink. You can also blend four large carrots and two Granny Smith apples together; it's delicious. Another option is to blend four large carrots with some vanilla soy milk—the result is better than delicious. Try some green drinks for energy; shop at

a health food store for any green drink powder, such as *Spirulina* or blue-green algae. Mix in a few frozen bananas and some apple juice, and you've got yourself a power booster.

Liquid Meals

Another good idea is to find an easy-to-stomach replacement meal, such as a liquid meal. The challenge here is to find one that doesn't taste awful. Remember, though, that when you're training heavy, replacement meals can feed your muscles. Your main concern is recovery; you do not want to feel like you're in low gear while you train. Your body relies heavily on carbohydrates—specifically, on stored carbs called glycogen—for power; your muscles use carbohydrate power. Not feeding your body can dramatically hinder your training.

Replacement drinks can do the trick. For the best results, down one within an hour of training. Look for a replacement shake that offers a good balance between proteins and carbs, plus additional minerals such as added electrolytes.

Keep a Log

Make a commitment to record your whole life diligently in your fight log—everything from what you eat to how many hours you sleep. Write down how your body feels every day, what injuries (if any) you suffered, and how you've been keeping up.

If you noticed, for example, that on some days you trained better than others, try to figure out why: Did you eat anything different on those days? Did you sleep more? Maybe you didn't train as hard that day. Your fight log will tell you. Your goal is to get the most out these eight weeks; an accurate fight log will help you alter your training, if necessary.

After the first week, you can change things up if you're constantly tired. You can certainly expect some muscle stiffness, but if you can't get out of bed, you need to reduce some of your training. Find a massage therapist or chiropractor to help relieve some of the stiffness. Plan ahead; if necessary, make weekly appointments for the next eight weeks. Purchase sea salt for your hot soaks. Besides being soothing, sea salt reduces minor swelling.

Most importantly, remember that not only is your performance on the line, so is your safety. Don't train so hard that you end up sick or—worse—injured. Use your log to gauge your training. Then you can adjust what needs to be changed.

It's all about you; this hardcore training is about personal improvement, not about winning per se. You'll challenge yourself; you'll push yourself. And after you're done, you'll be amazed at what you accomplished, even though you'll be drained. These weeks are about you, and how to make it as a top athlete.

Much of your training will involve overcoming mental barriers. Another suggestion, then (and this may sound a bit odd), is to pick a fighting name—the fight game is all about attitude. Pretend that you're the "Monster Masher" or "The Terminator." You're not Mr. Cleaver, waking up to go to your 9-to-5 job. Instead, you're a lean, mean, fighting machine, mentally masterminding your victory—completing these eight weeks. It doesn't matter if you're not entering the ring; you still need to pretend that the big event is weeks away. So much of this training is repetitive that you need to psych yourself up to be an elite athlete.

As a mental exercise, in your fight log, create lists of skill strengths and weaknesses. Be brutally honest about your techniques. If you can't determine, for example, what punches you need to improve, ask a trainer or another athlete to help you. You'll focus on improving your technique during the next eight weeks. Thus, this step is extremely important because your training will be based on areas that you need to improve and the strengths that you can enhance.

Pro-Elite

In this program, train six days a week. On Mondays, Wednesdays, and Fridays, you'll kickbox. Tuesdays and Thursdays will be reserved for roadwork and weight training. On Saturdays, you'll do sprints and interval work. You'll start each workout with a warmup. For example, you'll start your runs by walking, eventually working up to a 4- or 5-mile jog.

During weeks 1 and 2, you'll prepare your body for training every day. You'll focus on finding weaknesses in your form, movement, and technique. Does your hook lack power, for example? Can you land a side kick? It's very important that you know which techniques work and which don't. You don't want to make the same mistake a lot of fighters do, throwing moves that are not effective.

Refer back to your lists of strengths and weaknesses in your fight log. Delineate the listed items in a "bread-and-butter" list of techniques, the ones you execute the best. Then create a "Hail Mary" list, consisting of things you need to work on. Trust your instincts; you will naturally feel more comfortable about certain techniques than you do about others. Chances are that those techniques are your best. It's also important to split your list between kicks and punches; some fighters make the mistake of relying too much on either their kicking or punching game. If, for example, you go in just throwing kicks, your opponent will figure out quickly that he can knock your lights out by punching you.

You don't have to be a great kicker or have a lot of power in your punches to be effective. Develop your strong techniques to try to hide the weak ones. That's how you can develop a fight game plan for attack strategies: By going in prepared, knowing when and how to use your stuff is one less worry that you'll have in the ring.

189

Words for Warriors

Making weight means qualifying for a fight by registering on or below the specified weight class.

Pound for Pound

Fighters, are you going in heavy or light? Decide now because your training will be geared toward the weight class in which you plan to fight. The weight classes are detailed in the following list; they vary slightly, depending on the sanctioning bodies:

➤ Super heavyweight—more than 210 lbs.

➤ Heavyweight—190 to 209.9 lbs.

➤ Cruiserweight—180 to 189.9 lbs.

➤ Light heavyweight—169 to 179.9 lbs.

➤ Super middleweight—161 to 168.9 lbs.

➤ Middleweight—155 to 160.9 lbs.

➤ Super welterweight/light middleweight—148 to 154.9 lbs.

➤ Welterweight—143 to 147.9 lbs.

➤ Super lightweight—138 to 142.9 lbs.

➤ Lightweight—133 to 137.9 lbs.

➤ Featherweight—125 to 132.9 lbs.

➤ Bantamweight—120 to 124.9 lbs.

➤ Flyweight—117 to 119.9 lbs.

➤ Atomweight—less than 117 lbs.

Words for Warriors

Fighters qualify for a fight by registering to fight in a specific **weight class**. Your training, too, will be based on chosen weight. For example, if you're going up a class, you might want to add more weight training. If you're going in light, you'll have to watch everything you eat, in addition to doing more cardio work.

The outcome of your fight will be at least partially based on your choice of weight class. For example, if you're going in heavy, you'll have to gain a few pounds; weight training might do the trick. If you're going in light, you might have to hit the pavement to lose a few pounds.

Most fighters will try to fight in the lowest possible weight class without starving themselves. The reasoning behind this is the belief that small opponents have less power and reach (translation: It's easier to kick their butts).

Cutting weight is miserable, especially if you have to lose 10 pounds or more; it's like always being on a diet. If you can fight in a heavier weight class, the transition might be worth it. Not every fighter will benefit by going up, though. For example, a 5' 6" fighter, regardless of muscle mass, won't have the height to take on a heavyweight contender.

You can make a decision to go up or down after you've gotten in the best shape possible. Step on a scale; where does your weight fall? If it's between two weight classes, the decision will be yours, based on how you feel.

Training Heavy

Just about any performance will improve with weight training. Don't worry, though: This weight training won't make a muscle head out of you. Being strong will enhance your kickboxing, not slow down your kicks and punches as some fighters believe. It's important not to bulk up, however; your focus is on a total body workout.

If you're not a member of a weight gym, join one. As far as your routine goes, use the exercises outlined in Chapter 9, "Head to Heel Like Steel," or make up your own. Keep in mind that you'll be kickboxing three times a week (Monday, Wednesday, and Friday); you don't want to overwork muscles, such as your deltoids or shoulders. Therefore, the muscles you should focus on are in your back, chest, and legs. Don't kickbox and lift on the same day. Instead, lift on Tuesday and Thursday:

Two exercises for chest	Three sets. For example: barbell flat bench press and barbell incline press.
Two exercises for back	Three sets. For example: wide grip lat; pulldown and close grip lat; pulldown.
Three exercises for legs	Three sets. For example: squats and leg press.

On Track

Remember, the name of the game is not to get hit; your goal is to keep moving in a fight without petering out. So, you'll find ways to improve your cardio training. For example, you can cut down your pace times or increase your distance. You'll also have to do lots of push-ups and sit-ups. The push-ups will strengthen your punches, and those hundreds of sit-ups will toughen up your stomach, which will definitely take some hits during the fight.

Your long runs will be light work; your heart rate shouldn't get past a level 8 on the perceived exertion scale. To refresh your memory, you might want to turn to Chapter 8, "Be Your Own Coach." How long you run will depend on the weight class you're fighting in. If you need to lose a few pounds, your runs should last 45 minutes to one hour. If you're going in heavy, run for about 30 to 45 minutes. Don't forget to start by walking to get your body ready for its run.

Use these first two weeks to reflect on your training. You'll have plenty of running sessions, but it's particularly important to go over your training in week 1. Now is the time to change your regimen, if needed:

➤ Cardio work: Tuesday and Thursday

➤ 30 minutes of nonstop jogging to maintain weight

➤ 30 to 60 minutes of nonstop jogging to drop a few pounds

In Chapter 9, we explained the difference between anaerobic workouts (work without oxygen) and aerobic workouts (any exercise that uses oxygen in the body). In the ring, you are sometimes pushed to panting exhaustion; you'll most likely have to sustain that effort until the round ends. In order for you to work longer without suffering from the muscle burn and calling it quits, you'll train anaerobically. You'll also be doing some interval training so that your body becomes accustomed to the rhythm of a fight. For example, during the rest break between the rounds of a fight, your body flushes lactic acid, a byproduct of glycogen, from its muscles, so that you can get back on your feet for the next round. This is an example of interval training: hard work, rest, hard work.

As part of your anaerobic training, sprint work will be done on Saturdays. Start with a light, 30-minute run, and then move into timed sprints:

➤ Week 1: three 100-meter sprints

➤ Week 2: two 200-meter sprints; three 100-meter sprints

Fighting for Excellence

Everything you do, up to this point, will make you a better kickboxer including these workouts. In weeks 1 and 2, the focus will be on cleaning up and refining your kicks and punches, along with improving your overall conditioning. There is no question about it: You need to be able to finish the advanced one-on-one. In so doing, you can work on your punches, kicks, movement, and form.

Part of your routine will involve kickboxing three times a week. On Mondays, you'll work on improving your punches; on Wednesdays you can polish your kicks; and on Fridays you'll focus on conditioning. These workouts will be intense so you can fall into bed after you eat dinner. The following sections outline your kickboxing workouts.

Monday and Wednesday Workouts

➤ Advanced warmup

➤ Advanced ab routine

➤ Three rounds of shadow sparring

➤ Three rounds of kicking shield (Monday)/five rounds of kicking shield (Wednesday)

➤ Five rounds of focus mitts (Monday)/two rounds of focus mitts (Wednesday)

➤ Two rounds of Thai pads (Monday)/three rounds of Thai pads (Wednesday)

➤ Two rounds of heavy bag boxing only (Monday)/kicks and punches (Wednesday)

➤ 60 push-ups in sets of 30, 20, 10 (Monday)

➤ 100 sit-ups, 100 reps, done in sets of 25 (Monday)

➤ 60 Hindu squats in two sets of 30 (Monday)

➤ Two sets of conditioning drills for legs, abs, and upper body (Wednesday)

Friday Workout (Focus on Conditioning)

➤ Advanced warmup

➤ Advanced ab routine

➤ Three rounds of shadow sparring

➤ Three rounds of focus mitts

➤ Three rounds of kicking shields

➤ Three sets of conditioning drills for legs, abs, and upper body

➤ One 1-minute set of interval sprints

The End Result

We'll finish this chapter with a five-day overview; follow it for the next two weeks. Remember to stay in touch with your body. During these weeks, you should opt for changes if you feel these workouts are not for you.

Monday/Wednesday/Friday

6:00 A.M.	Wake up; drink fluids: water, or glass of juice
6:30 A.M.	Breakfast: Eat within 30 minutes of waking up
8:00 A.M.	Workout: none
10:00 A.M.	Snack: fruit smoothie or replacement shake
12:00 P.M.	Lunch: bulk of calories
3:00 P.M.	Snack: fruit, power bars, replacement shake
6:00 P.M.	Workout: kickboxing
8:00 P.M.	Dinner: very low fat; focus on protein and vegetables
10:00 P.M.	Good night

Tuesday/Thursday

6:00 A.M.	Wake up; drink fluids: water, or glass of juice
6:30 A.M.	Breakfast: Eat within 30 minutes of waking up
8:00 A.M.	Workout: weight train
10:00 A.M.	Snack: fruit smoothie or replacement shake
12:00 P.M.	Lunch: bulk of calories; watch fat and carbohydrates
3:00 P.M.	Snack: fruit, power bars, replacement shake
6:00 P.M.	Workout: aerobic running
8:00 P.M.	Dinner: very low fat; focus on protein and vegetables
10:00 P.M.	Good night

Saturday

8:00 A.M.	Wake up; drink fluids: water, or glass of juice
8:30 A.M.	Breakfast: Eat within 30 minutes of waking up
10:00 A.M.	Workout: aerobic run followed by anaerobic sprints
11:00 P.M.	Snack: fruit, power bars, replacement shake
1:00 P.M.	Lunch: bulk of calories
3:00 P.M.	Meal replacement
7:00 P.M.	Dinner: very low fat; focus on protein and vegetables
12:00 A.M.	Good night

The Least You Need to Know

➤ These eight weeks are for fighters, and for anyone who wants to train like a fighter.

➤ You'll wake up at 6:00 A.M. each day, eat at the same time every day, and train like clock work.

➤ You'll train six days a week. On Tuesdays and Thursdays, you'll train twice a day.

➤ To keep your energy level up, you'll eat five small meals a day.

➤ Drink 16 ounces of water per hour.

➤ These two weeks will be dedicated to finding weaknesses in your fight game.

Chapter 14

The Middleweight: Weeks 3 and 4

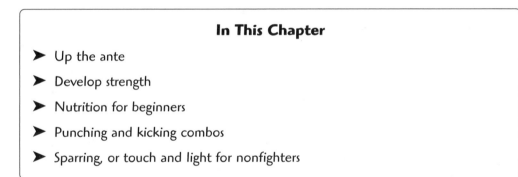

In This Chapter

➤ Up the ante

➤ Develop strength

➤ Nutrition for beginners

➤ Punching and kicking combos

➤ Sparring, or touch and light for nonfighters

Headed for the Olympic Games? Why not? We all dream of becoming an elite champion; we want to live out the fantasy of signing hundreds of autographs. Athletes everywhere have one thing in common: a *progressive training schedule*. This is a type of training that increases in intensity as the weeks go on; it's the type of training exemplified by your 8-week program. You're about to brave the workouts of weeks 3 and 4—the dog days of weeks 1 and 2 pale in comparison.

You're about to go from a maniacal, body sweating, weight training routine to intense sparring; you're moving away from the first two weeks, which warmed you up for weeks 3 and 4. During these two weeks, you'll intensely pump iron to gain physical strength; you'll grunt with every conditioning drill. Strength, not body size, is the focus of the weeks to come. As the physical demands of these workouts increase, so do the results. Remember, the end result is personal accomplishment.

Rounds 3 and 4

It's time to evaluate the first two weeks. As you shift from the lightweight routine to the more challenging middleweight, you should make some changes in your routine, if necessary. Maybe you need to eat more food, or perhaps you need to focus on finding the right foods. Are you sleeping enough to recoup from your training? So far you've only dipped your toes in the workout water, so to speak; the hardcore training starts now. Your life as you knew it is about to change. You'll start by learning how to take care of your body to obtain peak performance.

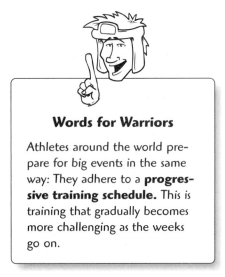

Words for Warriors

Athletes around the world prepare for big events in the same way: They adhere to a **progressive training schedule.** This is training that gradually becomes more challenging as the weeks go on.

Nutrition 101

We've asked you to eat five times a day—don't fret. You won't gain fat, especially if you know a thing or two about basic nutrition. Remember that eating every three to four hours revs up your metabolism, which is one way your body burns calories. Another way to burn calories is to—and this is the hard part—learn to navigate your way around bad fats.

Do you ever wish you had someone standing over you, saying, "Don't eat that, it's too fatty," or "Eat this, it's good for you"? Fat grams can sneakily add up, and the excess will almost always hamper your performance as an athlete. But do you have to turn your nose up at all fats? No; that, too, can curb your athletic dreams.

The American Heart Association says that we shouldn't get more than 30 percent of our calories from fat, and that only 10 percent of that number can come from saturated fat. What does that figure mean to you? Probably not much, unless you're standing by with a calculator. So what should we do, not put a morsel of fat in our mouth? That's not healthy, either. Fats help insulate vital organs, carry the fat-soluble vitamins (A, D, and E), and protect you from extreme hot and cold weather fluctuations. Fat is also the stored energy that you need for all those intense workouts.

The Bad Guys

The fats that you should eliminate are the omega-6 polyunsaturated fats, such as oils made from corn, safflower, sesame, and sunflower. Over the past century, evidence has steadily mounted, suggesting that diets high in these particular fats are dangerous to our health. For example, these fats are the quickest to turn rancid within the body. Furthermore, these oils are even deadlier when they are converted from a liquid to a solid or semisolid state, such as vegetable shortening or margarine, sometimes called trans-fatty acids or TFAs. These fats may be even more devastating to our health because nobody really knows what these fats will do once they're in your body.

The health risks associated with these oils range from heart disease and cancer to premature aging; researches haven't pinpointed the exact cause, but some studies suggest that these oils create *free radicals* within the body. One thing is for sure; these fats are not cardiovascular friendly.

You should also cut down on animal fats, also called saturated fats. You'll be able to easily recognize them because they're solid at room temperature. Coconut and palm oil are included in this group, as are beef, pork, lamb, and dairy products. Too much of these fats in the diet can clearly do a number on our arteries; they've been implicated in atherosclerosis and arterial disease.

Words for Warriors

Free radicals destroy cells in the body by damaging their membranes.

The Good Guys

So, after eliminating all that, what's left? There are also some good fats. For example, you probably want to eat more salmon and tuna; the fats in these fish, called omega-3 fatty acids, have been heralded as the good guys. Another source of good fats is flax oil or seeds. Try crumpling flax seed over cereal—it's delicious. You can purchase flax oil or meal at any health food store. Also good are monounsaturated fats. You'll find them in avocados, peanuts, almonds, hazelnuts, macadamia nuts, and olives. Canola oil is another option for good fats, as is olive oil; olive oil is also a healthy oil to cook with. Omega-3 fatty acids have been said to lower the risk of heart disease plus have tremendous effect on many other body functions, such as healing.

Kick-Tales

Some studies show that fish-eating communities have higher longevity and lower rates of heart disease than the non–fish-eating communities. Maybe that's why the Japanese can kick butt so well.

Your athletic performance will depend in part on your knowledge of the different kinds of fats. That means paying attention to the foods you eat; don't turn down an avocado thinking that it's too fattening, and then turn around and smear mounds of margarine on your roll. That's not the healthy option.

Don't Kiss Carbs Good-Bye

These days, it seems as if everyone is kissing carbs good-bye. This isn't a good idea, though, because carbs are your main source of energy. You've probably read somewhere that carbs make you fat, but it's just not that simple. For instance, the carbs in a candy bar might send you buzzing with a sugar rush; a multigrain bagel's carbs, however, slowly break down in the body, giving you a constant source of energy.

There are two categories of carbohydrates: complex and simple. Simple carbs include white sugar, cookies, candies, white breads, white rice, and some fruits. For complex carbs, eat foods such as multigrain breads, beans, potatoes, cereals, brown rice, and some fruits such as bananas and apples. Most fruits contain simple sugars as well; however, bananas and apples are top complex carbohydrate foods that can jump-start your workout. Vegetables are also broken down in two categories, starchy and complex; it's the starchy carbs that stay with you during your workout—potatoes specifically. Know this, fruits and vegetables provide precious nutrients that are frequently flushed from the body in the form of sweat when heavy-duty training. These foods nourish the body whole. Hey kickboxer, overindulge and sweat on.

You need to replace all white foods, such as white breads, with whole grain foods; substitute fruits for all those sweet candies; and trade in your junk food for wholesome, nutritious snacks. If you have to cheat, eat an oatmeal raisin cookie instead of chocolate chip. The message is simple: Don't dodge all carbs. If you don't have enough energy to get through your workout, if you're waking up tired, or if you can't keep up the pace that you normally do, you might not be getting enough carbs—you should rethink what you're eating. Besides the energy for your training, you need the fiber to keep your digestive tract healthy.

Kickboxing Buzz

Most fighters shy away from milk products, believing that their breathing is compromised during a fight; some also say that dairy products cause congestion.

Peak Power: Protein

Do you have a lingering sniffle or cold? Are you constantly tired? These are signs that you may not be getting enough protein. Besides making muscle, protein heals and repairs your body; it's the right stuff to fight off sickness. You have to eat enough protein daily to achieve peak performance.

Milk, fish, meat, and chicken are complete proteins, foods that meet the body's needs. Egg white is the perfect, complete protein. Then there are incomplete foods, such as beans, wheat, corn, rye, soybeans, nuts, and seeds; but you can combine these incomplete foods to make complete proteins. For example, rice and beans, when combined, provide protein—neither rice nor beans does this on its own. The general rule for combining is that most incomplete proteins combine with grains; for example, tuna and rice match up.

Planning Your Diet

Note that your need for fats, carbs, and proteins depends on your training and your body. With that in mind, meal planning will be part one of the most important aspects of your training. Use the information we've given you to acclimate yourself to balanced meals. And remember that we've given you this information to get you to eat right, not to eat one food group and avoid another.

Thanks to your fight log, you should have an idea of how your training is going. It's not too late to change things, especially if you're not happy with your performance. You may just need to slightly adjust your diet. On the other hand, you might want to hire a nutritionist. Through a computerized diet analysis report, she can tell you exactly how many fats, carbs, and proteins you need to reach peak performance.

Ringside Secrets

In addition to nutrition, there are a few things you need to know to be victorious in your training. Check out the following sections for some pointers on how to reach the top of your game, both in the ring and out.

Make a Fight Plan

If you're going to fight, make a fight plan—you have to have a strategy for a fight. Many fighters have lost their bouts for lack of a fight plan. Your plan can be as simple as keeping your hands up while you kick to protect yourself. In your fight log, write down your weaknesses, bad habits, and strengths as a fighter. Study yourself, and prepare yourself for the fight.

As part of your fight plan, you need to study the enemy as well as yourself. Your opponent, if he's a smart fighter, will have his own fight plan. That's right—he's evaluated you. Watch a few of his fights so he doesn't get an edge. If you can't go to a fight, send away for a video or ask around about his fight game. Trust us—fighters always gossip about other fighters.

Find weaknesses and bad habits in your opponent's fight game. You may be equally great fighters, but the belt will go to the one who makes the fewest mistakes. Also, pay attention to the techniques he throws most often. Earlier, we said that the fight game is nothing more than a guessing game: Where is the next punch going to land? Take the guesswork out of your fight—know your opponent's strategy as well as you know your own.

For example, if you can have a block ready for the vicious hook that's laid out his other opponents, you'll throw off his game. He's expecting you to go down just like the others, but you won't. Use his bewilderment: This is a good time to rain down a series of punches and seal the fate of fight. Or, maybe this fighter drops his hands while he kicks; what a great opportunity to take advantage of a bad habit. The winning of the fight goes to the fighter who stays on track with his game plan, while taking his opponent out of his.

Get Your Zs

Getting a good night's sleep is the best thing you can do while you're in heavy training. Setting a regular sleep pattern prepares your body for the workout that lies ahead. Without the right amount of rest, your body cannot recuperate from the physical demands of your training, and you might end up sick or injured.

Make it a point to get into bed at the same time every night so that you can establish a pattern. Evaluate your bedroom. Is it dark enough? Quiet enough? What noises wake you up at night? Can you stop them? Write down disturbing thoughts in your fight log so they don't keep you up at night. Use this time to make your bedroom sleep-friendly.

Going for Greatness

In this phase of training, you'll still train six days a week. On Mondays, Wednesdays, and Fridays, you'll kickbox. After you kickbox, you'll do your cardio work—a 30-minute run or the cardio-machines. On Tuesdays, Thursdays, and Saturdays, you'll weight train. You'll also do your sprints and interval work on Saturdays. For example, in the morning, you'll weight train, and for lunch, you'll do sets of sprints.

You'll start doing two workouts per day in week 4. For example, you'll weight train on Tuesday morning, and then take on full-contact sparring Tuesday night. Sunday is your one day of rest; don't lift a finger. Take this time to go over your progress. You need to come back on Monday refreshed and ready to train.

During the middleweight training weeks, you'll also spar. In week 3, you'll keep your head out of harm's way by body sparring. In week 4, however, you'll fight as if it's the real deal. As you spar, you'll practice the combos from Chapter 7, "'Float Like a Butterfly, Sting Like a Bee.'" While you spar, work on distance and angles of attacks. For those of you who feel yourself rising to a slow panic, note that you can touch or light spar if you do not plan to enter a fight.

Also during this phase of the training, you'll continue to improve on weaknesses in your form, movement, and techniques. You should train with a coach or training partner so he can point out such weaknesses. Developing your strengths will be your biggest asset in the ring—nobody wants to end up getting carried out on a stretcher. Finally, in these two weeks you'll continue to build strength, and the conditioning drills will intensify.

Solid as a Rock

A stronger athlete is a better athlete, plain and simple. If you're strong, you won't get pushed around in the ring, and you cut down on stress-related injuries. To increase your overall physical strength, during this phase of the training you'll add one more day of weight training.

The order in which you'll train your muscles changes with each workout. The idea is to not to overdevelop your muscles, but to strengthen the core muscles you'll use as a kickboxer. Try to get your workout done in the morning so your body can recover in time for your nighttime training. Weight train on Tuesdays, Thursdays, and Saturdays.

Tuesday Workout

Chest	**Flat bench press:** Three sets, 8 to 10 reps
	Incline bench press: Three sets, 10 reps
Back	**Wide grip pulldown:** Three sets, 10 to 12 reps
	Seated row: Three sets, of 12 reps
Arms	**Curl:** Three sets, 10 reps
	Tricep extension: Three sets, 10 reps
Legs	**Leg press:** Three sets, 12 to 15 reps
	Leg extension: Three sets, 12 reps
	Leg curl: Three sets, 12 reps

Thursday Workout

Back	**Close grip pulldown:** Three sets, 12 reps
	One arm rows: Three sets, 10 to 12 reps
Chest	**Dumbbell flat bench press:** Three sets, 10 reps
	Dumbbell incline press: Three sets, 10 reps
Arms	**Tricep extension:** Three sets, 10 reps
	Curl: Three sets, 10 reps
Legs	**Squat:** Three sets, 8 to 12 reps
	Leg curl: Three sets, 12 reps
	Leg extension: Three sets, 12 reps

Saturday Workout

Legs	**Squat:** Three sets, 8 reps
	Leg press: Three sets, 12 reps
	Leg curl: Three sets, 12 reps
	Leg extension: Two sets, 12 reps
Chest	**Flat bench:** Four sets, 10 reps
Back	**Wide grip pulldown:** Two sets, 10 reps
	Close grip pulldown: Two sets, 10 reps
	Seated rows: Two sets, 10 to 12 reps

The Unbeatable Bout

Let's pretend that your opponent is the new guy on the block. Tapes are sparse, and your fighting buddies don't have the scoop on his technique. All's not lost, though. You can be the unbeatable one. To do this, you'll sweat it out by practicing one combo after another.

Who, in their right mind, willingly walks into a buzz saw? That's what a combo can look like if it is thrown correctly. In the ring, throwing a series of combos is a little tricky for the simple reason that your opponent won't stand by and let you hit him— it's not like practicing on a heavy bag or kicking shield.

Throwing techniques in rapid succession will be your best strategy. Pay special attention, now. The more technique you can throw—fast—the more likely you are to land one. Your victory could depend on one of these strikes landing. Sure, you can get lucky with a one-shot knockout, but that's the exception, not the rule.

You'll work on driving a jab to the chin, followed by a really low kick. Varying your targets is important in the fight game: An example of a high target is the head; a low target is the calf; and then there is the gut, which is the middle target. With these combos, you need to focus on working your way up the body, or down and to the left or right side of the body. If you want to be the unbeatable one, keep your opponents guessing where the next strike will land.

You not only score points when throwing combos, you put together a valuable defense strategy. Nobody wants to get his lights knocked out, so he'll move to avoid what you're throwing. Thus, combos are a great defense strategy—especially if you lack good defensive skills such as bob and weaving.

By the way, after you launch an attack—three to four punch or kick combos—get out of the way. Standing around, admiring your handiwork may backfire, especially if you missed a shot. Your very annoyed opponent might come back swinging at you. Funny how that works!

Kickboxing Buzz

No one wants to get hit. Your opponent will bob, weave, catch, or parry so you can't land a strike. To increase your chances of connecting with your opponent, throw a variety of kicks and punches at all levels and angles. Your goal is to keep him guessing where the next strike will land. In the process, maybe you'll catch him off guard and knock him out.

Ready for the Ring?

In this phase of sparring, you can hit only to the body. The focus here is to practice the combinations that you'll use in the ring. You don't need the added pressure of trying to protect your head. If you're doing these workouts to get in shape, but not to fight, you don't have to body spar (but you can; it's up to you). Touch or light sparring will give you just as good a workout.

Your kickboxing workouts will include sparring. Notice that in the fourth week, you'll add a full contact spar on Tuesday night, along with a heavy-duty ab work drill. In addition, on Friday night, you'll add full contact sparring. On these days, you'll spar as if you're in an actual fight, with scheduled rounds and all. For the training sessions below, you'll be fighting a five rounder.

Monday Workout

➤ Warmup

➤ Ab workout

➤ Stretching

➤ Three rounds of shadow sparring

➤ One round of focus mitts

➤ One round of kicking shield

➤ One round of bag work

➤ Three rounds of body contact sparring (or light/touch sparring for nonfighters)

➤ Two rounds of focus mitts

➤ Three rounds of Thai pads

➤ One round of kicking shield

➤ Two sets of each kind of conditioning drills

Wednesday Workout

➤ Warmup

➤ Ab workout

➤ Stretching

➤ Three rounds of shadow sparring

➤ Three rounds of bag work

➤ Three rounds of body contact sparring (or light/touch sparring for nonfighters)

➤ Two rounds of focus mitts

➤ Four rounds of kicking shield

➤ Two sets of each kind of conditioning drills

➤ Stretching

Friday Workout (Week 3)

- ➤ Warmup
- ➤ Ab workout
- ➤ Stretching
- ➤ One round of focus mitts
- ➤ Two rounds of Thai pads
- ➤ Three rounds of body contact sparring (or light/touch sparring for nonfighters), three rounds of full contact sparring (week 4 only)
- ➤ Three rounds of focus mitts
- ➤ Three rounds of bag work
- ➤ Two sets of each kind of conditioning drills
- ➤ Stretching

Tuesday Spar Workout

- ➤ Warmup
- ➤ Stretching
- ➤ Three rounds of shadow sparring
- ➤ Three rounds of bag work
- ➤ Five rounds of full contact sparring (at an intense pace)
- ➤ 20 situps, two sets
- ➤ 20 frog kicks, two sets
- ➤ 20 crunches, two sets
- ➤ 20 medicine ball drop sit-ups, two sets
- ➤ 20 decline medicine ball sit-ups, two sets
- ➤ Stretching

Running Bleachers

Notice that you'll run after the kickboxing workout; you'll still hit the pavement three times a week and do sprint work on Saturdays. Keep in mind that you'll be tired from the kickboxing, so go slow. Just run for about 20 to 30 minutes on Monday, Wednesday, and Friday.

Find a set of bleachers. (Here's a tip: Most high schools have a track, complete with bleachers.) That's right, you'll run the bleachers. The pace needs to be quick, but you don't have to sprint up and down the bleachers. Your sprint training is about to intensify:

➤ Three minutes of stadium stairs

➤ Two 200-meter sprints

➤ Two 100-meter sprints

The End Result

Take a seat and reflect on your workout. How do you feel? You've put a great deal of thought and sweat into this training so far. Will you be able to go the full distance? Take Sunday to determine if you need to change things before you go on to the most grueling weeks of training, the heavyweight. Study the training you've just amazingly accomplished. And then, with your fight log by your side, make those changes. Lo and behold, you'll be geared up to continue—keep fighting on.

Monday, Wednesday, and Friday Workouts

6:00 A.M.	Wake up; drink fluids: water, or glass of juice
6:30 A.M.	Breakfast: Eat within 30 minutes of waking up
8:00 A.M.	Workout: none
10:00 A.M.	Snack: fruit smoothie or replacement shake
12:00 P.M.	Lunch: bulk of calories (watch fats)
3:00 P.M.	Snack: fruit power bars, replacement shake
6:00 P.M.	Workout: kickboxing and cardio-work
8:00 P.M.	Dinner: very low fat; focus on protein and vegetables
10:00 P.M.	Good night

Tuesday and Thursday Workouts

6:00 A.M.	Wake up; drink fluids: water, or glass of juice
6:30 A.M.	Breakfast: Eat within 30 minutes of waking up (make it carbohydrates)
8:00 A.M.	Workout: weight training
10:00 A.M.	Snack: fruit smoothie or replacement shake
12:00 P.M.	Lunch: bulk of calories (watch fat)
3:00 P.M.	Snack: fruit, power bars, replacement shake
6:00 P.M.	Workout: sparring (week 4 only)
8:00 P.M.	Dinner: very low fat; focus on carbs (week 4 only), protein, and vegetables
10:00 P.M.	Good night

Saturday Workout

6:00 A.M.	Wake up; drink fluids: water, or glass of juice
6:30 A.M.	Breakfast: Eat within 30 minutes of waking up (make it carbs)
8:00 A.M.	Workout: weight training
10:00 A.M.	Snack: fruit smoothie or replacement shake
12:00 P.M.	Workout: sprints
1:30 P.M.	Lunch: bulk of calories (watch fats)
3:00 P.M.	Snack: fruit, power bars, replacement shake
6:00 P.M.	Workout: none
8:00 P.M.	Dinner: very low fat; focus on carbs, protein and vegetables
10:00 P.M.	Good night

The Least You Need to Know

➤ All athletes train the same way—using a progressive training schedule. This type of schedule gradually gets more difficult.

➤ For peak performance, you need to eat balanced meals.

➤ You'll train six days a week. On Tuesdays and Saturdays you'll train twice a day.

➤ You'll increase your strength with weight training.

➤ You're getting ready for a fight by sparring.

Chapter 15

The Heavyweight: Weeks 5 and 6

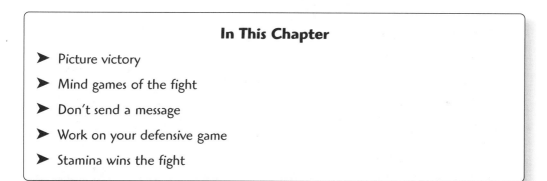

In This Chapter

➤ Picture victory

➤ Mind games of the fight

➤ Don't send a message

➤ Work on your defensive game

➤ Stamina wins the fight

It takes more than brute strength to send a message in the ring. Think back to the movie *Rocky*. The wicked set of jabs staggered him in the latter rounds; his head repeatedly snapped back as his opponent popped a series of right-handed bombs; his mangled face oozed blood as his opponent turned his brain to wallpaper paste. The fight still rings loud in most of our brains.

Rocky hung tough, barely surviving the fight. Why, then, did he eventually win? Rocky was on his last leg when, suddenly, he landed the right that put his opponent on the deck. Rocky was hungry for the win; Rocky had stamina.

Get hungry! Fighters, weeks 5 and 6 will make or break you. You'll battle mental and physical burnout. But that's what you'll be faced with in an actual fight. You might feel too exhausted to continue; you might gasp for breath; you might want to give up. But if you want to win, you have to have stamina—mental motivation and physical endurance. Don't think that you can't do it. Instead, think Rocky!

Rounds 5 and 6

Here's a warning: It will get lonely as you train; nobody will really want to be around you because you're probably not in the most pleasant state of mind. These weeks prepare you for the actual fight; the workouts are hardcore because you need to develop the mental and physical skills to stick it out, when all you want to do is quit.

As you train, you'll be pushed beyond your physical limits; the workouts are not pleasant. But keep in mind the end result—to hang tough and remain standing in the latter rounds of a fight.

You Are the Champion

Think of yourself as a winner. To get in this mindset, pick out a theme for yourself and your *cornermen*. For example, did you pick a name for yourself, as we asked you to in Chapter 13, "The Lightweight: Weeks 1 and 2"? Let's say that you're calling yourself the Monster Masher; you can customize your trunks, robes, warmups, T-shirts, or the cornermen's jackets. Or, instead of a name, you can pick your favorite colors and create a theme for yourself. Either way, you should look the part, bold and cocky; let your opponent see that you're a winner. You must feel like a world class champion the moment you step through those ropes.

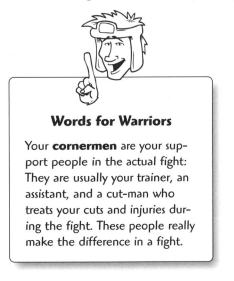

In addition to creating an intimidating first impression, you need to actually feel like the indisputable champion. Start today by talking to yourself. Look in the mirror and say, "Good morning, world champion." Say it as you train to get you through your workouts.

Words for Warriors

Your **cornermen** are your support people in the actual fight: They are usually your trainer, an assistant, and a cut-man who treats your cuts and injuries during the fight. These people really make the difference in a fight.

Feeding the Fighting Machine

Feed your ruthless, competitive body. Don't forget, you're eating five balanced meals a day. Your diet hasn't changed for this phase of the training, unless you're struggling to make your weight class. Now is the time to start cutting back on all fats; fat is still fat, good or bad. And eliminating all fats three weeks before a fight won't have long-term health consequences. For the next few weeks you might have to trim all fat from the meat you eat; choose lean cuts of meat such as round steak, sirloin, or extra lean ground beef. Use nonstick pans or sprays instead of oils. Steam all your veggies and eat dry baked potatoes; maybe sprinkle a few jalapeno peppers on top for some fat-free flavor.

On Sunday nights, plan out your meals for the week. Go shopping and buy only the items that are on your list. You may have to cut back on your portions. A good way to stick to this rule is to cook only a premeasured amount. That's what you'll be allowed to eat. Or, if you dine out, leave half the portion behind. Don't skip meals, though, because you're about to endure three ruthless weeks of training—you still need to feed your body. What you eat will affect the outcome of your training, so pick quality foods.

Sweet Dreams

Picture holding the belt; savor the taste of victory; hear the cheers of the crowd. What do you think about before you nod off at night, or when driving to and from work? Now you have something to think about. Instead of zoning out, use this time to program your brain; you're the indisputable champion.

Train Your Brain

Use your pre-sleep time to tell your mind that you're going to win. That way, your brain will have 7 or 8 hours to process your winning thoughts as you sleep. You can program yourself for success; if you can *visualize* yourself holding that belt, you will hold it.

Can you imagine your dense sweaty body in your favorite fighting shorts with your name—Monster Masher—embroidered on them? Go ahead, step into the ring and shake hands with your opponent. Picture the volley of straight punches to his face. Now, envision the turn kick that drops him to the floor. Feel his sweat as he staggers. Do you hear the crowd? They're cheering you on as the referee counts.

Words for Warriors

When you **visualize** victory, you're fueling your inner power to give you the outcome you want. You'll train the brain to physically respond. To do so, you must see yourself in the most positive way; you must hear positive comments. Imagine that you're winning; think it and you'll get real results.

Your visualization of your victory has to be real: Smell it, feel it, taste it, live it. You've traded war marks; maybe you have a few stitches over your eye, maybe he has a split lip. But you're the world champion. Sleep on this victory every night from this point on.

Train your brain; you don't just have to imagine the fight. Use imagery in your everyday life, especially if you're not going to fight. For example, you can imagine pushing yourself to complete some of these grueling workouts, making it through the next three weeks. Feel your body's natural power from head to toe as you imagine sprinting or sparring; tap into your physical strength as you pump iron. Project yourself in the gym; mentally correct bad form so that when you spar, your brain can help fix your technique. Replay in your head your coach's words.

Conjuring up such imagery may take some practice. At first, your mind may drift away from your training or the fight. Maybe you'll think about work or relationship problems. Most of us take our problems to bed, which can sometimes cause a fitful night's sleep. You need your eight hours, especially now. Write down those problems in your fight log so you don't bring them to bed. Instead, as you lie there, imagine the next three weeks or think about the fight. Focus on the business at hand.

It's Just a Job

Seasoned pros use this type of mind game to psych themselves up for a fight. After a few fights, the guesswork becomes less tedious, especially as the fighters become well-known. The fight community is pretty small; fighters read or hear the gossip about other fighters. However, just because you can predict your opponent's fight game doesn't mean the fight will be an easy one. In fact, the intensity level of the fight increases as you become a seasoned pro.

When you get paid to knock people out, after a while it becomes just a job. Once the thrills and the guesswork wear off, the actual fight becomes hard work. In most cases, pros don't make many mistakes. They are better conditioned and not easily intimidated by mind games. Fights become more brutal, and victory doesn't always come easily.

You should be thinking like a seasoned pro. Focus on ways to improve your game. Try not to get wrapped up in the excitement of being a fighter. Stay grounded, take care of business, and practice humility—go in as the underdog. Don't be deterred by mind games. But that's not to say that you shouldn't play a few of your own ...

Mind Games

In the ring, the mind games are endless. A few are fair; others are downright dirty. To tip the scale in your favor, you should have a few tricks up your sleeve. Why? Your goal is to keep your opponent off balance; you want him to second guess his fight plan. Most importantly, you need to send a message that you're not going to lose.

Start by referring to him in the past tense. Imagine victory, and make it known to him that you've already sealed the deal; it will drive him crazy to think that he's a thing of the past to you. You can also intimidate your opponent by staring him down as the referee lists the rules of the fight. For example, when the referee calls you both to the center of the ring for *last instructions*, try to stare a hole through him. If he looks away, you've got him—he's shaking in his gloves. Let him know you know that by smiling.

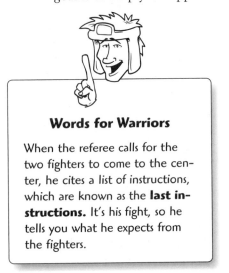

Words for Warriors

When the referee calls for the two fighters to come to the center, he cites a list of instructions, which are known as the **last instructions.** It's his fight, so he tells you what he expects from the fighters.

A seasoned pro won't be intimidated easily, so these mind games might not be too helpful. But you still have to do whatever it takes to win. For example, you may be down during the first couple of rounds, you may feel your own mental motivation slipping. Drastic action is needed: It might take getting mad, getting revenge, or proving something to yourself or your nation. Think about your children, your wife, or events in your life. Keep in mind that your opponent is probably as tired as you are. Don't quit! Do whatever it takes to regain your composure. It's not over until the end!

Superhuman Workouts

For this leg of your journey to kickboxing stardom, you'll train, again, six days a week. On Mondays, Wednesdays, and Fridays, you'll kickbox as usual. On Thursday nights, you'll add another sprint workout. In general, you'll weight train on Tuesdays, Thursdays, and the first Saturday (week 5). Keep up your light runs after kickboxing on Mondays, Wednesdays, and Fridays.

Sparring for the actual fight is the focus of this phase of your training. During week 5, you'll work on fight defenses. This time is not a learning period; it's a doing period. Now is the time to work on your best defense techniques; it doesn't matter if you *can't* do something—at this point, the focus is on what you *can* do.

In weeks 5 and 6, you'll work on slipping or blocking, depending on which skill is better. Defensive work will be your first round. In the next round, you'll focus on blocking kicks.

Ask your coach to work with you. For your punches, he may use focus mitts; or he may wear boxing gloves to throw a series of punches at you. As the punch nears, work on either blocking or slipping it. Practice blocking kicks in the same way: Have your trainer wear a pair of shin guards as he throws a series of kicks at you. You'll have to keep moving to fend off his kicks.

Stay in motion as he fires these shots at you; this will give you a good idea of how to make your opponent miss you. Remember, if he can't land a blow, he can't hurt you. As he tries, you'll tire him out. Then you have your chance: Now is a good time to fire a blow that he doesn't have the energy to block. That's good defense.

Kickboxing Buzz

Even if your defenses are terrible, you can work around them. For example, you can go in and throw punches and kicks, one after another. Eventually, though, you'll have to perfect your defensive game.

Headhunter

Most fighters are *headhunters*—they aim only for the head. Rookies are the worst about this. Most seasoned fighters anticipate attacks to the head, so they're prepared; you probably won't come close to landing a shot to their head. So, you need to modify your attack sequence. Aim for the body; you'll have a better chance of landing a head shot *after* firing a body shot. As your opponent goes to block the body shot, his

211

arms won't be able to come up fast enough to block his head, especially if you've committed several combos to memory. Practice different angles of attack in your kickboxing workouts.

Bear in mind that body shots will eventually weaken your opponent: They'll either wear him out or cause him pain. For example, a blow to the thigh can literally knock your opponent down; it can also cripple the strength in his kicks. Don't worry if he doesn't hit the floor immediately; these shots will take a toll on his strength in the latter rounds. Never forget that all your power comes from your legs; so does your opponent's, so practice aiming for the legs. Visualize landing these shots one after another.

Words for Warriors

Don't **telegraph** your opponent; don't give him or her any signals or hints about your technique, defensive strategy, or movement. Your opponent can figure out your next move just by watching your fight game. For example, you may hold your breath when you fire a jab, so he'll know it's coming. He'll be better prepared just by watching you fight.

Don't Send a Message

Work on your repetitive movements. Don't *telegraph* your fight game; that is, don't give your opponent any signals or hints about your technique, defensive strategy, or movement. For example, you might hold your breath before an attack or drop your left hand before throwing a hook. As you spar, ask your coach to point out these bad habits. Keep your movements flowing so your opponent doesn't recognize the attack.

Melting Iron

Weeks march on, but the mission remains the same; you're still going for total body workout. In week 5, you'll weight train three times a week—Tuesday, Thursday and Saturday—and then drop back in week 6 to twice a week. As the big event closes in, you'll cut down on your weight training and increase your sparring.

Tuesday Workout

Chest	**Flat bench press:** Three sets, 8 to 10 reps
	Incline bench press: Three sets, 10 reps
Back	**Wide grip pulldown:** Three sets, 10 to 12 reps
	Seated row: Three sets, 12 reps
Arms	**Curls:** Three sets, 10 reps
	Triceps extension: Three sets, 10 reps
Legs	**Leg press:** Three sets, 12 to 15 reps
	Leg extension: Three sets, 12 reps
	Leg curl: Three sets, 12 reps

Thursday Workout

Back	**Close grip pulldown:** Three sets, 12 reps	
	One-arm rows: Three sets, 10 to 12 reps	
Chest	**Dumbbell flat bench press:** Three sets, 10 reps	
	Dumbbell incline press: Three sets, 10 reps	
Arms	**Triceps extension:** Three sets, 10 reps	
	Curls: Three sets, 10 reps	
Legs	**Squats:** Three sets, 8 to 12 reps	
	Leg curl: Three sets, 12 reps	
	Leg extension: Three sets, 12 reps	

Saturday Workout

Legs	**Squats:** Three sets, 8 reps	
	Leg press: Three sets, 12 reps	
	Leg curl: Three sets, 12 reps	
	Leg extension: Two sets, 12 reps	
Chest	**Flat bench:** Four sets, 10 reps	
Back	**Wide grip pulldown:** Two sets, 10 reps	
	Close grip pulldown: Two sets, 10 reps	
	Seated rows: Two sets, 10 to 12 reps	

Step It Up

If you're still in pursuit of the perfect body weight, you might have to increase the duration of your runs after kickboxing on Monday, Wednesday, and Friday. If you're sitting pretty, just continue with a light 20-minute run after kickboxing. Regardless of these runs, however, everyone who reaches this phase of the training must do 2 days worth of sprints. On Thursday night, within 20 minutes after the sparring workout, you should run sprints. On Saturday, 1 hour after you weight train, you'll run the stadium stairs, plus timed *interval sprints*. In other words, you'll do some pants-on-fire type of running. Shoot your heart rate up by running, and then lower it by taking a walk—much like the rhythm of a hard-fought match.

Thursday Night

➤ Two 200-meter sprints

➤ Two 100-meter sprints

➤ Ten 10-meter sprints/walking intervals

Saturday Afternoon

➤ Three minutes of stadium stairs

➤ Four 100-meter sprints

➤ Four 50-meters

➤ Ten 10-meter sprints/walking intervals

➤ Two minutes of running stadium stairs

Words for Warriors

In doing **interval sprints,** you'll run as fast as you can, and then stop on a dime. Run again, and then stop. You're raising the heart rate up to the point at which you can't talk; then, rest before the next interval sprint.

Superior Sparring

Now you're getting down to brass tacks; you're a 100 percent fighter. In this phase, the sparring picks up in both intensity and frequency. In week 5, the Monday, Wednesday, and Friday kickboxing routines don't change too much; you'll focus on your defensive game. On Tuesday and Thursday, you'll spar only.

The workouts for week 6 change a little. For example, Monday, Wednesday, and Friday workouts focus on a specific area of fighting. On Monday night you'll focus on your boxing techniques; Wednesday night will be your kicking day; on Friday you'll finish up with Thai pad work. Tuesday and Thursday nights are still reserved for sparring.

Week 5 Workouts (Monday, Wednesday, Friday)

➤ Warmup

➤ Ab work

➤ Stretching

➤ Three rounds of shadow sparring

➤ One round of slipping and blocking drills

➤ One round of kick blocking drills

➤ Three rounds of full contact sparring

➤ Three rounds of focus mitts

➤ Two rounds of kicking shields

➤ Two rounds of Thai pads

➤ Two rounds of bag work

➤ Two conditioning exercises for each body group

➤ Final stretching

Week 5 Workouts (Tuesday, Thursday)

➤ Warmup

➤ Stretching

➤ Three rounds of shadow sparring

➤ One round of slipping and blocking drills

➤ One round of kick blocking drills

➤ Five (or as many rounds as the fight is scheduled) full contact sparring rounds

➤ Ab work

➤ Final stretching

Monday Workout (Week 6)

➤ Warmup

➤ Ab work

➤ Stretching

➤ Three rounds of shadow sparring

➤ One round of slipping and blocking drills

➤ One round of kick blocking drills

➤ Three rounds of boxing sparring

➤ Six rounds of focus mitts

➤ Three rounds of bag work (boxing only)

➤ Two conditioning drills for each body group

➤ Final stretching

Wednesday Workout (Week 6)

➤ Warmup

➤ Ab work

➤ Stretching

➤ Three rounds of shadow sparring

➤ One round of slipping and blocking drills

➤ One round of kick blocking drills

➤ Three rounds of sparring (both kicking and punching)

➤ Six rounds of kicking shield

➤ Two conditioning drills of each body group

➤ Final stretching

Friday Workout (Week 6)

➤ Warmup

➤ Ab work

➤ Stretching

➤ Three rounds of shadow sparring

➤ One round of slipping and blocking drills

➤ One round of kick blocking drills

➤ Three rounds of sparring (both kicking and punching)

➤ Five rounds of Thai pads

➤ Two rounds of bag work

➤ Conditioning drills

➤ Final stretching

The End Result

By now, you should feel strong: tired, but strong. The good news is that you've only one more week of hardcore training, week 7. So take this time to reflect on the last two weeks, and to visualize the big event. Remember, you're the world champion, so keep replaying the victory in your head. The following sections detail your daily schedule for this phase of training.

Monday, Wednesday, and Friday Workouts

6:00 A.M.	Wake up; drink fluids: water, or glass of juice
6:30 A.M.	Breakfast: Eat within 30 minutes of waking up
8:00 A.M.	Workout: none
10:00 A.M.	Snack: fruit smoothie or replacement shake
12:00 P.M.	Lunch: bulk of calories (watch fats and carbs)
3:00 P.M.	Snack: fruit, yogurt, power bars, replacement shake
6:00 P.M.	Workout: kickboxing and cardio work
8:00 P.M.	Dinner: very low fat; focus on protein and vegetables
10:00 P.M.	Good night

Tuesday and Thursday Workouts

6:00 A.M.	Wake up; drink fluids: water or glass of juice
6:30 A.M.	Breakfast: Eat within 30 minutes of waking up
8:00 A.M.	Workout: weight training
10:00 A.M.	Snack: fruit smoothie or replacement shake
12:00 P.M.	Lunch: bulk of calories (watch fat and carbs)
3:00 P.M.	Snack: fruit, yogurt, power bars, replacement shake
6:00 P.M.	Workout: sparring with anaerobic work (Tuesday); sparring only (Thursday)
8:00 P.M.	Dinner: very low fat; focus on protein and vegetables
10:00 P.M.	Good night

Saturday Workout

8:00 A.M.	Wake up; drink fluids: water, or glass of juice
8:30 A.M.	Breakfast: Eat within 30 minutes of waking up
10:00 A.M.	Workout: weight training (week 5 only)
11:30 A.M.	Snack: fruit smoothie, yogurt or replacement shake
12:00 P.M.	Workout: sprints
1:30 P.M.	Lunch: bulk of calories
3:00 P.M.	Snack: fruit, yogurt (week 5 only), power bars (week 5 only), replacement shake
7:00 P.M.	Dinner: very low fat; focus on protein and vegetables
10:00 P.M.	Good night

The Least You Need to Know

➤ The fight game is won by stamina.

➤ Visualization is training your brain for a positive outcome.

➤ Mind games are played to throw your opponent off balance and make him question his game.

➤ Telegraphing your moves means sending your opponent signals or hints about what you're going to do.

➤ Most rookies aim for the head; they're known as headhunters. It's a bad habit.

➤ You can regain your composure by mentally motivating yourself during the fight: Get mad, or even defend your country or your honor; think about your child or spouse.

Chapter 16

The Super Heavyweight: Weeks 7 and 8

In This Chapter

➤ Kickboxing: a mental chess game

➤ Week 7 is hard

➤ Train your brain

➤ The day of the fight

You're a leading candidate to fight The Terminator, reigning K-1 heavyweight champion. Imagine the prefight pep talk from your coach:

Don't worry about his elusive right bomb; don't fear his powerful left leg. You'll loop him if you take him out of his game.

Don't go out swinging, or he'll stay in the middle of the ring and wait for you to come to him. He might even draw you near the ropes so he can pound on you. If he maneuvers you into the corner, he'll fire punch after punch to wear you out; the guy is a real banger.

Stay light on your feet, and don't let him land a shot. Make him wear himself out—just keep dodging his swings. Have patience; he'll eventually get tired. That's when you can use your combinations to out-point him. Don't count on a knockout unless you get a lucky shot.

He's a street fighter; you've got good technique. The fight will go the distance, and the winner will be the one who can also go the distance.

Rounds 7 and 8

Let's finish the last week with a bang; it's the toughest training you'll do. Then, in week 8, you'll train just to keep active, nothing hardcore.

There is no more weight training and, unless you're struggling with a few pounds, you won't run as much. In the next two weeks, you'll practice as if you're actually fighting—these weeks are sort of like dress rehearsal. You'll combine all of the training you've had up to this point; you'll rehearse your game plan, combos, and defensive moves; and you'll commit to memory your opponent's game plan. Is he a *banger?* A *technician?* The *counter fighter?* The *spoiler?* Following is a list of some of the different types of fighters:

➤ A **banger** is a fighter who uses more power than speed. He'll rough you up with his quasi-legal moves: He might try to draw you to the ropes so he can bang away on you, or he might push you with the palm of his glove.

➤ The **technician** fights with clean, smooth skills; rarely does he make a mistake.

➤ The **counter fighter** is skilled at making you "miss" your techniques so that he can counter; he's the most dangerous type of fighter. If he can throw you off balance, get you to lean into him, he'll strike—using his own power plus your momentum.

➤ The **spoiler** is skilled at making you look bad, no matter how clean you fight, because he fights with bad technique. That's his goal—to get you to fight like him.

You'll spar six days this week to make sure that you can go the distance in a real fight. During these workouts, practice as if you're fighting. Here is a word of caution, though: Sheer exhaustion might cause you to become accident prone. Be careful—it would be a real shame to have to withdraw from the fight because you get hurt during practice.

Outside the Ropes

Think about your opponent's fight game. The trick is to take him out of his game by drawing him into your fight plan. Again, visualize the prefight pep talk.

At this point, your stamina shouldn't be an issue. You should be in tiptop shape; otherwise, you might not survive the fight. To ensure that you can hang in there, you'll be doing a lot of sparring during week 7. At the beginning of the week, the sparring will be intense; as the week goes on, it will taper off. Use this time to hone your techniques and your attack and defense strategies. What you're really doing is building confidence in your fighting. The more you rehearse the moves you want to use to fight, the better you'll be able to recall them in a split second. If you think that you'll be able to do it, you will.

Mental Tune-Ups

Preparing for a fight requires a tremendous amount of physical conditioning, as you know. However, much of the game will also take brain power; it's a constant battle between the logical and emotional sides of the brain. The logical side recalls all those perfectly executed strikes you've practiced, whereas the emotional side strikes without regard for the consequences.

Becoming a mentally strong competitor will take actual ring time. The good news is, you can train your brain just like you train your body.

Emotions

Emotions run wild in a fight. (Taking a chunk out of another fighter's ear is a good example of the emotional side of the brain run amok.) After all, you're in the heat of battle with an opponent who wants to kick your butt. Because you're re-acting in a split second, you might not always do the right thing. In most cases, after you have a few fights under your belt you'll master the art of self-control. However, you should learn several mental exercises to help you control fear and other negative thoughts in the ring.

> **Kickboxing Buzz**
>
> You will be using tools such as visualization and rehearsal of your moves to secure an edge over the competition. These drills and techniques take about 20 to 30 minutes per day—not much of a sacrifice for an effective tool against mental screw ups. Remember that mind and body have to work hand in hand in order to perform well in kickboxing.

Fear

During a bout, and especially in a self-defense situation, fear is very strong. Every fighter will feel it—don't deny it. In fact, there's an old saying in the fight game: "A courageous man is not one without fear because he's too ignorant to know better. A courageous man is a man who has fear but faces it anyway." But fear can be a good thing, especially in the ring—it can motivate you to move very quickly and perform better.

Superstition

On the other hand, fear can cripple you, freeze up your mind, burn up vital energy, and hinder your performance. Can you ease this fear? Some fighters do so by practicing some pretty strange rituals.

Fighters are among the super-superstitious. Have you ever met a superstitious person? For example, do you know someone who won't leave home without some sort of luck charm? That's sounds pretty normal, right? Well, fighters have superstitious rituals, too.

For instance, some fighters have been known not to wash their groin protectors. Although this sounds gross to a non-fighter, most of us are not dealing with the fear involved with stepping in a ring to battle it out for several rounds. Fighters thus figure out their own ways to deal with fear; it's a mental game to make them feel better, to make them feel they have an edge in the fight.

Kick-Tales

Here are some real-life fighters' rituals:

Some fighters will only wrap their hands with a specific tape. They'll wrap the left hand first, and then the right hand.

Some don't ever wash their fighting shorts.

Then there are the fighters who wear the same boxer shorts the night before the fight; it's true, there are fighters who won't go to bed the night before the big event without putting on their Winnie the Pooh boxer shorts!

Training Your Mind

Understanding and being able to control fear and other negative thoughts in the ring will come in handy. For example, let's say you've been leading the fight. Then, suddenly, your opponent comes alive. You start to panic. As soon as you do, your opponent senses that he's got you. What you're thinking can make or break the fight. Could you have controlled your thoughts? You bet!

By taking the following five steps, you'll learn how to deal with the emotional—mainly fearful—side of the fight game. Take 20 to 30 minutes per day to train your brain. Move from step to step, in the correct order. Do every step—skipping ahead really won't speed things up.

You can practice these steps after your workouts or before you go to bed. For instance, maybe you'll want to stretch and practice these mental exercises in the morning. Then, at night, before going to bed, practice these exercises again. Remember, the belt will go to the fighter who can think on his toes.

Step 1: Relax the Body

Train your body to relax; your mind will soon follow. A good time to practice relaxation is while you're stretching after your workouts. Inhale as you stretch the muscle; exhale to release the stretch and say good-bye to tension.

You can also practice this technique while you're in the pre-sleep stage. As you lie in bed, start with your toes. Contract them. Hold the contractions for a count of three or four, and then release. As you release the contraction, mentally picture the stress flowing away from your body. Work your way up your body; contract each muscle. You should feel pretty relaxed. Don't be surprised if you doze off before completing the exercise—that's a sign that you're doing it right.

Step 2: Control Your Breathing

Control your breathing—you do it every day. You may be asking, how tough can this exercise be? But there's a specific way in which you can breathe to help you remain calm, stay focused, and conserve energy.

Use controlled breathing during those nail-biting moments before you climb into the ring. Try this technique to slow down your super-hyper breathing and racing heartbeat:

1. Inhale for four to five counts; as you exhale, count to 10, or blow out as slowly as possible.

2. Breathe through your nose for a count of four, and then exhale for a count of eight through your mouth. Don't blow your breath out forcibly, though.

3. Think calm. Talk your heart rate down. Keep repeating this cycle until you feel relaxed.

These exercises can be done with your stretches, or at any other time—especially when you feel that your nerves are getting the best of you. The point is to train your body to relax, so use these exercises for the big event.

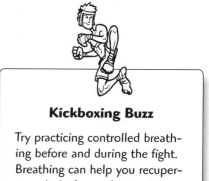

Kickboxing Buzz

Try practicing controlled breathing before and during the fight. Breathing can help you recuperate a little faster after each round. In a fight, your goal is quick recovery. You don't want your heart rate racing any more than it has to.

Step 3: Focus

Concentrate! Focus! Tune out your surroundings! This is tough to do when nervousness seizes your body. A match between two equally skilled fighters will be won by the fighter who concentrates on his fight plan, so you need to learn to focus.

Sit in a comfortable position in front of a mirror. Look at yourself. Now, pick a spot on the mirror and stare at it until you reach a trance-like state. Nothing should break this state of trance: no amount of noise, commotion, or bright light.

Now, pretend you're walking through the roaring crowd to the ring; reporters are pushing and cameras are flashing. So you don't get caught up in the moment, stay in a trance-like state. You can count on this trance-like state to help you remain focused on the fight.

Step 4: Visualization

We've already touched on visualization, but now you need to use it to win the fight. Imagine your best performance. Use visualization now to taste, feel, and smell victory. Remember, visualization is a clear and realistic mental picture of your performance, so take five minutes to picture the knockout turn kick—take five minutes to picture your victory.

Step 5: Mental Rehearsal

Take five minutes to rehearse mentally what you'll do in the following situations:

➤ What if he gets you on the ropes?

➤ What if he draws you into his game?

➤ What if he lands a clean shot?

➤ What if he lands more shots then you had planned?

Take some time to think and reenact all kinds of scenarios. Try to stick to your fight plan as much as possible, rehearsing how you'll act if your opponent does this or that. On the morning of the fight, mentally rehearse your fight plan, round by round. Everything that you can do physically should be rehearsed in your head.

Good-Bye, Asphalt

Now to the physical workout .... At last, there is no more aerobic running, unless you're struggling to make your weight class. If that's the case, keep running after your kickboxing workouts. Otherwise, you'll add some intense anaerobic running at the end of this week (Thursday, Friday, and Saturday):

➤ Five minutes of stadium stairs

➤ Two 200-meter sprints

➤ Two 100-meter sprints

➤ Four 50-meter sprints

➤ Ten 10-meter sprints/walking intervals

Staying Power

The week starts with intense sparring, gradually tapering off as time goes on. By now, you're a lean, mean, fighting machine. Your goal is to push your body to maintain an actual fight-pace through all the scheduled rounds. You have to train at the level at which you'll be fighting. For example, if you're fighting a world champion fight, you'll have to find a world champion-quality training partner—it won't do you any good to train with people who can't take it to the next level. You'll need to know before entering the ring that you've got the staying power to survive a full-length fight. The fight may not go the distance, but you need to think that it will and be prepared for it!

Week 7 Workouts: Monday through Wednesday

➤ Warmup

➤ Abs routine

➤ Three rounds of shadow sparring

➤ Three rounds of heavy bags

➤ Seven rounds of sparring (or two rounds more than the scheduled fight)

➤ Two rounds of focus mitts

➤ Two rounds of kicking shield

➤ Conditioning drills (three of each kind)

➤ Final stretching

Week 7 Workouts: Thursday through Saturday

➤ Warmup

➤ Abs routine

➤ Five rounds of shadow sparring

➤ Three rounds of heavy bags

➤ Four rounds of sparring

➤ Three rounds of focus mitts

➤ Three rounds of Thai pads

➤ Stadium stairs, sprints, intervals

➤ Final stretching

Let's Get Ready to Rumble!

Your hardcore training comes to a halt in week 8—you need this time to recuperate. You'll still kickbox, but with no sparring, from Monday through Thursday. Friday is your day off. Take time to mentally prepare yourself for the fight. Saturday is fight night. Go kick some butt!

Week 8 Workouts: Monday and Tuesday

➤ Warmup

➤ Five rounds of shadow sparring

➤ Five rounds of touch sparring

➤ Three rounds of focus mitts

➤ Three rounds of Thai pads

➤ Two rounds of kicking shields

➤ Ten minutes of jumping rope

➤ Final stretching

Week 8 Workout: Wednesday

➤ Warmup

➤ Five rounds of shadow sparring

➤ Three rounds of light bag work

➤ Five rounds of touch sparring

➤ Five minutes of jumping rope

➤ Final stretching

Warning Warriors

Many fighters resist rest. But you need it; besides letting the body recover, you need to restore your glycogen level for the fight. Don't listen to that panic feeling that tells you more is better— more training often results in sickness. Instead, use week 8 to recover. You'll be in shape if you followed the training program. The key is train hard without overdoing it. That's why proper sleep and eating right go hand in hand in training.

Week 8 Workout: Thursday

➤ Stretching

➤ Five rounds of shadow sparring

➤ Three minutes of jumping rope

➤ Final stretching

Fill Your Tank

Are you still struggling with a few pounds? If so, cut back on calories in week 8. Don't cut the amount of food, just the calories. Don't allow any fat to pass your lips. Here's the really unpleasant part: The day before you weigh in, you'll have to reduce your water weight by sweating it out. This means lots of cardio work and some time in the steam room. But don't worry, water can easily be replaced after weigh-in.

After you weigh in, start *carbo-loading* with starchy foods such as potatoes, rice, and oatmeal. When carbo-loading, be sure to drink lots of water, especially if you've dropped water weight for weigh-in. Carbs retain water, which can protect you from dehydration during the fight. Keep in mind that having *glycogen* (stored carbohydrate) in your body directly affects your performance: Low glycogen stores can cause you to tire out from fatigue; you may even have to stop the fight. Boosting your glycogen stores means more energy for your fight.

You'll carbo-load up to the event. Watch your fat intake on the day of the fight because it can slow you down. After the fight is feast time. Focus on protein as your post-fight meal.

Warning Warriors

If you're struggling to make weight, don't skip meals. Cut the fat. Going without food the day before the fight will directly impair your performance. A better bet is to drop the water weight, which can be easily replaced after weigh-in.

The Night Before the Fight

7:00 P.M.	Weigh-in
7:15 P.M.	Drink lots of water
7:30 P.M.	Press conference
8:00 P.M.	Dinner with a high carbohydrate content
10:00 P.M.	Replacement drink with high carbohydrate content

The Day of the Fight

Be sure to drink water all day!

9:00 A.M.	Breakfast: high protein and carb
11:00 A.M.	MR drink: high in carbs
1:00 P.M.	Lunch: medium protein and high carb
3:00 P.M.	Snack: low protein and high carb
6:00 P.M.	MR drink: high carb
8:00 P.M.	The fight (one hour)

Words for Warriors

Think about feeding your muscles for the high-intensity fight. Store away a baked potato; it can help you perform better. Eating this way is called **carbo-loading**. **Glycogen,** or stored carbohydrate, is your main source of energy during any high-intensity activity. You'll need to rest the day of the fight to help restore your glycogen level; it takes 24–48 hours to rebuild.

The Right Stuff?

In the morning, go through your equipment—it's the last thing you want to worry about later. You don't want to forget anything, because chances are your cornermen won't have it either. Remember, you're nervous. Make a list of your equipment. Then, lay each piece out on your bed. As you pack it, cross out each piece until the list is complete. Don't forget a few comforts from home, such as your pillow and blanket. Here's your checklist:

➤ Gauze and tape

➤ Groin protector

➤ Fighting shorts or pants

➤ Robe

➤ Mouthpiece

➤ Lucky charms

➤ Shin pads (for full contact rules only)

➤ Foot pads (for full contact rules only)

➤ Competition headgear (amateur competitions only)

➤ Jump rope

➤ Warmup sweats

➤ Cross-trainer shoes and mat shoes

➤ Bag gloves

➤ Thai pads or focus mitts

Cornerman's Equipment

➤ Petroleum jelly

➤ Cotton swabs

➤ Ice packs or bags

➤ Water bottles

➤ In-swell

➤ Bandages

➤ Scissors

➤ Bucket

➤ Steri-gel

➤ Towels

➤ Water

TCB: Taking Care of Business

You're here to TCB—to take care of business. That's how fighters psych up for a fight, and that's what you'll do as part of your job. But before you run off to work, you'll have to undergo a series of TCB procedures. For example, the referee will ask to inspect your equipment; it doesn't matter whether you're fighting as an amateur or as a world champion. This safety precaution is done to protect all the fighters. During that time, the referee will go over the rules of his fight; he runs the show so he'll tell you what he expects. The rules will vary, depending on the referee. So, it's a good idea for you to find the referee early on; ask if he'll inspect your equipment and talk the talk so you can settle in and focus on the fight.

After the referee has seen you, it's a good idea to inspect the ring. Climb into the ring to feel the surface. Walk around to find out if there are any hollow parts that can trip you. Make a mental note about the surface: Is it vinyl or canvas? Push up against the ropes to test the springiness. Will it pop you back hard or soft? Get a good feel for the ring—you don't want any surprises during the fight.

Warning Warriors

For safety reasons, your wrapped hands will have to be inspected by the referee or a boxing official. The referee will ask you to hold out your hands. He'll look to see if you taped your knuckles on the wrap (which is illegal), and he'll check for any other foreign objects stuffed away in the wrap that could inflict serious damage on an opponent. Every fighter must have his hands examined. If the wraps have been tampered with, you can get fined or disqualified from a fight.

No Funny Business

You'll actually show your wrapped hands to the referee or another boxing official. They'll examine them to ensure that no "funny business" is going on. (For example, you can't put a piece of steel inside the wraps to inflict severe damage to your opponent.) After the wraps are examined, the official will sign off by making a big X on the top of the wraps and signing his name. If the X doesn't match up, he'll know that the wraps have been tampered with.

You won't use your practice wraps. For a fight, you'll have to use gauze material and tape. For the fight, you need a stronger and tighter wrap to help protect your hands and wrists.

Getting Warm

You'll warm up about 40 to 50 minutes before show time. Figuring out when you're fighting is the hard part. Sometimes you're the first fighter, sometimes you're the tenth. The time is hard to gauge because you never know when there will be a string of knockouts. You may be up sooner than you expected. Your coach will pay attention to what's going on outside; meanwhile, you should be mentally rehearsing your fight plan. Your warmup may go something like this:

➤ Jump rope for 5 minutes, and then rest for 5 minutes. Jump rope for 3 more minutes.

➤ Get a 10-minute upper body massage from your trainer.

➤ After the massage, stretch your upper body, and then rest.

➤ Get a 10-minute lower body massage from your trainer.

➤ After the massage, stretch your lower body and back, and then rest.

➤ Start to shadow spar.

➤ Shadow spar for the same amount of time the fight is scheduled to last.

➤ Briefly rest after your shadow rounds, and then start working the mitts or Thai pads.

➤ After a few rounds of mitt work, take a breather.

➤ Rehearse the fight in your head and make sure you see yourself as the winner.

Warm up slowly to bring yourself to a light sweat; don't overdo the warmup. You should feel good and loose, not out of breath. Before walking out to the ring, practice your controlled breathing to help calm your nerves. Don't forget, walk out in a trance-like state.

The Grand Entrance

After you've walked the hall to the ring, take a minute to inspect the ring. Look for wet spots on the ring surface from previous fights. Check the ropes once again to see if they have lost any spring. Mentally store this information away; it may play an important role in the fight later on.

Go! Fight! Win!

You're about to go in there and do battle; you've prepared for this moment like no other warrior. This training got you here; it produces winners. However intense the training, though, if you don't really believe that you're a winner, no amount of training can prepare you. Now is the time to show your loved ones, your trainer, and yourself what dreams are made of.

Monday through Wednesday Workouts (Weeks 7 and 8)

8:00 A.M.	Wake up; drink fluids: water, or glass of juice
8:30 A.M.	Breakfast: Eat within 30 minutes of waking up
11:00 A.M.	Workout: none
1:00 P.M.	Lunch: bulk of calories (watch fats and carbs)
3:00 P.M.	Snack: fruit, yogurt, power bars, replacement shake
6:00 P.M.	Workout: kickboxing with sparring; kickbox without sparring (week 8)
8:00 P.M.	Dinner: very low fat; focus on protein and vegetables
10:00 P.M.	Good night

Thursday through Saturday Workouts (Week 7)

8:00 A.M.	Wake up; drink fluids: water, or glass of juice
8:30 A.M.	Breakfast: Eat within 30 minutes of waking up
11:00 A.M.	Workout: none
1:00 P.M.	Lunch: bulk of calories (watch fats and carbs)
3:00 P.M.	Snack: fruit, yogurt, power bars, replacement shake
6:00 P.M.	Workout: kickboxing with anaerobic work
8:00 P.M.	Dinner: very low fat; focus on protein and vegetables
10:00 P.M.	Good night

Thursday Workout (Week 8)

8:00 A.M.	Wake up; drink fluids: water, or glass of juice
8:30 A.M.	Breakfast: Eat within 30 minutes of waking up
11:00 A.M.	Workout: none
1:00 P.M.	Lunch: bulk of calories (watch fats and carbs)
3:00 P.M.	Snack: fruit, yogurt, power bars, replacement shake
6:00 P.M.	Workout: shadow spar
8:00 P.M.	Dinner: very low fat; focus on protein and vegetables
10:00 P.M.	Good night

There is no workout on Friday of week 8. Saturday of week 8 is the big night—fight night.

The Least You Need to Know

➤ In week 7, you'll spar as you'll fight in the actual fight.

➤ There are five steps to becoming a mentally tough competitor: relaxation, controlled breathing, focus, visualization, and mental rehearsal.

➤ You'll train very lightly in week 8.

➤ Carbo-loading the day before the fight can help rebuild your glycogen levels.

➤ Your main source of energy is glycogen.

➤ To make weigh-in, you'll have to drop the water weight by sweating it out.

Part 5

Protect Yourself

Here's your battle cry: The best defense is a strong offense! Remember, you're a survivor, not a victim! What will you do if you're confronted by a stranger? In this part, we'll prepare you mentally and physically for the eventuality of being attacked by a stranger. A good self-defense program consists of three parts: awareness, mental preparedness, and defensive skills.

Chapter 17

The Fight Game

In This Chapter

➤ Are you ready to fight?

➤ Amateur and pro kickboxing

➤ Rules and regulations

➤ The K–1

➤ Pitfalls of a fighter

You and your trainer have endured months of training: You've taken hundreds of lessons, sparred with the best of them, and tolerated the aches and pains. And now it's down to this: Do you dare step into the ring? Your training is about to be seriously tested. Are you ready for real competition?

Competition kickboxing is growing just as fast as fitness kickboxing is. You don't have to go pro to fight; you can also compete at the amateur level. Competition gives you a purpose whether you're a young warrior, ready to show off your stuff, or a fighting-fit jock who needs to know that those years of training are about to pay off. Competition gives you an incentive to move on to the next level of fitness. But before you climb under those ropes, you should have an idea of what to expect from the fight game.

So, You Want to Fight?

Listen up, adventurous athletes! Why not join the ranks of amateur kickboxing? You can enter the ring as early as 10 years old and stay as long as your pain tolerance allows. No matter what your age or level of fitness, amateur competition is open to all kickboxers. Do note, though, that once you're older than 35 you'll have to have a physical examination before every fight. Relax—it's the same for the pros, no matter their age.

Amateur kickboxing is at an all time high in the United States. Ten years ago, amateur fights were hard to find. Back then, Asia and Europe dominated the kickboxing world. But times are changing—which is very exciting for all you kickboxers who love this sport.

Big time world competition is no longer an unattainable dream; amateur fights can be a means to turn pro. Or, if you just want to push yourself, amateur fights provide a safe environment in which to test your skills. In other words, you don't have to go pro; your fights can be a reward for all your hard training. Once you step into the ring, you know what it's like to be a real fighter—it's all about the fear and anxiety, the thrill of victory or the agony of defeat.

Where Do I Sign Up?

Ask your personal coach or the coaches at your martial arts or kickboxing gym where the next amateur fight in your state is scheduled to take place. They should be in touch with local and statewide fights.

If your coach doesn't keep up with the fighting world, you can join an amateur sanctioning body. Joining a sanctioning body keeps you informed about what's happening in the kickboxing community. However, make sure that you find one that is either regulated by the state athletic commission or nationally or internationally known. There are too many organizations that promote and sanction amateur competitions; you might want to look into joining the World Kickboxing Association (WKA) and the International Sport Kickboxing Association (ISKA) because they both sponsor many international competitions. Competing abroad is an excellent way for young warriors to gain fighting experience and worldwide recognition.

Sorry, fighters—at the amateur level, you don't win money, only experience (and sometimes fame). Fighting for an organization as an amateur will give you some exposure, which will help when you turn pro. Within each sanctioning body, you can compete for certain national or world titles. Most organizations send out newsletters that rank amateur fighters and promote fights. In this way, you can keep up with the fighting world. The fee may run anywhere from $10 to $20, depending on the organization you choose to join.

Keeping Score

You'll be scored on a 10-point system: The winner of each round will get 10 points. The loser of the round gets nine points. You lose points for knockdowns and certain fouls. For example, you can lose one point if you're knocked down but get up to fight. If you're dazed by a blow, you can lose one point. The referee will give you a standing eight count; he'll get directly in your face and count to eight. If you snap out of your daze, you can continue to fight, but you'll lose a point. Most fights are over if a fighter is knocked to the ground three times. The winner will be the one with the most points at the end of the match. Note that the winner is usually the more aggressive fighter, the one who threw the most effective techniques.

Amateur Rules

Almost all amateur fights are three rounds; championship bouts consist of five rounds. Each round lasts two minutes, and you'll have 1 minute to rest between each round. Now you know why, in training, your interval sets are 2 minutes exercise and one minute rest—to get you ready to fight in the ring. Sometimes, amateur Thai boxing rounds last 3 minutes; but the fights still go three rounds. In children's fights, the matches go three rounds, and each round lasts 1 minute.

Amateur Gear-Up

As amateur kickboxers, you're required to wear 12-ounce boxing gloves if you weigh 160 pounds or more. The lighter weights will wear 10-ounce boxing gloves. Under no circumstances do you want to forget your groin protector or mouthpiece—they're required safety gear. So are your shin and footpads, and your headgear. Amateur fights are particularly strict with headgear, requiring that you wear amateur competition headgear.

Warning Warriors

Make sure that you have a qualified coach and sparring partners before you attempt to enter this competition. The ring is the last place to find out that your coach does not have real kickboxing experience.

Hardcore Kickboxing

American kickboxing wasn't an overnight success. The competitions were few and far between, and the money wasn't great. However, earlier kickboxing celebrities such as Bill "Superfoot" Wallace, Maurice Smith, and Benny the Jet thrilled spectators as they won match after match. Slowly, kickboxing attracted more and more crowds here in the United States. But American kickboxers were still forced to travel overseas for more money and better fights.

At first, American kickboxers got clobbered by the Thai and European kickboxers. Why? The problem seemed obvious—American kickboxing rules were not the same as in the rest of the world.

The most brutal form of kickboxing, Muay Thai, directly influenced European fighting. These International Rules, as they later became known, were physically more challenging than the American rules. U.S. kickboxers were not learning how to fight like the rest of world; they were not prepared for the brutality of worldwide kickboxing. For example, Thai boxers use every part of the body—they can even throw elbow strikes—when fighting in the ring.

There are international kickboxers who are superstars in countries such as Holland, where fights rake in big bucks. Holland, in fact, produces some of the best kickboxers in the world. Thailand has some of the greatest feather or lightweights. Japan breeds many middleweight champions. But what about the United States? In order for American kickboxers to make a name for themselves within the sport, they had no choice but to learn to fight like the rest of the world. Fame and fortune came with each victory. Furthermore, one of the most successful kickboxers, Maurice Smith, mastered the rules abroad to become one of the best kickboxers and the longest reigning American heavyweight champion in the world today.

Full Contact Kickboxing

In the early 1970s, a new form of karate fighting was launched. This new form involved using formed rubber hand and foot pads so fighters could safely hit the body and face. Shortly after that, American kickboxing, which is sometimes called full contact karate, evolved into a sport.

Words for Warriors

Who's the **world champion?** That depends .... World championship titles are determined by the sanctioning body. Often, fighters are champions of several sanctioning organizations.

Today, the same rules apply to the sport—with one exception. Back then, fighters wore foam rubber hand protectors rather than the regulation boxing gloves of today. Now, all competitors must wear competition weight boxing gloves: 10-ounce boxing gloves are required for fighters who weigh 160 pounds or more; anyone weighing less than that must wear 8-ounce gloves. All fighters must wear shin and foot pads, a groin protector, and a mouth piece.

Full contact matches vary in rounds, depending on whether it's a world title fight or a contender's match. *World titles* go twelve rounds, and *contender's* matches vary from four to ten rounds. All kicks must be thrown above the waist. In other words, you can't kick to the legs or fire a knee strike. Furthermore, you must throw eight kicks per round. If you don't throw eight kicks, you can expect a one-point penalty for each missed kick. You must make a real attempt to land your kick; otherwise, you lose one point.

Whether you will be able to prance around the ring while showing off the World Champion belt may depend on your punching game. Because full contact rules permit kicks above the waist only, your target areas are reduced. Your hands, then, might become your best weapons. Most of the competitions in the United States and Canada use the full contact rules at the amateur level. Most professional fights overseas, on the other hand, adhere to international rules.

Words for Warriors

The word **contender** refers to a fighter who is ranked in the world, or to a potential fighter who is waiting for a shot at the world title.

The following are the American Rules for kick-boxing:

➤ You must throw eight kicks per round, minimum.

➤ You will spend 2 minutes fighting, 1 minute resting.

➤ There are 12 rounds in a world title fight.

➤ All kicks must be above the waist.

➤ No knee strikes are allowed.

➤ Boxing gloves, shin and foot pads, groin and mouth protectors are required.

International Rules

Most contenders fight the international way because of the money involved. Furthermore, because the international rules are used around the world, more fighters have the opportunity to fight. Depending upon what countries you choose to fight in, you might have to learn two sets of rules (full contact and international rules).

World title fights held in the United States and Europe go 12 rounds. Each round is 2 minutes long with a 1-minute rest. Competition weight boxing gloves and safety gear such as a mouth piece and groin protector are still required. However, you don't have to wear shin and foot pads.

The biggest difference between full contact and international rules is that with international, you can kick anywhere. For example, you can kick to the legs, which gives you more ways to take down your opponent. You can also throw as many kicks as you want during the fight; there isn't a kick requirement. With international rules, you have more angles of attack, which makes the fight more challenging.

The following are the international rules for kickboxing:

➤ There is no kick requirement.

➤ You can kick anywhere but the groin.

➤ You will fight for 2 minutes, rest for 1 minute.

➤ A world title match consists of 12 rounds.

➤ Boxing gloves and groin and mouth protectors are required.

➤ Shin and foot pads are optional.

The Other International Rules

Okay, let's up the ante: In Asia and Europe, you'll use a different set of international rules. For one, all professional fights, including world title matches, last five rounds. And here's the killer part: Each round lasts 3 minutes, with a 1-minute rest.

The safety equipment is the same, though: regulation boxing gloves, groin protector, and mouth piece. You don't have to wear shin and foot pads. Most fighters will fight barefoot or with a white cloth wrapped around their ankles for support.

In both sets of international rules, fighters can use all the punches and kicks, and are allowed to land kicks anywhere. In addition, they can use knee strikes. Furthermore, while throwing a knee strike, fighters are allowed to grab or clinch their opponents for 3 to 5 seconds.

Following is list of the other set of international rules, effective in Asia and Europe:

➤ There is no kick requirement.

➤ You can kick anywhere but the groin.

➤ There are 3-minute rounds, with 1-minute rests between them.

➤ All matches (world title and otherwise) are five rounds long.

➤ Knee strikes are allowed.

➤ Boxing gloves and groin and mouth protectors are required.

➤ Shin and foot pads are optional.

Words for Warriors

Neck wrestling is a type of clinching you can use to throw your opponent off balance.

Muay Thai Kickboxing

The most cold-blooded form of kickboxing originated in Thailand; it's called Muay Thai, or Thai boxing. Any kickboxer worldwide can compete using Muay Thai rules—but he'll probably have to travel to Thailand to do it. Every now and then, promoters will sponsor a fight in Japan, Europe, or, on a very rare occasion, the United States.

Thai boxers are required to wear a groin protector and regulation boxing gloves. A mouthpiece is optional in Thailand. Shin and foot pads are not allowed.

All matches, including title fights, last five rounds; each round is 3 minutes. What makes Thai boxing so brutal is the relentless and legal kicking, punching, and kneeing to the head and body (you can hit anywhere except the groin). Elbow strikes are also allowed, as is *neck wrestling*. This is a type of clinching used to throw an opponent off balance—and remember, kickboxing is all about balance. Once your opponent is wobbly, you can land knee strikes more effectively or throw him to the ground.

Sometimes, you'll see fights outside of Thailand that use modified Thai rules. In such fights, elbow strikes are not allowed.

Following are the rules for Thai kickboxing:

➤ There are no kick requirements.

➤ You can kick anywhere but the groin.

➤ There are 3-minute rounds, 2-minute rests.

➤ All fights (including world title fights) last five rounds.

➤ Knee strikes are allowed.

➤ Elbow strikes are allowed.

➤ Boxing gloves and groin protectors are required.

The Five Big Organizations

The purpose of associations, organizations, and federations is to unify kickboxers worldwide. In most cases, these organizations sponsor kickboxing competitions: regional, national, and world title fights. They set safety standards and the length of fights. Likewise, they rank fighters, set pay standards, and establish qualifications for referees and judges. A sanctioning body makes a sport a sport. For the fighters, they provide a means to compete with one another, similar to traditional martial arts competitions. This active sportsmanship creates a camaraderie and unity among kickboxers that keeps kickboxing alive and vibrant. There are many kickboxing associations, but here is a list of the most recognized:

➤ **WKA**—World Kickboxing Association is the most prestigious kickboxing organization in the world. It sanctions international style rules only.

➤ **ISKA**—International Sport Kickboxing Association sanctions full contact rules and international rules.

➤ **WKC**—World Kickboxing Council sanctions fights in international rules and full contact rules both in the U.S. and Europe.

➤ **IKF**—International Kickboxing Federation sanctions international style fights including Muay Thai rules outside of Thailand as well as full contact and international rules.

➤ **USAKA**—The United States Amateur Kickboxing Association sanctions fights in the United States only.

Kick-Tales

The WKA is the oldest sanctioning body, and the first to be recognized internationally. In the U.S., the PKA (Professional Kickboxers Association) sponsored the first kickboxing match. The ISKA was later formed from the PKA because the latter went bankrupt.

Words for Warriors

A **fight purse** is how much money you make from a fight; the amount is determined before you fight. Most beginner pros are paid by the scheduled amount of rounds. For example, if the fight is scheduled for five rounds, and the purse is $100 per round, the purse would be $500.

Going Pro

You've paid your dues as an amateur fighter. These days you're hungry for the big time—professional kickboxing. It's not as easy as you think. Besides being a good fighter, you have to be fairly well organized and stay on top of your career.

That's why you should find a manager. Your manager will help you guide your career. His two biggest responsibilities are getting you fights and making sure you get paid. Your manager makes money off of you, so he has a real incentive to fulfill these responsibilities. Most managers get anywhere from 10 to 30 percent of a *fight purse*.

There is no question about it, a good manager can help establish your fighting career. Here's a word of caution, though: You should look for a manager who is concerned about your well-being, not just the money. You might even want to manage your own career, a task that is not impossible—unless you get too busy.

A Permission Slip

Most states require a fighting license. Sounds silly, doesn't it? Think of this license as a permission slip given to you by the state athletic commission or state labor board. All fighters who want to compete in prize fights must be registered in the state in which they want to fight. It's like a driver's license; every state will have a few different requirements.

You'll also have to pass a doctor's physical examination. Most states require that you be tested for hepatitis, HIV, and AIDS. In a sport that draws blood, this testing is extremely important to protect fighters from transmitting these diseases. Your fighter's license tells other fighters that you've passed the physical and medical requirements to compete safely.

Warning Warriors

It's a big deal to lose your license! If you lose your license in one state, you might not get licensed in any other state.

Note that your license can be revoked if you don't follow the rules of a fight; thus, the license keeps fighters in line during a match. If you break the rules during a fight, you can be fined or, depending on what you did, lose your license to fight and your money for that fight. Be aware that the state doesn't have to give you your license back, and is entitled to withhold a certain percentage of your fight purse.

Not only does the state licensing commission make sure fighters are fit enough to compete and abide by the rules of conduct, they also license the fight promoters. A fight promoter finances the fight and is responsible for sponsoring a safe fight that upholds traditional kickboxing rules. The ring and all the safety equipment must be in excellent condition. The state commission board insures that these fights are legitimate and that the promoter pays you, the fighter. Finally, referees must also be licensed through the state. The state commission is responsible for assigning referees to specific fights.

Kickboxing Buzz

Most referees are former kickboxers. They have to understand the rules and pass a test that is devised by the state and a sanctioning body.

The World's Best

Now we come to the prestigious K-1 Grand Prix. The letter *K* stands for the fighting styles of kickboxing—karate, kung fu, and kenpo. The number 1 refers to the best fighter in the world. The K-1 was the brain child of the Japanese karate and kickboxing master, Kazuyoshi Ishii. His dream was to bring the biggest and the boldest stand up martial arts—kickboxing, karate, kung fu, tae kwon do, kenpo, and Muay Thai—into one competition. K-1 now determines the world's best kickboxer.

Rules Made Simple

Most tournaments are spread over a few days; the promoter decides the title of the fight. The K-1, however, is set up differently. Competitions feature eight men, and all fights are held in one day. There are three fights only. All fights of the tournament last three rounds, each of which is three minutes long. No elbow attacks are allowed, and all fighters must wear 10-ounce boxing gloves. After slugging it out, the exhausted winner is crowned the champion.

Following is a list of the K-1 rules:

➤ There is no kick requirement.

➤ You can kick anywhere but the groin.

➤ There are three 3-minute rounds, each followed by a 1-minute rest to determine the World K-1 champion title.

➤ Knee strikes are allowed.

➤ No elbow strikes are permitted.

➤ Boxing gloves and groin and mouth protectors are required.

K-1 Frenzy

The K-1 debuted in 1993; it was a huge success, attracting competitors from Holland, the United States, Thailand, Australia, and Japan. Because the response was overwhelming, K-1 now promotes about 10 fights a year. Not all these competitions are tournaments, but fighters still have a means to show off their stuff.

Fights are held all over the world; the biggest—the ones that pay the most money—are held in Japan. The winners of the K-1 U.S.A. and the K-1 Europe travel to Japan to fight in the K-1 Grand Prix tournament.

As you can probably imagine, the K-1 ranks as the number one fighting sport in Japan. That's amazing, considering this country loves martial arts sports. The K-1 Grand Prix fills the Tokyo Dome, which holds 80,000 people; it is watched by many more on Pay-Per-View television. K-1 fighters in Japan are like movie stars in the United States—they are idolized.

As more fights are promoted outside Japan, the K-1 becomes more and more popular. Europeans have always loved kickboxing; with the K-1, kickboxing is becoming a national pastime in many countries. Even in the United States, the K-1 is growing. The first tournament showed a lot of potential. Now, it's gone even farther: The American fight audience seems to be switching gears from traditional boxing to kickboxing.

The grand prize for winning the K-1 Grand Prix is $300,000—more money than you can make in any other kickboxing event. And every year, the "show money" seems to be greater. Indeed, fighters get paid for just fighting in the K-1. They should be compensated, though—it's a tough fight.

Sign Me Up, K-1

If you're a young, tough kickboxer weighing in at over 200 pounds, you may be invited to fight in the K-1. That's right, you have to be a heavyweight male kickboxer. Sound unfair? It's just like boxing—the heavyweights claim the fame. However, don't give up hope. There are other events in the works for lighter fighters, such as the K-2 for the light heavyweights and the K-3 for the middleweights. There's even some talk about a K-tournament for women.

As for qualifying, you'll have to be invited to compete in one of the events. More than likely, you'll have to be some kind of hotshot or a fighter in other K-1 tournaments. Obviously, winners of the other K-1 events get to fight in the K-1 Grand Prix. Make no mistakes: The K-1 offers the greatest opportunity for young fighters; it's an honor just to be invited to qualify.

Kickboxing Buzz

The biggest worldwide kickboxing event is the K-1; it attracts champions from around the world. The winners of the K-1 America and K-1 Europe get to compete in the K-1 Grand Prix in Japan. The fight purse for the winner is about $300,000—that's big money.

Watch Out—The Fight Game

For every success story, there are hundreds of hard luck stories. Attention, young fighters: You should always follow your dreams, but you should also be aware that there can be a downside to this sport. Perhaps it you're aware of some of the bad things that can happen to you in this business, you're better armed to deal with misfortune.

Your Manager

It's very important that you hire a manager who has your best interests at heart. When choosing a manager, make sure that you talk to him about your career. Listen to what he has to offer you; you want a strategic game plan for your career. Make sure he has the connections to get you good fights, endorsement deals, and enough publicity to keep you growing within the sport.

Money, Money, Money

Despite all the flashy deals made for the big time fights, the money is not great. Many young fighters think that the big payday is right around the corner, but that corner may be a long time coming.

If you're a fighter, you may have to get a second job until you prove yourself in the ring. Fighting on a regular basis takes time; even then, sometimes the money still can't put food on your table. You may have to be a kickboxing trainer as you wait to make it big time. Or, you might want to consider traveling abroad to fight. (Japan pays the best. Try to get the attention of the Japanese promoters because they'll ask you to fight in Japan, often all expenses paid.)

Don't despair! As kickboxing reaches new heights, more opportunities will pop up in the United States, and the prize money will get better. For example, big time boxing promoter Don King had a kickboxing match on the under card of one of Evander Holyfield's boxing matches. With this type of mega-exposure, who knows? Maybe kickboxing will be the next super sport!

Your Big Mouth

Don't let your mouth write a check that your butt can't cash.

An overinflated ego can set you back as a young fighter. Early success in the ring can leave you feeling overconfident. The next time, you might bite off more than you can chew. Needless to say, you should always enter the ring as if you're the underdog; and be a gracious winner.

The Least You Need to Know

➤ You don't have to go pro to step into the ring. Amateur competitions are a great way to strut your stuff.

➤ Amateur competitions vary from four to twelve rounds; each round lasts 2 minutes, with a 1-minute rest between rounds.

➤ As a pro fighter, you can compete in three different rules: American (or full contact) or two different sets of international rules. On rare occasions, you may compete with Thai boxing rules.

➤ The five big kickboxing organizations are WKA, ISKA, WKC, USAKA, and IKF.

➤ The K-1 event determines the world's best kickboxer. Fighters can earn big money if they're invited to fight in the K-1.

Chapter 18

The Perfect Self-Defense

In This Chapter

➤ Mentally prepare yourself for an attack

➤ A three-step plan to self-defense

➤ Trust your instincts

➤ Recurrent training

Happy holidays! No, it's not exactly the holiday season, but we want to prepare you early. Picture this scenario: You don't want to scramble to finish your shopping. No one wants to fight the wall-to-wall crowds and walk for miles to the car. But you do it anyway; you waited until Christmas Eve to do your shopping.

Par for the course, the only parking spot is a good distance from the mall. You're in a power shopping mode—dawn to dusk—because you haven't yet bought a single present. You've got to buy for a family of 10, plus 20 of your closest friends ....

Mission accomplished; it's finally closing time and you've got the goods. Now you have to get home to wrap all these presents before your guests arrive for Christmas dinner. It's pitch black, and your car is parked in the last parking spot in the lot. No one else is in sight.

Deep down inside you know that walking through an empty parking lot, with your arms full of bags, might not be a good idea. But you have all these unwrapped presents, the turkey (which sits without its trimmings in the refrigerator), and the house— what a mess. Pressured by tight time constraints, you reason that nothing will happen; 'tis the season to be jolly, happy, giving ... so you go for it.

Don't Give Them a Reason

When you least expect it, danger can strike you. Imagine that you're approached by a gang member who thinks Christmas came early. He values your packages over your life; you mean nothing to him. What will you do to save your life?

Welcome to your three-step self-defense plan. We'll talk about awareness first. Because kickboxing and self-defense tactics can't be learned overnight, you need to prepare yourself mentally for a "what if" situation. After that, you'll learn a few striking tactics, similar to your kickboxing moves. Finally, you'll learn how to defend yourself while on the ground.

You're probably thinking that kickboxing should be enough. But the reality is that you never know what a would-be attacker is going to do. You have to be prepared for the unknown, so you can't rely 100 percent on kickboxing. A realistic self-defense program includes a little punching, kicking, and some fighting on the ground. And, most importantly, a little awareness on your part.

Kickboxing Buzz

Most local police departments offer self-defense seminars. Most police think that the martial arts are a good choice for protection. In the meantime, however, you need to prepare yourself mentally for what might happen to you some day.

The Facts

Do you think you're immune from crime because you live in a nice neighborhood? Think again. Your income bracket doesn't insulate you from crime. If someone can shoot the president of the United States, who has the best security in the world, you are certainly not protected from a would-be attacker.

In fact, one in four violent crimes occurs near the home. Including these, almost half occurred within a mile from home and 73 percent within five miles. Only 4 percent of victims of violent crime reported that the crime took place more than 50 miles from their home, according to the U.S. Department of Justice.

Every minute, several muggings, beatings, rapes, sexual assaults, robberies, thefts, household burglaries, and motor vehicle thefts take place in the United States. The odds are very good that you could be involved in some sort of violent crime. Not all bad things happen at night in the seedy bar areas of town. In fact, most burglars hit you when you're not home, between the hours of 9:30 A.M. and 2:30 P.M.

Most women don't like to think about rape. They shrug it off, thinking that it can't happen to them. Unfortunately, it can—at home, at school, at a party, anywhere. One in three females will be a victim of a sexual assault attempt at some time in her life. Rape just doesn't occur in high-risk situations such as walking alone at night, hitchhiking, or going to a party given by strangers. Rape can happen anywhere.

Approximately one-third of all rape victims are attacked in their own homes. In more than half of reported rapes, women know their attackers.

Think about what you do in your life; you don't want to go through life afraid, but these are the facts. Have a plan.

First Things First

Don't dismiss your instincts: If you get the feeling that walking to your car alone is stupid, don't do it. You need to listen to your feelings. Walking to your car with an armful of packages at night, praying that someone doesn't notice you sends a message to a would-be attacker: "I'm scared! I'm a victim! Come get me!" There are a few things that you can do in this situation, such as call for mall security or 911. But first, you need to get in the "awareness" mindset.

Code White

A would-be attacker can easily spot a potential victim: Most of the population walks around in *code white,* meaning that they're aware of their surroundings only from their fingertips in to their bodies. In other words, you're only aware of your groceries, your kids, and the cell phone that is attached to your ear.

If a would-be attacker were to approach, you wouldn't have time to react. If you are caught off guard, often it's too late. A thug will invade your personal space, and you'll act like a victim instead of someone who knows what to do. Attackers look for victims who are completely oblivious to their surroundings.

Kickboxing Buzz

Not all bad things happen at night. In fact, most residential burglaries happen in between the hours of 9:30 A.M. to 2:30 P.M. Most people have the same daily work schedule; unfortunately, most burglars will stake out people's homes to figure out when they come and go.

Words for Warriors

If you walk around completely oblivious to what's happening around you, you're suffering from **code white.** You see only from the tips of your fingers to your body: You're a good target for a bad guy.

Bad guys can pick a victim out a mile away: walking with head down, making no eye contact. You may walk by a bad guy as he pretends to open the car door. In reality, he's watching you talk on your cell phone or fidget with your car keys. The next thing you know, he's grabbed your purse, and you're face down on the asphalt, wondering what happened.

Code Yellow

Be aware: Your instincts tell you when something is not right. Don't go to your car by yourself. Instead, call mall security and ask them to escort you to your car. Or wait for a group of people to come out and walk with them. You can always call the police department as a last resort. Sure, waiting to be safe may take more time than making a run for it, but your life is worth every minute.

Most police officers operate in *code yellow*. In other words, they don't look like victims, even when they wear their street clothes. Stay in touch with what's happening around you. If you step out of a building, pause for a moment to look around before walking to your car.

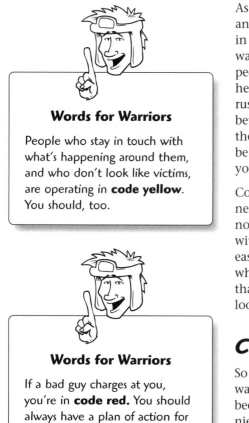

Words for Warriors

People who stay in touch with what's happening around them, and who don't look like victims, are operating in **code yellow**. You should, too.

Words for Warriors

If a bad guy charges at you, you're in **code red.** You should always have a plan of action for such situations; how will you get yourself out of code red alive?

As you walk to your car, continue to scan the area for anything that does not seem right. Look behind and in front of you to watch what's going on; stand tall, walk with a mission, and make eye contact with the people around you. Don't walk to the car with your head down, looking at your keys. If someone were to rush you, you might not see him coming. You've a better chance of defending yourself while observing the area. It's not 100 percent foolproof; you can still be surprised. But at least if you see someone coming you prepare yourself for the next move.

Code yellow is often called a relaxed state of awareness. It communicates to a would-be assailant: "You're not going to sneak up on me!" If you're eye to eye with a bad guy, he's thinking that you're not such an easy target. Why would he want to pick on someone who can defend herself? It's a crap shoot—"I can take that guy, but I don't know about her .... No way, she looks like a fighter."

Code Red

So what are you going to do if that gang member wants your packages? Are you going to say, "No, I've been shopping all day and I'm exhausted. My little nieces and nephews are coming tomorrow for turkey dinner and my house is a mess. Won't you go pick on someone else, please?" Maybe you'll get lucky, and your mugger will have a heart. Realistically, though, it's never your lucky day with a mugger; he wants your stuff. You have to have a plan for such occasions; that's where *code red* comes in.

What If ...

You're tucked in bed, sleeping soundly. Then you hear it—a noise in the kitchen. Not sure if it's a dream or real life, you listen again. Sure enough, someone is walking up the stairs to your bedroom ...

You're driving home late one night. The same white van has been behind you since you left the highway. Now, it's still following as you turn onto the side streets, headed toward your home ...

You're jogging on the same path that you always jog on. You're in the zone, focusing on your jog. Someone jumps out from behind the brushes and pushes you to the ground ...

In each of these instances, you have only two options—fight or flight. Do you think you can take him on? Do you want to? Maybe it's best to call 911. You'll have to do whatever it takes to get out of this situation alive, and hopefully unharmed. That's why you should have a plan for such situations—the time to think about what you'll do is not when you're faced with a crisis.

Jot down a few responses to the preceding scenarios so you're not wondering how you'll react. You may want to write down five scenarios of your own. Later in this chapter, you'll learn tips and tactics to take care of yourself in a life-threatening situation.

Recurrent Training

Kickboxers use the same types of moves—both offensively and defensively—in practice as they would use in combat. As Bruce Lee once said, "The reason that sportsmen such as boxers, kickboxers, and wrestlers have a higher success rate in self-defense situations over other martial artists is because they will fight in the same manner as they train." For this reason, it's important that you repeat, over and over again, the punches, kicks, and patterns of movement that could save your life; this is called *recurrent training*. In other words, what you practice in class will pop into your head in a life-threatening situation.

Repetition is the key to following through in a scary situation. The more you condition your mind and body to the techniques of kickboxing, the more likely they are to come back to you in a street fight. When you are faced with a street situation, your mind goes in a million directions. The way you react in such a situation usually comes from your subconscious. The more you kick, punch, knee—even in your workouts—the better prepared you are for a real-life situation; training provides constant reinforcement of defense moves.

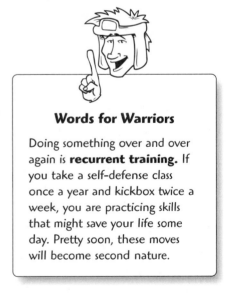

Words for Warriors

Doing something over and over again is **recurrent training.** If you take a self-defense class once a year and kickbox twice a week, you are practicing skills that might save your life some day. Pretty soon, these moves will become second nature.

Smell Trouble

Trust your instincts; if you don't feel comfortable with something, don't do it. The very second you think someone is following you, chances are, you're right.

Are we aware of these warning signals, these red flags? You bet. But we tend to sweep them under the rug. Just remember the Christmas shopping scenario discussed earlier—most of us will run to our car, even though the situation is potentially dangerous. We talk ourselves out of common sense and into trouble. Listen to those very first instincts; you'll never deceive yourself.

No Way Out!

When you are in a dangerous situation, you need to be thinking, "How do I get out of this situation unharmed and alive?" Your job is to be prepared for a real-life threat. If someone comes up and surprises you, your reaction should be, "Oh, I'm way ahead of you—I've got a plan!" It may be kickboxing, spraying him in the eyes with mace, fleeing the scene, spitting on him, gouging his eyes out, faking an epileptic fit, or behaving like a crazy person—just make sure you're ready.

For a split second, you'll probably be paralyzed by fear. A few seconds later, though, you'll act out your plan. Life-threatening situations are unpredictable; the best way not to look like a victim is to remain calm, cool, and collected. Don't wait until you're rolling around on the ground to figure out your next move; you risk making the wrong decision, or worse, acting like a victim.

Everyone will have her own plan; the idea is to be prepared for all the "what ifs" in life.

Warrior Women

Okay, you've done everything right. But somehow you've found yourself in a not so good situation. Can kickboxing help? You bet. No, you don't have to turn into a gladiator. You just have to get mad enough to jab him in the nose so you can run; you can learn how to distract him or take him off guard so you can get the hell out of there.

Remember, a woman is attacked every five minutes; most attackers will play the odds. If their chosen victim puts up too much of a fight, they will let her go, hoping the next girl who walks by will not put up a struggle.

If you're thinking that a criminal will show some mercy because you didn't put up a fight, think again. The FBI surveyed violent criminals and found that only one percent of the criminals would hurt their victims more for resisting. Or, to put it another way, an attacker has decided whether to hurt you before he ever even attacks you. Fighting back doesn't sway his decision. According to the statistics, you really have nothing to lose if you fight back.

Don't act scared—fear will immobilize you, giving your attacker the upper hand. There are no guarantees as to how you will react in a panic situation; however, by seriously training, you'll be better prepared for anything. In addition to preparing you mentally, kickboxing can make your body stronger, which in turn will help you deal with a real-life situation.

Narrow Body or Wide Body?

Rapists prey on the weak and feeble. As kickboxers, we're neither weak nor fragile. Kickboxing gets you in good shape: Ninety percent of the fight business is about good conditioning.

Sure, your fighting body will turn some heads, but you'll also be able to fight longer if your attacker hangs on. All the fancy moves in the world won't help you if you can't fight for more than 30 seconds. Bear in mind that most attacks last about a minute—but they feel more like an hour. You're super charged and hyped up; your mind races with fear, which drains your body's energy reserves. No one can guarantee the results in a street situation, but you can certainly stack the odds in your favor.

Kickboxing Buzz

In the United States, a woman is assaulted every 5 minutes. In years past, women were taught not to fight back in a rape or assault. Today, the statistics say something different. Statistics from the FBI (1993) say that three out of four women who fight get away.

In other words, 75 percent of women escape their attacker. Don't be afraid to use your kickboxing skills: Those women didn't go 12 rounds with their attacker; they just resisted enough to make it difficult, and to get out alive.

Beware!

Over the years, we have signed up for martial arts classes, thinking that we'll learn how to protect ourselves. Yes, you're doing something to improve your chances of surviving an attack. However, an overinflated sense of self-confidence can get you into trouble. You really want to avoid a real-life self-defense situation if at all possible.

If, however, you are confronted by a real-world attacker, you can save your life—particularly with kickboxing. Remember that kickboxing's roots extend back to the ancient fighting arts, in which hand to hand combat was taught to the soldiers to prepare them to kill their enemies.

You should seek out a self-defense program that mimics real-life fighting; your cardio-kickboxing class won't do. Even though it gets you in the mood to hit someone, you really want to understand the fighting system and how it may save your life someday.

The Instructor

You want to find an instructor who can teach you survival skills. For starters, you should look for someone with a real-life self-defense background—police, military, or accomplished martial arts.

Find an instructor who has, for example, trained police or private businesses in self-defense and safety tactics. Make sure that he teaches techniques that can increase your chances of survival.

A real-life threat is unpredictable; you may be able to strike him and run, or he may drag you to the ground—you have to learn how to push a 200-pound man off you. Avoid instructors or schools that claim that their martial arts are the best in a self-defense situation. Instead, you want to find a system that is grounded in reality—and the reality is that no two attacks are the same. Modern day survival techniques range from street smarts to being in tip-top shape. You may have to take out your attacker, so you want to be physically prepared for anything!

Oh No! Code Red

You want to stall for time, distract your attacker, and make him sorry for picking on you. He might even flee the scene, if you make the attack really difficult for him. The point is, you're not acting like a victim if you have a plan. Again, trust your instincts on what to do if you're attacked. How you get out of a situation will depend on the surroundings and your attacker.

Right now, think about your options and test your plan. Call the local police or fire department, and talk to them about personal and home safety. Check to see if your windows and doors are locked. Even that door that leads from your garage to the house should be locked—don't think for a second that a burglar doesn't know about that door.

A clever burglar will stake out your house to watch your every move. He'll strike when you're not home; that unlocked garage door could be his winning lottery ticket into your house. Or worse, imagine that you're home, resting from a cold. You hear a strange noise, but you're groggy from the cough medicine you just took. The burglar thinks that you're at work. What do you do?

You're a trained kickboxer, but you don't have all the facts. Does he have a gun? How many burglars are there? What will he do if you see his face? Remember, he thinks that you're working. Do you really want to stick around? Can you get out of a window safely? Can you hide in a closet? Maybe you can get out of the house; maybe you have to lock yourself in the closet. If that's the case, do you have time to dial 911 or take a cordless or cell phone with you? These are questions you should be asking yourself. Don't wait until you hear someone coming up the stairs—it may be too late.

How will you react, waking up from a groggy sickness sleep to find two strange men standing over you? Now may be a good time to use kickboxing tactics. The point is, you must mentally prepare yourself for such a situation. You don't want to act like a victim.

Plot out a few getaways. Go over them in your head. Share these ideas with your family members. And certainly contact your local authorities; they can give you the best advice on how to handle self-defense issues in your area. The time to wonder about self-defense is not when you're standing eye-to-eye with some creep. Be prepared! Think about your everyday moves and ways to make you safe.

Some cities have an enhanced 911, meaning that you're immediately logged into the system when you call 911. So, in case of an emergency, if you only got as far as dialing 911, the police or fire department can immediately be dispatched.

Don't misunderstand; these tips are not meant to scare you. Self-defense is not just about kicking butt; it's also about mentally preparing yourself for an attack. Think through several life-threatening situations, so you can act quickly and smartly. You want your attacker to be sorry for messing with you.

Up Close and Too Personal

You're pretty confident that you can kickbox your way out of any situation. However, unless you're a natural born fighter, why would you want to? That's why we're talking about ways to avoid getting into a sticky situation. Are these plans foolproof? Hardly. That's why you should also learn how to defend yourself physically. A well-rounded self-defense class should prepare you mentally as well as physically to increase your chances of surviving a real attack.

Fighting this creep should be your last resort. And it *does* matter how tough you think you are—someone is always bigger and tougher. The street is no time to try out your skills; there are too many factors working against you.

Kick-Tales

A police officer told me the following story: One of his female students was a marathon jogger. She jogs the same trail every day. One day, an attacker jumped out and pushed her to the ground. He unzipped his pants while she was on her knees; she started to grab handfuls of grass and shoved it into her mouth while she growled. The attacker probably thought that she was nuts as he ran away. Who cares what he thinks? We can't act like victims. After he ran away, she spit the grass out and ran to call 911.

Do you recall that the brain is the ultimate weapon? Use it. Don't put yourself in harm's way. But if it comes down to defending yourself, win.

The Least You Need to Know

➤ Always trust your instincts; if you feel that you shouldn't do something, don't.

➤ If you're completely oblivious to your surroundings, you're suffering from code white.

➤ A relaxed state of awareness is code yellow.

➤ Staring eye-to-eye with some creep in a self-defense situation is code red.

➤ A good self-defense plan involves three steps: awareness, striking moves, and a few ground fighting tactics.

➤ Prepare a mental escape plan for your everyday situations, just in case you're attacked.

Chapter 19

The Complete Martial Artist

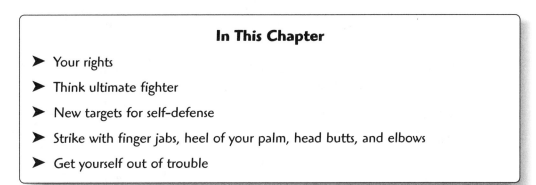

In This Chapter

➤ Your rights

➤ Think ultimate fighter

➤ New targets for self-defense

➤ Strike with finger jabs, heel of your palm, head butts, and elbows

➤ Get yourself out of trouble

Do you think that you could hit someone if you had to? Before you answer that question, really think about it. Many people have never hit someone, nor have they been hit.

Maybe you were only interested in the calorie burn when you started kickboxing; you probably didn't think about what could happen to you someday. But do you have any idea what a blow feels like? Have you ever been hit, or hit someone? What would you do if you were pushed to the ground? How would you react if someone jumped out at you? Would you freeze with fear? Would you stand there in a state of shock? These are reasons for you to step in to the ring—not to fight, but to practice hitting and getting hit.

In addition, we wanted to provide you with a few helpful tips and instructions on how to get out of a sticky situation. The fact is that attacks *do* occur; it's best not to wait until that moment to decide on a course of action. We recommend that anyone who is interested in self-defense fight in a controlled setting, so you learn what do in a life-threatening situation. We don't want to be helpless, and you shouldn't, either.

What Are Your Rights?

If you believe that you're in danger, you have the right to defend yourself. Verbal threats might not fit under that rule; for example, if someone shouts that he is going to kill you but walks away, so should you. However, if he lunges for you, you have the right to do whatever is necessary to get out of that situation. But let's say that your punch scares him, that he cowers and runs from you. Even in a state of rage, you shouldn't run after him. When the threat is over, so is the fight.

At that point, it's best to let the police fight for you. Your attacker could always say that it's your word against his. Every state is different, so you should check with your local authorities regarding self-defense laws.

The Ultimate Fighter

Even though you're a kickboxer, you can't rely 100 percent on your kicks and punches to save you in a real-life attack. You'll have to learn a little bit about ground fighting moves such as *grappling* and *takedowns*.

As kickboxers, we are taught to strike. But what if you can't kick or punch? For instance, say your attacker gets you on the ground—now what? How are you going to defend yourself? How will you get back on your feet so you can get the hell out of there? Remember, no one can predict what will happen in a real-life attack; your goal is not to freeze up and act like a victim, but to be prepared for the unexpected. Don't worry—you're not going to learn how to become a pro wrestler. But adding a few wrestling moves to your arsenal certainly can't hurt.

Words for Warriors

Ever watch a wrestler? He's using **grappling** and **takedowns** to win the match. He never strikes, only muscles his opponent to the ground. The takedown is when you take your opponent to the ground; whereas, grappling enables you to control your opponent with certain techniques to keep him on the ground.

On the streets, you'll fight like an Ultimate Fighting Champion—no rules, no holds barred, full contact brawl. First, you'll learn how to adjust your kicks and punches so you can use them in a self-defense situation. Keep in mind that your strikes are still your best bet. Your punches, for example, are your quickest form of defense. You can act very quickly with your hand strikes—and that's what you should always keep in mind. Use your kicks for power. If a kick is thrown correctly to the groin, for example, you can take the wind out of your attacker. Then you can run. Remember, kicks are your long-range weapons, so use them to keep your attacker at a safe distance.

Without a doubt, you must learn how to throw your kicks and punches correctly; you really don't want to end up on your back. But if you find yourself looking up at your attacker, you'll learn how to escape. You'll also learn how to push your attacker to the ground in the hope of knocking the wind out of him, or maybe even breaking a bone or two. The best advice, though, is to practice these moves so that they settle into your subconscious. That is, you need to think like the Ultimate Fighter.

Down and Dirty

A wise coach once said, "It's not the size of the dog in the fight, but the size of the fight in the dog." Obviously, a 200-pound man will have more strength than a 105-pound woman. The fact that you may be weaker than your attacker doesn't mean that you can't outwit him. You should automatically assume that you're not as strong; then, you're not surprised by what your attacker will do, and it's an added bonus if you have the strength to take him down.

The ultimate goal in self-defense is to win, either by taking that creep out or outlasting him in the fight. Obviously, you need to be strong and in good condition, just in case the fight drags on. Remember, your chances of escaping are better if you can wear him down. If he is hanging in there, however, your best chance is to fight him. You're going to show this idiot that he made a big mistake by messing with you.

So, in a self-defense situation, it's fair to get down and dirty. Think about three new targets: the groin, the throat, and the top of the foot.

The Groin

You can kick, knee, even throw a punch to the groin. No words can explain the pain that comes from a square shot to the old manhood. Keep in mind, however, that although a groin shot can slow down an attacker, you shouldn't rely on it as your only self-defense strike. For example, he may be wearing a cup or some other sort of protection. If that's the case, consider another target.

The Throat

The throat is a great target if the groin shot won't work; it's soft and open for an attack. Contrary to common belief, killing someone with a blow to the throat is extremely difficult. Yes, it can be done, but your chances of winning the lottery five times in a row are better than your chances of killing someone in this manner. So go ahead, strike the throat to stun your attacker. Then you can run.

Kickboxing Buzz

In a self–defense situation, you'll have three new targets: groin, throat, top of the foot. All three are extremely vulnerable if attacked.

The Top of the Foot

The third target is the top of the foot. The bones on the top of the foot are very delicate—that's one reason why you never use the top of your foot when you throw

259

kicks. So, in a self-defense situation, try stomping on the top of the attacker's foot for a quick escape from a hold. Be sure to stomp hard enough to stop him from walking or running after you.

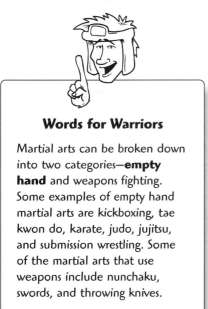

Words for Warriors

Martial arts can be broken down into two categories—**empty hand** and weapons fighting. Some examples of empty hand martial arts are kickboxing, tae kwon do, karate, judo, jujitsu, and submission wrestling. Some of the martial arts that use weapons include nunchaku, swords, and throwing knives.

The Empty Hand

In reality, you're not going to have a weapon ready to fire if you're attacked. Instead, you'll have to depend on your hands to defend yourself. Martial arts that don't use weapons—such as kickboxing, tae kwon do, and karate—are often called the *empty hand* fighting arts.

In a self-defense situation, the rules of empty hand sports don't apply. Remember, anything goes on the street, and you have to do whatever it takes to get out of the situation. Notice the similarities between the strikes below and the ones you have already learned—jabs, crosses, and hooks. Instead of the traditional closed fist, you'll use your fingers and the palm of your hand as striking surfaces. Thus, by slightly modifying the moves you've already learned in kickboxing, you suddenly possess a handful of self-defense moves.

The Finger Jab

Strike the eyes of your attacker. This move is similar to a jab, but you'll use your fingers as you throw the punch (see the following figure). Leave your first two fingers extended, and use the tips of those fingers to poke at the attacker's eyes.

A finger jab to the eyes.

Head Butt

The head butt can be used as a great escape move. We know, the idea of hitting some-one with your head might not sound like a great idea, but it is. The top part of your head is very hard; you can throw your head back or forward to break your attacker's nose (see the following figures). With a little speed, you may even knock him out.

The front head butt (left) and the back head butt (right).

Back Elbow

If your attacker is close enough, throw an elbow strike (see the following figures). To get the best of him, throw the strike with the bony point of your elbow. Aim for the soft tissues: nose, eyes, throat, solar plexus, or groin.

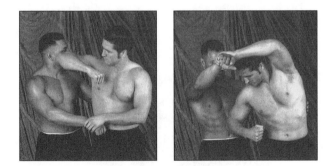

A back elbow to the face (left) and a back elbow to the body (right).

Palm Strikes

Another good self-defense move is the palm strike. Throw a punch; instead of a closed fist, though, open your hand. Strike with the front part of the hand, and ideal-ly with the lower part of the hand, near the wrist, to inflict serious injury. There are three types of palm strikes: a jab palm heel strike (see the following figure, left), a cross palm heel strike (see the following figure, center), and a hook palm heel strike (see the following figure, right). When throwing a hook palm heel strike, be sure to extend your arm a little more than you do with a regular hook.

The jab palm heel strike (left), the cross palm heel strike (center), and the hook palm heel strike (right).

Using palm strikes increases the striking surface to help guarantee that you land a shot. You'll also cut down the chances of injuring your hands by hitting with an open palm. Finally, with your hands open, it's easier to grab your attacker.

The Foot Stomp

This particular technique may not be brain surgery, but it can be highly effective in a self-defense fight. It is basically like throwing a side kick to the ground (see the following figure). This move is great for hitting your attacker's feet—or any other body part that happens to be on the ground.

The foot stomp.

The Fight of Your Life

The following sections detail a few acts of violence. They are not meant to scare you, only to give you a few ideas about how to react if you're ever in that situation. Keep in mind that your punches and kicks are still your best form of defense.

As you read each self-defense scenario, remember that you have two choices: flight or fight. Even though the following sections show a series of self-defense tactics, if you can get away, do. You don't have to complete the series, maybe the thug will run with the first strike. However, if he persists and you think that you can take this attacker on, assume the fighting position. Who knows? Maybe he'll run.

Self-Defense Scenario # 1: The Wrist Grab

One common self-defense scenario involves an assailant grabbing your wrist and trying to drag you away. A side kick to an open target—the knee—is just the first in a series of moves you can use to make your attacker release his grip.

If an attacker grabs your wrist, lower your weight to make it harder for the assailant to pull you by turning your body sideways to help create a good angle for a kick. Then, use his pulling momentum to amplify your power when throwing the side kick. Aim slightly above the knee (see the following figures). This side kick should knock your attacker off balance.

Resist a wrist grab with these steps.

Self-Defense Scenario #2: Front Grab or Choke

When the assailant grabs you from the front, step one foot back for balance, and bring your hands up to the fighting position. Now, throw a knee to the groin area, and then take your right arm and circle over your attacker's arms. At the same time, step through with your right leg and turn your body away from the attacker. You'll have his arms trapped, which will pull him off balance. Finish by throwing a series of back elbow strikes to his face. (See the following series of figures.)

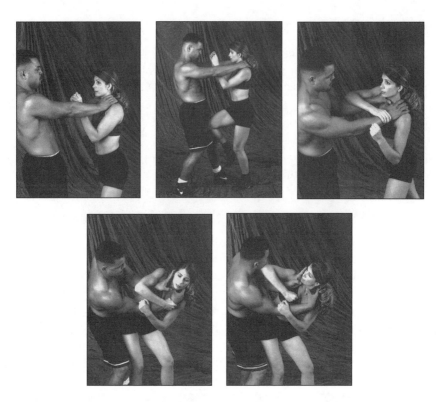

Stun your attacker with a kick to the groin. Then complete the job with an elbow strike to the chin.

Self-Defense Scenario #3: The Choke from Behind

If an attacker grabs you from behind to choke you, know that he can kill you immediately with this choke hold. Drop your chin immediately to prevent your attacker from choking you to death. Then, use your right hand to grab his choking arm to release some of the pressure from the choke (see the following figure, left). Next, use the foot stomp to smash the top of his foot; this should help loosen his grip. Then, take your left elbow and throw a back elbow strike to the solar plexus or groin (see the following figure, center). As you pull free, finish him off with a side kick to prevent him from grabbing you again (see the following figure, right).

Self-Defense Scenario #4: Bear Hug from Behind

Imagine that your attacker grabs you from behind, with his arms in a bear hug around your chest or stomach (see the following figure, left). Lower your weight to make it difficult for him to pick you up. At the same time, stomp on his foot. Use your middle knuckles to strike the back part of the attacker's hands—this really hurts. Next, lower your head to your chest and swing it backward, delivering a back head butt to his face (see the following figure, center). Turn around. Face your assailant and launch a leg kick to your opponent's left leg (see the following figure, right). Now run away.

An elbow to the gut will break your attacker's choke hold. Don't let your attacker grab you again; fire a side kick.

Stomp, back head butt, and kick your way out of a bear hug.

Self Defense Scenario #5: Hair Grab

Your attacker may grab your hair to control you. He may also hold your hair so that he can better strike you. When the attacker grabs your hair, reach up and interlock your fingers to grab his hand (see the following figure, left). Press his hand to the top of your head to help stop the pain and to control the grab. Bring your elbows together to protect your face from getting punched. Step back. With your best kicking leg, throw three front kicks to the shin, groin, and solar plexus (see the following figure, center). Finally, launch a jab to the face, followed by a cross (see the following figure, right).

Free yourself from a hair grab with these steps.

Self-Defense Scenario #6: Front Grab

In this scenario, your attacker grabs the front of your clothes (see the following series of figures). Turn your body slightly and bring your hands up. Strike a double palm strike to the ears, and then throw a jab to the face, followed by a cross. Finish by grabbing the back of the assailant's neck to launch two knee strikes. Aim for the groin or solar plexus.

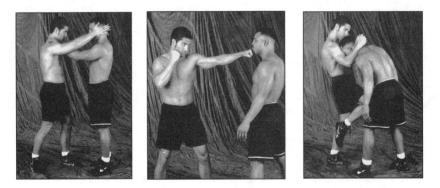

Deliver a palm strike to stun your attacker; follow with a jab, and then use a knee to the groin to finish him off.

Self-Defense Scenario #7: Side Head Lock

Your attacker has grabbed you and put you in a side head lock (see the following figure, left). Throw a hook to the groin, and then stomp his foot. Throw a knee strike to the back of his thigh and pull yourself out of the head lock (see the following figure, center). Finally, push the attacker off balance (see the following figure, right).

To maneuver your way out of a side head lock, throw a hook to the groin fol-
lowed by a knee strike at the back of the attacker's thigh. Finally, push the
attacker off balance.

Dealing with More Than One Attacker

One, two, maybe three attackers—how will you
survive this nightmare? The best way to deal with
this type of situation is to remain on your feet.
Keep on the outside of your attackers—never get
between two attackers. Kickboxing teaches you to
keep moving, which will come in handy when
you are facing more than one person at a time. If
you focus your attention on one attacker, the
other can come from behind. Instead, stay in
front, and try to focus on both of them at all
times.

In this situation, it's best to flee, not fight, especially if you're a 100-pound woman. If you're
forced to fight, the best strategy is to hit and

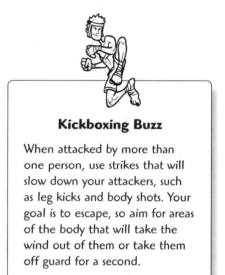

Kickboxing Buzz

When attacked by more than
one person, use strikes that will
slow down your attackers, such
as leg kicks and body shots. Your
goal is to escape, so aim for areas
of the body that will take the
wind out of them or take them
off guard for a second.

move. Do not stay in one place. And don't worry about where your strikes are going to
land; it's your opponents who need to worry about your hapless strikes. Furthermore,
your attackers have to worry about hitting each other in the fight, you don't.

Self-Defense Scenario #1: Frontal Attack–Bear Hug from Behind

Attacker #1 has grabbed you from behind in a bear hug (see the following series of
figures). Attacker #2 comes at you from the front. The first order of business is to escape from the hold and get out from between the attackers.

Use a front kick to the groin on attacker #2, and then use a backward head butt on attacker #1. Stomp on the foot of attacker #1 in order to secure an escape. Next, throw a right roundhouse kick to the thigh of attacker #2 and move behind him. From behind attacker #2, push him into attacker #1 and escape.

You may have to execute your entire arsenal of kicks and strikes when breaking away from more than one attacker.

Self-Defense Scenario #2: Double Frontal Attack

When attackers #1 and #2 come at you from the front, step back and circle to the right (see the following sequence of figures). With this move, one attacker will be in the way of the other. Strike attacker #1 with a side kick to legs or stomach, and then push attacker #1 into attacker #2. Now, launch a 1-2 combo—the jab and cross—into attacker #1.

When attacker #2 attacks you, fake a jab to the face and throw a roundhouse kick to the thigh. Grab attacker #2 to throw a knee strike into the legs or groin. While still holding attacker #2, strike with a finger jab to his eyes. Finish by pushing the temporarily blinded attacker #2 onto attacker #1. Escape.

Follow the series of strikes to take down two attackers. Notice the fake jab, followed by a roundhouse kick to the thigh. Along with using your arsenal, you may have to fake out your attackers.

Self-Defense Scenario #3:
Bear Hug from Behind–Front Grab

Attacker #1 has you in a bear hug, and attacker #2 is in front of you, holding your hands (see the following sequence of figures). Knee strike attacker #2 in the groin, and then front kick attacker #2 to the chest and push him away. Next, foot stomp attacker #1 and back head butt him in the nose. Strike attacker #1 in the back of the hand that's holding you around the waist to make him release you. Step away and circle around the two attackers. Escape.

269

Show no mercy with these debilitating shots.

The Least You Need to Know

➤ Anyone who is interested in self-defense should fight in a controlled setting to prepare for a real-life threat.

➤ You have the right to defend yourself if you fear for your life or the life of someone you love.

➤ The Ultimate Fighter uses all the fighting arts and the matches are very similar to real-life street fights.

➤ Your punches are your quickest weapons.

➤ Your kicks are your most powerful weapons.

➤ Self-defense targets include the groin, the eyes, and the top of the foot.

➤ In a self-defense situation, you'll strike with the heel of your hand, fingers, and elbows.

Chapter 20

The Fight of Your Life

Brace yourself for a fact: A would-be attacker won't stand by and let you kickbox him to death. As scary as that may sound, it's the truth. You're entering the unknown; your attacker, on the other hand, knows the drill—he's a real pro.

An attacker wants to control you. He'll try to throw you to the ground or push you into his car. On the ground, he can hold your hands so you can't hit him, or he can put something in your mouth so you don't scream. If he gets you into his car, you may never be seen again. You, however, must put up a fight; you don't want to be rolling around on the ground, and you never want to get in his car.

How are you going to defend yourself if you're taken to the ground? You don't have to be an expert wrestler, but you should have a little training in this area. For example, the most common mistake is to roll onto the stomach, clutching the head. You might think that you're protecting yourself, but you're really giving your attacker an opportunity to control you. We're going to show you how you can defend yourself if you're thrown to the ground.

Ranges, Again!

Nothing has changed as far as the ranges of your weapons. Kicks are your long-range weapons—they keep your attacker from getting too close (great for women!). Punches are your medium-range weapons. (Punches are not so good for women because most men are stronger in the arms.) Elbow and knee strikes are your short-range weapons. Use them when your attacker is in your face.

Remember the Christmas shopping/empty parking lot scenario from Chapter 18, "The Perfect Self-Defense"? Well, we're going to reenact it a few different ways. Don't worry—because you've got the training, you'll get away.

Imagine that you're walking through the parking lot, hands loaded with presents. You're looking around, noticing what's going on around you—good move. A gang member charges towards you. You see him coming, though, so you drop your bags and assume the fighting position. He stops, stunned that you're ready, or at least that you look like a fighter. He approaches you. You, then, turn into the Tasmanian devil, hurling kicks his way. For keeping this creep at a distance, your kicks are your best weapon. He tucks his tail between his legs and runs away—mission accomplished! He thinks you're a crazy woman, but who cares? You're okay.

Now imagine that this thug assumes the fighting position as well. Don't panic—it might be a bluff. But think about your punches: the finger jabs and the open hand cross. He's getting a little too close now. You throw a kick, but he's not fazed. He fires a cross; you successfully block it, coming back with the two finger jab to the eyes. In a state of shock, he runs away; to him, you didn't look like a kickboxer.

Now imagine that the finger jab didn't bother him; he closes in to restrain your hands. But it's not his lucky day—you drive your knee into his groin. As he falls to the ground, cupping his privates, you run away.

Finally, imagine that he's down, but by this point you're so angry that you want to stomp on his groin again. But he blocks your foot and flips you onto your backside. What now? You're on the ground, and he's about to spring on top of you.

In the Dirt

Kickboxing this creep into submission would have been nice. But now he's tackled you to the ground and you've got to get to your feet as quickly as possible. We'll cover two ground strategies: offense and defense. Ground offense is pretty straight-forward—you'll learn how to shove your attacker to the ground. Ground defense, unfortunately, takes a little more time. Because you're in a weak position, you've got a few more things to think about, including how to put your attacker in a position that makes it difficult for him to move while staying out of the way of his strikes. You also don't want him to flip you onto your belly. Finally, you want to escape as quickly as possible.

It's not a great situation to be on the ground, at the mercy of an attacker, but you can work it to your advantage.

The ground fighting art, *judo*, uses defensive guard positions. Using these positions is the best way for you to either control your attacker or maneuver an escape. There are many guard positions that you can learn, but we will just work on the basics. Following are a few different scenarios.

Words for Warriors

Judo is the art of self-defense. It's a martial art that teaches you how to turn your opponent's strength against him by using techniques such as throws, take-downs, and submission holds.

The Closed Guard

For the closed guard position, wrap your legs around your attacker's waist, and lock them together with your heels. Grab the attacker's head with your free arm. Then, take your other arm and grab the attacker's arm; hold it tight. The closed guard will keep your attacker close to you so that he can't hit you or move. However, notice that you can't hit him, either. This is a neutral position, used in an extreme situation. In this position, you want to hold on tight because your attacker will fight you. Let him burn up his energy and get tired: Hang on until someone can help you or until you have the opportunity to escape.

The Open Guard

The first open guard position keeps your attacker between your legs, but not in a leg-locked position. There are three types of open guard positions: open guard #1, #2, and #3.

Open Guard Position #1

The open guard #1 is used to keep your attacker from taking advantage of you while you're on the ground. Since he's standing, he's got the power and mobility to harm you. Stay on your back. No matter where he moves, keep him trapped between your legs by spinning on your back. He'll try to flip you over, but you don't want to end up on your stomach—that's a weak position. As the attacker tries to close in, use your legs to kick at his shins or knees to keep him away from you. Do not kick both legs at the same time; alternate your kicks. You always want to have a free kicking leg, just in case your attacker grabs one of your legs. A determined attacker will try to work past your kicks. As he closes in, you can strike him in the head (see the following series of figures).

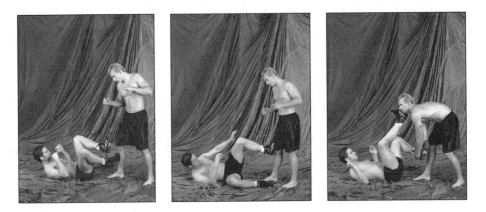

Use the open guard #1 to keep your attacker from taking advantage of you while you're on the ground.

Open Guard Position #2

Use this open guard position to control the distance between you and your attacker. Here's the scenario (see the following sequence of figures): You're on your back with your knees bent into your chest. The attacker is on his knees, facing you. As the attacker attempts to strike or get closer, bring your knees together and clamp your feet around his waist. If he tries to push past you, keep pressing against him. Lift your hips off the ground to make it tough for your attacker to throw any strikes.

To keep your attacker from getting too close to you, bring your knees together and clamp your feet around his waist.

Open Guard Position #3

In this guard position, you have more control over your attacker and a free hand to strike your attacker while you are on your back.

Dig your heels into the attacker's hips. Your knees are pressed against his sides, and your hands are either grabbing the back of his head or blocking your face. If your attacker fires a strike, push with your feet. You'll keep him away by either sliding back or pushing him away.

The Proper Stand-Up

Standing back up after being knocked down in a street situation is very important. Why? Because if you get up wrong, you can put yourself back into a vulnerable position. Remember, your attacker is a real pro; he's waiting for you to make a mistake. He wants to knock you back down, or knock you senseless with a punch. Don't let him.

Here's the scenario (see the following sequence of figures): You're on your back, and your attacker is standing over you. You got him in an open guard; kick him anywhere you can to keep him from getting any closer. Now, you can turn your body sideways to stand up and move away.

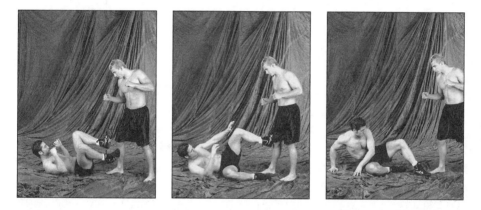

You can buy a few seconds by kicking your attacker. Now stand up and get ready to fight.

Ground Scenario #1

Your attacker is ready to pounce on you. So, hold your attacker in the open guard position #1 (see the following sequence of figures). As your attacker grabs your left leg, pull it in to bring him closer to you. When he gets close enough, strike his face with the heel of your right foot. Next, turn your body sideways, with the left hip down. Take your left foot and hook it behind the attacker's right ankle. Then, side kick with your right leg to the attacker's kneecap to force him to the ground.

Stun your attacker with a heel strike so he doesn't get on top of you.

Ground Scenario #2

You're holding your attacker in the open guard position #2 (see the following sequence of figures). As he stands up to get a better angle to strike you, grab both his ankles with your hands. Thrust your hips forward; at the same time, pull his ankles to knock him down. Get up and take a mount position to strike at him with a finger jab to the face.

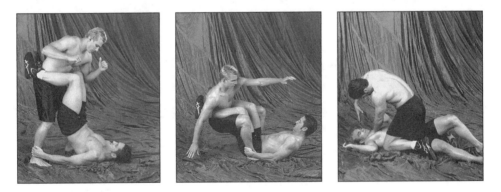

Use this scenario to reverse positions with your attacker.

Ground Scenario #3

What will you do if your attacker is on top of you? Use the open guard position #3. In this guard, you will hold your attacker by the back of his head to throw him off balance (see the following sequence of figures). Use a right elbow strike, in a downward motion to the back of his head and neck. Release the back of his head enough so that you can finger jab his eyes. When the attacker rears back, throw a kick to his chest with both legs to knock him backward. Then, get up.

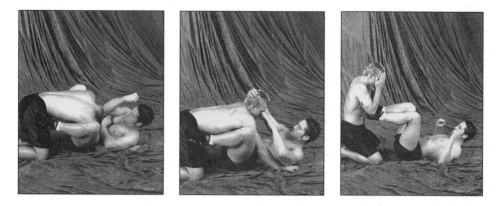

In this guard, you can throw very effective techniques in order to get away.

The Ground Offense

In a ground offense attack, you're buying time—enough time so that you can run. These take downs should help. Even so, you still have to think through the situation. Just because you pushed him to the ground, will he run after you? Then what?

Remember, you never want your attacker to get too close. But what happens if he does? What if you can't punch him or strike him with a knee or elbow strike? Try pushing him to the ground. Again, you have only two choices, flight or fight. If you think that you can outrun him, go for it. Or, you may have to get in the fighting stance and protect yourself.

The Leg Sweep

Leg sweeps are a pretty good tackle tactic. Use them to throw your attacker off balance so you can run away from him or strike him. You don't have to wait until he drops to the ground; when he's off balance, he's open for an attack. Even if it's for a second only, you'll have the perfect opportunity to strike so that he doesn't run after you.

A leg sweep can be done from either the front or rear leg; the strongest sweeps are off the rear leg. Start by facing the attacker in the fighting position (see the following sequence of figures). Move your body in the same motion you use for a roundhouse kick, and strike the attacker's right leg at the ankle. Instead of recoiling the kick, keep it straight and swing through it (like a baseball swing). This motion creates the momentum to knock your attacker off balance.

Kickboxing Buzz

Leg sweeps knock your attacker off balance, and that's when you can strike. You don't have to wait for your attacker to fall to the ground.

Sweep your attacker to the ground.

Keeping the Attacker on the Ground

You should absolutely run when you have the chance; however, you've got to make sure that your attacker stays on the ground at least long enough for you to get away. But note that he may be able to outrun you. Then what? You may have to continue the battle, even when he's down. Leg sweeps take your attacker down, but probably not for long. You should have a backup plan, and be ready for anything. Once your attacker hits the ground, you can use the following pins to hit him without leaving yourself open to being hit.

The Knee-on-the-Stomach Pin

You've swept your attacker to the ground. Now, keep him pinned by placing one knee—and your entire body weight—on his stomach. Move to the side of his body, leading with the left knee; place your left knee on your attacker's stomach. Bring the right knee up to a 90-degree angle to the side of his body, keeping your hand ready to throw punches. Your hands are free to finger jab or to smash his nose with the heel of your palm.

The Mount Position Pin

The second position is the mount position pin, in which you'll straddle your attacker. In this position, you should use your body weight to keep him in position so that you can strike him in the face.

After you've swept your attacker to the ground, move to the side of his body. Leading with your left knee, move across his stomach, placing your hands on his chest for balance. Place your left knee on the other side of your attacker's body. You should be facing him when you straddle him (see the following figure). Be sure to clamp down on both sides of his body with your legs, and be ready to strike.

Straddle your attacker with your legs and get ready to strike.

Kids Kicking Butt

Parenting … it's hard enough. But in this day and age, you probably feel that you can't safely let your child out of your sight without feeling a bit panicky. How, then, can you protect your child? It's you, Mom, who needs to tell your child not to get in a car with a stranger. It's you, Dad, who can give him a few tips on how to teach the class bully a lesson or two. And it's the teacher, telling your child to look out for strange people hanging around the playground.

Following are a few tips on how to protect your child in a threatening situation. This information shouldn't replace the advice of your local authorities (such as the police department), and we are probably not telling you anything new; however, it is always a good time to review safety with your child.

The same principles apply to your children as to you. We told you to make a plan; now do the same for your kids. Role play with your children—there are a hundreds of events that could happen, and you want them to be ready. Make a plan for scenarios that go along with your child's everyday schedule. For example, what if …

➤ a stranger offers your child some candy?

➤ your child gets lost in the mall?

➤ a stranger enters your home?

➤ a strange man stands by watching your children play in the park?

➤ mommy/daddy passes out in the kitchen?

Rehearse each situation with your child. That way, if a threatening situation comes up, he won't panic; he'll know to act out what you told him.

Talk to Your Children

You should make your child repeat her full name, address, and phone number. Show her how to call 911, both on your home phone and on a pay phone. You can even use a play phone with your child for practice; pretend that you are the operator, and quiz your child about her full name, home address, area code, and phone number.

Also, walk your child through the neighborhood; make sure that he knows which neighbors he can go to for help in case of an emergency. (For example, tell him to run out the back door and to your neighbor's house if a strange man enters the house.) Use this time to point out areas in the neighborhood that may threaten your child's safety. For example, abandoned buildings, overgrown shrubbery, vacant lots, and busy streets are all dangerous areas for children. Certainly, go over the dangers with your child, and report suspicious activity in the neighborhood to the local authorities.

When we were children, our mothers warned us never to take candy from a stranger. Unfortunately, today, kidnappers are much more creative. Some will use puppies as a ploy to get your child near the car; others might say, "Your mother's sick, won't you come with me so I can bring you to her?" Who knows? But you must warn your children not to go near a stranger's car. To make sure that they understand you, ask them if they know what a stranger is. A good definition of *stranger* is someone that your children don't know well. It doesn't matter if it's a woman or a man, or if they are dressed well or in a fancy car—a stranger is a stranger. For practice, you might have your child point out to you all the strangers in a crowded fast food restaurant.

If your child gets lost in a shopping center, tell her to trust only security. You want to stress that she go to the nearest security or checkout counter to make a public announcement. Tell her not to wander the parking lot looking for you. Have a backup plan for where to meet in case you're separated.

Teach your child to stay alert to what's going on around him and to walk confidently. Enrolling your child in kickboxing can also help; in most cases, instructors will teach self-defense moves. Kickboxing will do for your child what it does for you: It gets you in great shape, ingrains punches and kicks, and instills that *don't quit* attitude. Best of all, it gives you the hope that your child will remember what to do if she is ever faced with a life-threatening situation. Maybe you can sleep a little better at night knowing that you've done everything within your power to protect your child from harm.

"Help!"

Teach your child to shout "Help!" over and over again if he is grabbed by a stranger. Tell him to make a lot of noise, to scream, to do anything to attract attention. Make sure that he knows to bike or run away to the nearest place where people are around.

Kids are easy targets. Tragically, we hear about kidnappings, sexual molestation, child-care beatings, and school shootings in the news just about every day. We have stressed that you should take a self-defense class in addition to reading this book, and that you should use your kickboxing workouts to rehearse the skills that you learn. Do the same for your children. Following are a few self-defense tactics; practice them with your children.

Break Away from a Front Grab

If an attacker grabs the front of your child's shirt (see the following sequence of figures), he should deliver a front kick to the attacker's shin to get him to let go. Then, the child should throw a left cross to the chest area and push the attacker to the ground.

If your child is defending himself against the schoolyard bully, it's best for him to strike to make a point, not severely injure the bully.

Break Away from a Wrist Grab

If an attacker grabs your child's wrist (see the following figures) and the child can't free herself, she should grab the attacker's hand (the one that is holding the child's wrist) and deliver a side kick to the stomach.

Side kicks are a very effective weapon against wrist grabs.

Break Away from a Side Head Lock

Imagine that an attacker has your child in a head lock (see the following sequence of figures). The child should stomp on the top of the attacker's foot. Then, he should throw a series of right and left punches to the attacker's upper thigh. These tactics should cause the attacker to loosen his grip, so the child can pull free.

A simple way to get your head free from an attacker's lock.

Break Away from a Bear Hug

If an attacker grabs your child from behind and holds her in a bear hug (see the following sequence of figures), she should stomp down on the top of the attacker's foot. The child should then use the middle knuckles of her left hand to strike the backside of the attacker's hand. Then, the child should reach down between her legs and grab the attacker's foot, lifting it to make him fall down.

Three steps to take the attacker to the ground.

Break Away from a Front Choke

As an attacker grabs your child in a front choke, the child should step back to maintain her balance (see the following sequence of figures). Then, the child should raise her arms above her head, interlocking her fingers. She can then bring her arms down on the attacker's arms to loosen the hold around her neck. Next, she can grab the sides of the attacker's arms and throw a front kick to the chest area. The child should keep kicking until the attacker lets go.

A choke hold could kill you. Execute these fast kicks to get away.

Hey Men!

At this point, you men probably feel a little left out: We know that we've focused, to some extent, on self-defense for women and children. But self-defense is self-defense, regardless of age or gender. Obviously, you'll handle a real-life threat a little differently than a woman might: Women want to get away as quickly as possible, whereas men might take on a much more aggressive style of self-defense. Following are some reasons why you might want to think that through, however.

If a mugger comes up and demands your wallet, give it to him. If he takes it and runs, don't run after him to pummel him—he can sue you if you do. As crazy as that may sound, it's your word against his, and he was technically running away when you attacked him (which rules out self-defense). If he assaults you, however, you have the right to defend yourself.

You may be faced with the same situation in a barroom brawl. You can't strike the drunk who slurs obscenities at you, but if he takes a swing, you can swing back to knock him down. However, you can't get on top of him to destroy his face once he's down and not making any further move to hurt you. Again, if you do you'll end up liable. That's not to say that a barroom brawl cannot escalate into a life or death situation, though. You have the right to defend yourself, but there's a fine line between protecting yourself and inflicting major pain on someone.

Finally, don't confuse control with hesitation: If you hesitate in a fighting situation, you could get hurt. So, it's a good idea to spar so that you will develop self-control in tandem with self-defense skills. Therefore, sparring, even light contact sparring, can better prepare you for the real thing. In addition, this type of exercise gives you the edge in a real-life fight, helping you to sharpen your punches and kicks so that the punch you throw to take down an attacker can't be construed as a violation of his rights.

Whatever the case may be, be prepared for the worst. Think about it this way: The time to try a new technique is with your trainer. The time to learn that a new maneuver doesn't work is not during a street fight—it might cost you your life.

The Least You Need to Know

➤ Kicks keep your attacker at a distance, and punches are your fastest weapons; use your elbows and knees if your assailant gets in your face.

➤ The guard is a judo move used to tire your attacker so you can get up off the ground.

➤ Leg sweeps help you knock your attacker to the ground.

➤ Your kids can learn a few self-defense moves as well.

Part 6

After the Lights Go Out

Climbing the ranks from beginner to world champion is the best way to gain a supreme sense of self-esteem. But how does a champion, or anyone else, stay challenged in the field of kickboxing? In this part, we'll explore other avenues of kickboxing and martial arts.

Find out if you can be the coach who gives life to the sport of kickboxing, and determine if you have the skills and patience to teach the little ones. And finally, we'll answer that dreaded question that plagues most of professional kickboxers, "Do I say good-bye to kickboxing?"

Chapter 21

Be the Perfect Trainer

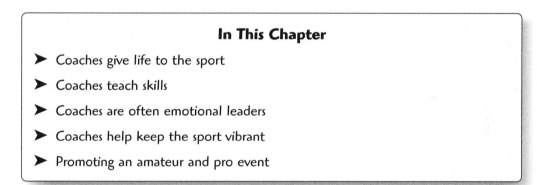

In This Chapter

➤ Coaches give life to the sport

➤ Coaches teach skills

➤ Coaches are often emotional leaders

➤ Coaches help keep the sport vibrant

➤ Promoting an amateur and pro event

Kickboxing is not the easiest sport to master. At first, most students feel stupid. Can you be the coach who stays after class to help those students? Your fighters need constant encouragement because they'll continually doubt their ability—fighting is hitting, and hitting causes fear. Can you be the coach who motivates these kickboxing students even after a knockout? Your kids want to play. Can you make kickboxing fun?

Do you love to put a smile on your students' faces? Do you feel fulfilled by teaching, by sharing your passion? Kids kickbox because it's fun; parents kickbox because it's a challenge; fighters kickbox for greatness. As a coach, you'll influence many lives—it's your job to preserve the integrity of the sport. As a coach, it's your job to groom and promote fighters; it's your job to share what you love—kickboxing!

Superhuman

They call it coaching, giving life to a sport. Coaches have a genuine concern for the students they teach; they have a strong desire to share their kickboxing skills and secrets, and the patience and understanding to let each student grow at his own pace.

Oftentimes, the coach acts as an emotional leader, a counselor, a friend, maybe even a substitute parent. For the competitive athlete, the coach is a leader, a role model, and a disciplinarian. Coaches hold the key to the athletic dreams of their students.

As a coach, you'll play the single most important role in your student's life; it doesn't matter if the student is there for fitness, self-defense, or sport. A good coach is there to witness the successes and failures, the satisfactions and frustrations, and the joys and disappointments of kickboxing. The coach is a technician and emotional leader, driven by the love of the sport.

Good Coaching

Sure, you've got an edge on the technical end if you're a kickboxer. But good coaching doesn't stop there. If you want to stay on top, think of new ways to keep kickboxing current. For example, add in some cardio-kickboxing moves. If you remain open-minded to new ways of training, your students will become better kickboxers. Maybe you will want to suggest cross-training; give them a workout that includes some weight or endurance training, some yoga, or some type of power stretching. Good coaches also need to understand the basic principles of nutrition. If you train fighters, you need to step it up: Know about high-performance nutrition so your students can achieve peak performance. Finally, try to learn everything about training responsibly, mixing light days with some heavy workouts. You don't want to over-train your students; otherwise, they might end up hurt.

In addition to all that, a coach is an emotional leader. Maybe you have the natural ability to instruct; perhaps you have to work at it. Regardless, know that successful coaches have two things in common: patience and affection. Show your students you care by following these simple rules:

➤ Get to know your students.

➤ Make kickboxing their own.

➤ Coach them.

➤ Control your emotions.

➤ Be positive, and be sincere with your compliments.

➤ Don't bore your students with long speeches.

➤ Say important facts three times.

➤ Watch your body language.

For the Love of Teaching

Make an effort to get to know your students. You can better coach them if you know about their backgrounds; home situations; spouses, girlfriends, or boyfriends; and general pressures from their schools, jobs, and families.

Don't be surprised if you end up masquerading as a therapist. Your students, especially the ones taking private lessons, may end up spilling their guts as they strike the bags. Just listen. It's important to maintain a high level of professionalism. Don't betray their trust by spreading their woes all over the gym. Instead, use the information they offer to better train them.

Tailor-Made

Treat each member as an individual. Based on what you know about the person, you can suggest a particular workout. You can say something such as, "This is what I see in you, so you should be doing this particular workout." Individualize their workouts. Take every situation into account: their goals, their background, their time commitment, and their money situation.

Maybe your students won't be able to tell you their goals at first. Work with them for a few minutes; ask questions while you train. Most clients will give you enough so that you can come up with the best approach to meeting their goals.

Kickboxing Buzz

You might want to start each class by saying, "I commit." To achieve excellence in kickboxing, there is but one choice: There is no guarantee of success, but by choosing the attitude of "I commit," your students won't settle for "I'll try."

Coach Them

Don't train all your members one way; that's coaching the lazy way. At the same time, however, you should have a set program that doesn't lack substance, and that provides consistency. First, develop a program. Then, individualize it for your students as you go. Remember that there's no set way to train: You should do whatever yields the desired results.

Students like to measure their success, whether it's by fitting into a smaller size of clothing or being able to spar with a 200-pound man. So make sure you have a step-by-step development progression; otherwise, you risk boring your students or—worse—taking away their incentive to learn new things. Your training methods are not set in stone; you should be on a constant lookout for new and better ways to train.

Remain Calm; Kickboxing Is Hard

Empathize with students who are trying to learn new moves. When correcting their form, and you'll do a lot of that, make sure that you keep the negative comments to a minimum. Giving corrective feedback is a big part of your coaching job from the get go, so keep calm. Don't fly off the handle if your students don't get it—they won't, at first. After all, these are not pros, but students who are hungry for a challenge.

Also keep this in mind: Nobody loves a nag. Don't bore your students with long lectures on how to do things correctly, and don't ramble on and on. Instead, collect your thoughts and break them down to the simplest words before giving instructions. State directions and corrections clearly and simply. The fastest way for you to turn off a member's enjoyment is to focus on every little mistake he makes.

Keep an upbeat and positive tone while you correct. Kickboxing is difficult to learn. Your students will need constant encouragement because they'll always question their own ability. Remember that beginning students will have no idea what you're trying to say if you speak fighter lingo—speak their language.

Keep Up the Good Work

People love to hear when they're doing well. They also love it when you use their name. ("Hey, Helen! Great side kick!") Tell them what they do well, but don't cover up mistakes. Praising someone's technique is an effective way of getting him to repeat it: Positive feedback helps motivate people to work on more difficult skills. Say it loud, and say it often.

Watch Your Body Language

Watch yourself. The quickest way to know what someone is thinking is by "reading" his face or body language. Teaching can get monotonous, especially when you train beginners on a regular basis. Don't act bored: Don't roll your eyes or let out a sigh of boredom, and don't forget to smile.

Watch your body language. Resting your hands on your hips may indicate that you are bored, for example. Be careful not to send the wrong message: A smile from the coach goes a long way, regardless of whether you're teaching children or fighters. You should always try to carry yourself in a pleasant, confident, and ready-to-work attitude. And send your students the message that you love teaching them.

No Roots in Kickboxing?

You can still teach kickboxing even if you don't have a professional kickboxing background; however, it's your responsibility to understand the proper bio-mechanics of kicks, punches, and blocks. You need to learn everything you can about kickboxing. Take classes, or train under a former fighter. (If you're really lucky, you might be able to find an ex-kickboxer in your area who is offering some type of apprenticeship.) You don't have to fight to be able to teach.

Looking for Work

Probably the best way to learn kickboxing is by training with a former kickboxer. That's what they do in Japan: Young fighters pick a fighter to train under. This apprenticeship gives them an opportunity to live, eat, sleep, and breathe fighting; it grooms future fighters. Today, apprenticeship programs train instructors.

This type of hands-on training provides the student with a real appreciation for the techniques. Not only will you learn about kickboxing, you'll train like a fighter. In other words, you'll get in shape, mentally and physically. A good apprenticeship program will offer a true understanding of kickboxing, in order to prepare you for all aspects of the sport.

Kick-Tales

There's no particular time limit on how or when you will be certified or allowed to teach on your own; that's dependent on you, on how well you pick it up. For example, learning how to cardio-kickbox, which is less demanding, usually takes 10 hours of instruction. During those 10 hours, you'll learn cardio-kickboxing techniques, class format, and class design. Then you'll have to teach approximately six to eight classes under the supervision of the head trainer. If you pass the requirements, the head instructor will certify you for teaching on your own.

When searching for an apprenticeship program, ask yourself the following questions:

➤ Will you develop a complete understanding of all techniques?

➤ Will you be able to demonstrate techniques?

➤ Will you be taught how to design training programs?

➤ Will you pass a physical fighting-fitness test?

➤ Will you complete all requirements of sparring?

➤ Will you know how to use all the training equipment?

The Winner in All of Us

Think of each student as a winner. She may be a housewife throwing a side kick for the first time; a business executive stepping into the ring to spar with you; or a teen you've groomed since his tiny tot days—the warriors looking for the next fight. How far do you push them?

Being a good coach means fulfilling your student's goals, not yours. Not everyone wants to fight in the ring, and not everyone will share your passion for kickboxing. The reality is that most students are there to get a good workout, and to feel good about their body and health.

Words for Warriors

Apprentice programs are designed for future instructors who want to teach private clients or classes in kickboxing. They're not meant for people who want to train fighters for the ring. Fighting in the ring takes ring experience.

That's another part of your job: You must make your students feel that they are doing something good for themselves. Sure, you'll push them, but you've got to know when to quit. For example, pushing young teens into competition can actually do more harm than good. The fighters will let you know that they want to compete; follow their lead.

Some coaches, especially ex-fighters, feel a special thrill and a sense of pride when watching their students compete. You can get that same thrill by helping your clients meet and surpass their own personal goals. Every goal or achievement in life tends is fueled by competition, even if you're competing against yourself. So don't lose sight of what your client wants; create a challenge so they keep coming back for more kickboxing.

Teaching "Can-Do" Athletes

High-performance competitors need instruction, too; their level of training is just heightened. But taking your training to the next level requires that you mentally prepare your athletes. It's important to teach fighters to control their thoughts—some thoughts can fuel an athlete's performance.

There's a strong link between success and self-confidence; the feelings of competence and high self-esteem that accompany a win can follow a fighter to his next fight. So how do you motivate the fighter who is four losses deep? How do you teach him not to give up? The negative impact of those losses might replay in his mind, affecting his muscle control and overall confidence. In other words, negative thoughts lead to negative feelings, which directly affects performance. How do you turn these thoughts off?

Use self-talk and affirmation to combat negative thoughts. Teach self talk to correct bad form, to get your fighter focused on the big event, to focus his attention, to build his confidence, and to create a positive attitude. By teaching affirmation, you're teaching your athlete to believe in his abilities—pep-talks are a great example of this: Have your fighter tell himself, "Hey, I'm a good fighter, I can take this guy."

As a coach, you've got to bolster your fighters emotionally. Even though the infliction of pain is part of fighting, all fighters fear getting pounded on—even if they don't admit it. Thus, because of the fear, the pain starts long before the fight does. Think back to the eight-week progressive training program (covered in Chapters 13–16): Maybe you didn't think you'd make it through all the throbbing, aching, dizziness, and numbness. That's how a fighter feels before a fight. Self-talk and self-affirmation become great ways to reduce fears and negative thoughts; these are ways to enhance self-esteem and self-worth.

Often, competitive fighters (especially real pros) just need a little tweaking, not a lot of technical work. Sometimes they just need the mental training to push them into a spectacular performance; As a coach, you can provide that training.

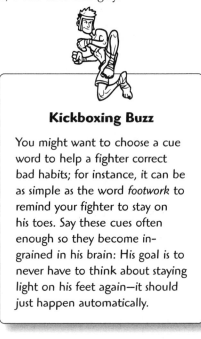

Kickboxing Buzz

You might want to choose a cue word to help a fighter correct bad habits; for instance, it can be as simple as the word *footwork* to remind your fighter to stay on his toes. Say these cues often enough so they become in-grained in his brain: His goal is to never have to think about staying light on his feet again—it should just happen automatically.

Up and Coming

Why leave it up to Hollywood to promote kickboxing? It should be up to coaches. So why not organize and promote a fight or tournament? Besides your making a little extra money, sponsoring fights helps keep the sport alive. As a coach, your goal should be to secure a successful future for your young fighters. Competitions are limited in the United States, and young fighters need fight experience. By hosting fights, not only do you promote your young fighters, you promote yourself as well, which protects the future of kickboxing.

More fights mean more exposure, which could ultimately result in a better future for the entire kickboxing industry. As a coach, you have a responsibility to protect the future of the sport. In Europe and Asia, kickboxing is a national pastime. It could be here, too: Who knows? Kickboxing may eventually give American boxing a run for its money ....

Kickboxing is growing in popularity, but for the most part, professional fighters don't have a lot of opportunity to gain real fighting experience. Kickboxing needs a big push—a push that could start with amateur fights.

Promoting Amateur Fights

To promote an amateur fight, you must first contact the State Athletic Board to learn the requirements for the state in which you live. In most states, it's fairly easy to get approval to host an amateur *fight card*. Then the fight promoter will have to get the bouts sanctioned by one of the kickboxing organizations.

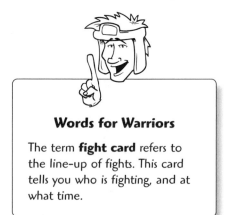

The sanctioning organization works hand in hand with the state to make sure that the fight meets state laws. You'll have to pay the sanctioning organization a fee, ranging from $50.00 to $150.00. The state commission will make sure that there is medical staff on hand—such as paramedics and an ambulance—in addition to checking the fighters' safety gear to ensure that it's in good working condition.

Amateur events can be held anywhere from a school gymnasium to a local martial arts studio. In most states, the athletic commission will be less strict in regard to an amateur event, so it is up to the promoter and sanctioning body to keep an eye on the event.

The Big Time

Having a pro-card fight involves a great deal more. Both the sanctioning body and the state will be more visible, for one thing. In addition, a pro-card means making money, so rules must be upheld. First, you'll have to buy a promoter's license. You'll also have to pass a background check; the State Athletic Board strives to weed out unscrupulous people seeking to make a quick buck, so they try to make it as difficult as possible. If you pass, you'll probably have to come up with a hefty security bond to ensure that the fighters get paid even if the event is not financially successful.

Furthermore, the fighters and the cornermen will have to be licensed by the state. The state also usually assigns referees and judges, but often the promoters are permitted to handpick their own as long as they are licensed by the state. Finally, the state commission will have a representative at the fight to handle complaints, to correct any problems, and to assess fines. These officials stand by to make sure that the fight adheres to the following rules:

➤ The fighters' safety equipment is in good working order.

➤ Hands are wrapped correctly.

➤ Fighters and cornermen are licensed by the state.

➤ A medical staff is on the premises.

Finding a Sanctioning Body

After you've done the legwork, you need to find a kickboxing sanctioning body that will publicize your fight as a legitimate contest. Most sanctioning bodies welcome this opportunity for two reasons: to get their name out and to promote kickboxing. As you might expect, there is a sanction fee for the contest; this fee rises with the level of the fight. A heavyweight championship match, for example, commands a big fee.

Sanctioning bodies represent the fighters. In most cases, a particular sanctioning body will promote the fight; representatives of the sanctioning body will be on the premises to make sure that the rules of the fight are upheld and the conduct of the fighters is acceptable.

Finding a Place to Fight

Next, you must find a place to host the fight. Think about what kind of crowd you want to attract, and how many fans. Think small if this match is your first. As you get your name out there, you can rent a bigger place. When negotiating the deal, ask who will pay the following costs to put on the big show:

➤ Security

➤ Parking

➤ Ticket collection

➤ Concessions

➤ P.A. and sound system

➤ Clean up

➤ Venue insurance

These costs add up. Find out who will cover these costs: the venue or you? Are some of these costs included in the deal, or will they cost extra? Take a walk through the venue to make sure there's enough room for separate dressing areas; fighters need a lot of room. Each cornerman will also need his own dressing room. Are the restrooms equipped with showers? Is there a warmup area, or at least enough room to make one?

Venues are different around the country. Keep in mind that not only does the venue have to be accommodating for the fighters, it must be safe for the audience. As a promoter, you'll make your money promoting a spectator sport, and without fans, you may not stay in business too long—so take the fans into consideration when booking a venue.

You'll also have to create a fighting atmosphere outside of the venue to draw in crowds. Unless it's a heavyweight championship belt fight, the fights can't always keep the audience revved up. Adding lights, sound, music, and smoke will help keep the fans on their toes, waiting for more; it's a show just as much as a fight. In fact, most promoters say that they're in the "entertainment business; kickboxing is just part of it." If the matches are not colorful and the fighters not entertaining, the fight may not be successful.

Matchmaking

Another aspect of a fight is the *matchmaker*. A matchmaker's job is to match up fighters. The matchmaker sets up the bouts and picks the matches and the fighters. In the spirit of fairness, they pick fighters who are equally skilled. Matchmakers have a difficult job: They'll lose all credibility if the fight is a big mismatch. Plus, the fighters could get injured. Matchmakers also have to think about pleasing the crowd by making the bouts exciting.

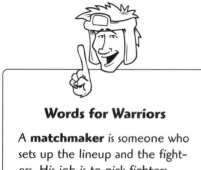

Words for Warriors

A **matchmaker** is someone who sets up the lineup and the fighters. His job is to pick fighters who are equally skilled and to produce an exciting fight.

For matchmakers, having a crystal ball helps because fighters often are unpredictable. Some perform; others are about as exciting as watching paint dry. It's hard to predict what the fighter will do in the ring. So when you're looking for a matchmaker, make sure he has experience, that he is someone who has seen a lot of fights and fighters. The matchmaker is supposed to remain impartial and have no real interest in the fighters in order to guarantee the equality of the lineup and match.

Getting the Word Out

After all that, you have to promote the fight. Depending on the fight, you could bring in a large crowd. Some world championships attract over 20,000 fans, especially in Japan. The bigger the fight, the more publicity you want. Think about ways to attract national and local attention. Getting the word out by television can be very expensive, but if you have fighters who have a lot of market appeal or TV exposure, this type of promotion could mean a lot of money for everyone involved. Remember, the idea is to keep the sport alive. Another strategy is to stage tournaments with some seasoned pros, at the same time introducing some of the new fighters. Following is a quick checklist of ways to get the word out:

➤ Send and pass out fight posters and flyers.

➤ Come up with computer web sites and Internet announcements.

➤ Do radio and TV commercials.

➤ Print ads in newspapers, news magazines, and martial arts and kickboxing magazines.

➤ Set up interviews with newspapers, TV news, and so forth.

Sponsorship

Finding sponsorship can offset the expenses of promoting your event. Hire someone; there are many publicists who are experienced in finding money for sporting events. Your best bet, though, is to find a sponsorship that is linked to kickboxing fights; for example, check out boxing equipment companies.

Make up a sponsorship package, detailing what the sponsor will receive in return for giving you money for the event. Sponsors will almost always want exposure in return for their financial generosity: They benefit by having a captive audience who have nothing to do between matches except read advertisements for their gear. Maybe they'll want the fighter to wear their clothing. You would probably be surprised to learn what companies would be interested in sponsoring the event.

Pulling in the Big Bucks

How much should you charge for admission? That depends on several factors: rent, fighter's purse, promoting fees, profit, and staff. That's one reason why financial sponsorship is so important; it helps offset these expenses. You, too, want to make money.

The more experience you have, the better your ability to predict the potential revenue from your paying fans, commonly called live gate. At first, just figure that 50 percent of the crowd will be a paying crowd—that's a safe number. As you gain experience, you'll become a better judge of both running a show and knowing the particular market.

Understanding the target market is particularly important because you don't want to charge too much per ticket. In Las Vegas, you can put on a large and expensive show because people will pay a lot of money to see a great fight. However, in small town U.S.A., you might not want to go all out. For one thing, fans might not be interested in all the fanfare; or there may not be as many fans. Furthermore, it will not cost as much to put on a fight in a small town. But you can count on one thing: No matter where the event is held, fans will want to see a great fight. Give them that, and kickboxing will soon become a national pastime.

The Least You Need to Know

➤ Coaching means giving life to a sport.

➤ Coaches have a genuine concern for the students they teach, as well as a passion to share kickboxing experience.

➤ Good coaching requires meshing physical and mental training.

➤ A good coach listens to his students.

➤ You don't have to have a professional kickboxing background to coach. You can always attend an apprenticeship program to get hands-on training.

➤ Coaches should strive to advance kickboxing by promoting events and tournaments, both amateur and pro.

Chapter 22

Kid Kickboxers

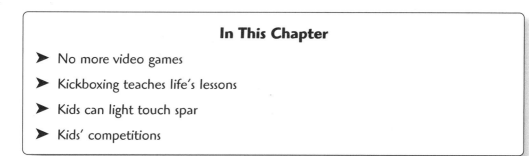

In This Chapter

➤ No more video games

➤ Kickboxing teaches life's lessons

➤ Kids can light touch spar

➤ Kids' competitions

Kids ... those cute little creatures that spend all their time glued to the TV, playing video games, at the same time screaming "Mom ... I need this. Dad ... I need that, please." And, Mom and Dad, you're probably dreaming of tub-therapy—Calgon, take me away!

We've got the perfect cure: kickboxing. Of course, you'll miss the little darlings as they backpack it to class. But think about it this way: Your children will learn some of life's valuable lessons—hard work and determination pay off. Your kids will learn to respect themselves and others. They'll use their body in productive ways and grow up liking it.

Do we have you? Raising a healthy, happy kickboxer is not always easy, so you've got to do your research. Take a look at the sport. We've given you a general overview of how the program works; you'll have to do some checking of your own, however, because gyms will vary. When searching for your child's gym, remember that safety must be stressed at all times.

This chapter answers such questions as, "Is kickboxing for my child or for me?" It's not just the coach's responsibility to make sure that your child has a positive experience—you, too, can make all the difference in the world.

Inspector Clouseau

Nothing but the best for your child, right? Although there are plenty of new *dojos,* or gyms, on the market, figuring out which ones are good for your child is a difficult task—especially if you have Power Rangers or Teenage Mutant Ninja Turtles on your mind.

Kickboxing wasn't always so popular; it traditionally took a back seat to karate and tae kwon do. Today, though, gym owners are trying to profit from the kickboxing craze, so you have to be careful. You don't want your child to have a bad experience. So get snoopy! Look for a safe and fun program; it may take a fair amount of snooping around, but good gyms are often recognized in the community. Always ask about a potential coach; other parents love to brag about their children's coaches.

A good coach doesn't come easy, either, but you should take your time finding one. Children look up to their coaches, especially if they were former fighters. They take on a superhero status in your child's eyes. So find a coach who you respect. Is he in good shape? Is he a nonsmoker? Does he practice what he preaches? What's his background in kickboxing?

Whether the coach has any real experience in kickboxing will be directly linked to what your child will learn. For example, a lot of karate coaches are trading in their starched uniforms to teach kickboxing. But remember that karate is a semi-contact sport, and kickboxing is contact. You've got to make sure that the coach takes precautions during sparring: Are the children wearing well-fitted safety equipment? Does the coach tell your child how to put the gear on and secure it? Other martial arts instructors may be good teachers, but their knowledge and experience of kickboxing may be limited. When evaluating potential coaches, ask questions specifically relating to kickboxing:

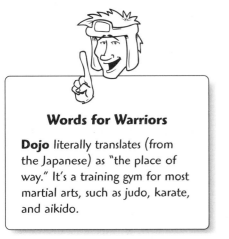

Words for Warriors

Dojo literally translates (from the Japanese) as "the place of way." It's a training gym for most martial arts, such as judo, karate, and aikido.

➤ Does your coach insist on proper conditioning?

➤ Some children can bend like rubber bands; does the coach correct bad form that may hurt them?

➤ Most children have bottomless energy; does the coach put that energy to good use?

➤ Does the coach do warmup and stretching exercises before every class?

➤ Does the coach offer disciplined playtime, such as relay races?

➤ If your child loses, does the coach stress good sportsmanship?

➤ Does the coach teach good technique for punches and kicks?

➤ Is the coach knowledgeable about competing or does he have contacts with other training gyms?

Sit through a class to watch how things are done, paying special attention to the sparring session. Most accidental injuries happen while your child spars. Safety should be emphasized at all times. Is your child being taught to fall correctly? Are the classes challenging? Are the other kids enjoying themselves? How does the instructor handle the little ones who cry or act up? Trust your instincts. If you do not feel comfortable, don't sign up.

Most coaches will ask you to watch a class before signing your child up. Snoop around so you can get a general feeling about the gym, its instructors, and its students. Sure, kickboxing is fun, but it can be challenging—especially early in the program. You must be able to trust your coach because he's grooming not only future kickboxers, but your children.

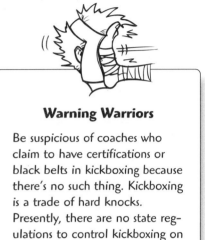

Warning Warriors

Be suspicious of coaches who claim to have certifications or black belts in kickboxing because there's no such thing. Kickboxing is a trade of hard knocks. Presently, there are no state regulations to control kickboxing on the instructional level.

Tiny Tots

Kickboxing programs shouldn't accept children under the age of eight. However, you can start your children in karate as early as age four; it's a noncontact martial art. Kids under eight may be a little too scared to throw a punch, and most little ones fear getting hit. There's no reason to rush a child who is still afraid of being whacked by a soccer ball into kickboxing.

Kickboxing is like playing full contact chess; it's a blend of physical and mental challenges. In other words, kickboxing combines physically demanding sport conditioning with the philosophies of traditional martial arts. Kickboxing teaches your child to deal with fear. Eventually, with real training—and maybe a few tears—your child won't fear getting hit. The same child who wouldn't play soccer because he winced as the ball came at him might turn into the daredevil of the team as a result of his kickboxing training. Every child will be different, though; it's best to talk to the coach. By starting them in karate at a young age, they'll learn the basics—kicking, striking, and balance—which often makes the switch to kickboxing easier.

Safety: Can They Spar?

Your child won't shun sparring—most children love it. Injuries in martial arts account for less than 1 percent. In other words, the chance of your child getting hurt is very slim. Rid your mind of the image of a child slugging it out: He'll only light touch spar. With the proper equipment and coaching, children are rarely hurt; if a child *is* hurt, the injuries are usually minor (bloody noses and fat lips). The sport couldn't survive if it wasn't safe. Besides, kids do what's fun, and being injured isn't fun.

Student sparring with his coach.

If your child dreams of competing at a junior level, it's another story. He'll have to practice full contact sparring occasionally. He might, then, suffer more than a bruise; he might even shed some tears. However, that's part of the game.

Pee-Wee Workout

Kids' programs don't differ too much from those of adults. They'll start by warming up. They'll stretch, and then they'll learn new strikes and blocks in the review and learning interval. After that, they'll shadow spar to practice the techniques they've just learned. The class usually ends with light contact sparring and some easy conditioning drills. The heart of the class should always center around technique.

Keep in mind that programs may vary from gym to gym. However, shy away from signing your child up for boot camp kickboxing; it's not healthy for their growing bones. Kids don't need to burn off calories or pump iron; instead, they want to have fun. Look for a gym that offers in-gym competitions such as boys against girls or team sparring against the coach. Sprint or relay races are also fun. Or maybe the coach will host a pee-wee tournament: one round bouts to put some fire in the little ones' bellies and get them ready for competition. As they grow with the sport, they'll become stronger, improve their flexibility, and develop coordination. As your child's body matures, power and strength moves can be added to prepare him for junior competition.

Respecting the Coach

Your child will learn in a highly structured and safe environment. Depending on the coach, there are a number of tactics that can be used to teach self-discipline. For example, a coach can give a child who misbehaves a sit-out period; the coach can then make it really fun for the other kids as the rascal sits and watches. Most kids hate to see the other kids have all the fun; they usually think twice before acting up again.

Most children are too young to understand that they're learning some of life's valuable lessons in kickboxing. Respect, for example, will be demanded from day one. Children need to be told what to do; in kickboxing, they have to play by a set of rules. They are rewarded only if they play by these rules. If they break the rules, they can't practice. You can't argue with a system that's worked for hundreds of years—this type of system turns out some pretty incredible kids, who respect not only themselves but others.

What about teenagers? Is there one alive who listens to his parents? Well, he'll listen to the coach—and most coaches will do what the parents ask. If, for example, your child is failing English, the coach can encourage better grades by requesting a report card. At that point, it's up to the coach to pick the reward or discipline. Most coaches will work with your child's limitations; let them know how they can help.

Parents! Can We Talk?

As your children grow, what will they bid farewell? Homework, schoolyard bullies, exams, and curfews. What will they remember? Rolling around on the floor, sparring with the coach, running sprints, and being able to beat up on that schoolyard bully. Why not share kickboxing with your child? Make it a real family experience, one they will remember.

Be involved: You can take a one-on-one lesson as your child takes class. If that's not appealing, how about assisting the coach, volunteering for carpool duty or generating fundraising causes for competitions. Stick around to watch them in class. Praise their athletic abilities. Even if you can't give much time, show up to as many practices as possible. Children love having their parents in the background for support. Let your child know that you are supportive by asking the coach for a few tips on how to make kickboxing an enjoyable experience for your child. (For example, you might ask about equipment: What kind is the best to buy? How often should you inspect it for wear and tear? When should you replace equipment?) Show that you care by talking with your child about safety: You should talk to your child about mouthpieces and how they work to protect their teeth, or discuss why their headgear needs to be buckled.

Kickboxing is not just a babysitting program; your child is physically active. By becoming involved, you're setting a great example for your kids.

Good Job

If your child asks for feedback, tell him the truth. Be sure to make positive comments along with the constructive criticism to encourage them to continue. Also, consider using the *sandwich method*, which is recommended by many sports psychologists: Compliment the child, and then suggest areas that can be improved, followed by another positive comment. For example, say, "Nice front kick, but recoil it so you get a little more power. You'll get it next time, and it will look as good as your round kick. Good job!"

Be careful: Don't constantly give your child pointers. Leave this to the coach. If you're not careful, your child might think that he's not good enough for you, that you're critiquing his every move.

Parent Aid

Teach your child to listen to his body, to hear the difference between serious pain and a bruise. Make it known that his body will send him messages that you can't hear. Encourage your child to listen to his own judgment when he's hurt, and make sure that he understands that accidents *do* happen. However, recurring pain is not normal; your child should tell you or the coach about any pain or injury, just in case he needs medical attention. Tell the coach immediately if your child is injured.

When enrolling your child in a class, don't neglect to tell the coach if your child has a preexisting problem such as asthma. The coach needs to know what to do if your child has an asthma attack during practice. Does he call 911 or administer some type of first aid? One more thing: Don't send your child to class sick. Besides getting all the other children sick, her chances of injuring herself become greater.

Training year round may help cut down on injuries. Most children are couch potatoes all summer long, only to go back to school out of shape. And children are notorious for not pacing themselves. They may be raring to go, but if they're out of shape, their bodies may just flop around—that's how children get hurt. But not in kickboxing; besides keeping them off the couch, kickboxing keeps your child in shape, ready for any activity.

Finally, you should tend to any emotional injuries your child may receive as well. Kids typically can't understand emotions, whether it's being picked on at school or witnessing an argument between his parents. But they *do* know something is not right. As a parent, listen to your children. Talk about these feelings with them. Insist that they get a good night's rest—fatigue and emotional stress can affect a child's concentration in class, which may lead to injury.

Coaches: Do You Really Want to Work with Kids?

Are you up for the challenge? It takes a lot of patience to work with children. Sometimes they cry; other times, they don't pay attention or they act up. But then there are days when their eyes light up with excitement because they accomplished something new. This is not a job to be taken lightly.

Teaching children can be some of the most rewarding work you'll ever do because you're passing on some of life's lessons. Through your training, you can teach these children to use their bodies in productive ways and grow up liking their bodies. As they grow up, they'll come to understand this and think of you fondly.

The Money Factor

Kids will be a big part of your business. Approximately 60 to 80 percent of a gym's revenue can come from teaching the little ones. Make it fun and safe for them: Your business will grow exponentially if you have a good reputation in town and develop a good rapport with parents.

Handling Mr. Mouth

What do you do if a parent screams on the sideline, "Kick his butt!"? What if he heckles the other opponent: "C'mon, you can take him, he's nothing." What will you do if he screams obscenities as he watches his child lose?

The bad news is that you can't kick his butt, coaches. If he continues to insult or use abusive language, try talking to him. You may want to write down a few of his comments, just to refresh his memory, and then have a talk with him. Call Mr. Mouth at home so his child can't hear. Start with positive comments; then you can talk about his antics. For instance, tell him it's great that he devotes all his time to watching his child, but that the other children really don't need to hear such comments.

Mr. Mouth may not have realized that he's upsetting the other students. Wait to see what he says. Maybe he'll apologize, and that will be that. If he continues, you still can't knock his lights out; you'll have to try a more drastic approach. Threaten to drop his child from the program. Parents, no coach wants to take such a drastic measure. So don't scream from the sidelines; you'll only make the people around you miserable. Most importantly, you shouldn't show your child this ugly side of you.

The Makings of a Pro

Kids can compete at an amateur level; these events are strictly regulated and set up by most state athletic commissions. Tournaments must comply with health and safety standards established for each individual state. Your child will need your permission to compete.

Kids must wear the same safety equipment that is required for adult competitors: 12-ounce boxing gloves, headgear, shin and foot pads, a groin protector, and a mouthpiece. Junior bouts consist of three 1-minute rounds, with a 1-minute rest in between rounds. Following are the rules for kids' kickboxing:

Kickboxing Buzz

Most junior tournaments are strictly regulated. Kids are not allowed to go in there and pummel each other to death. Referees are quicker to stop a match if a young fighter appears to be hurt. In most cases, referees limit the amount of hard contact.

➤ Six kicks per round minimum

➤ Three 1-minute rounds, 1-minute rests

➤ All kicks above waist

➤ No knee strikes

➤ Boxing gloves, shin and foot pads, groin and mouth protectors, and headgear required

The fighting divisions are age, sex, and weight. Age divisions are broken up by two years. Boys compete against boys, and girls compete against girls. Weight divisions balance the scale; opponents have to be within 6 pounds of each other.

Is Your Child Ring-Ready?

Follow yourchild's lead: Does he love the sport? Does he want to train three or four days a week? Does he have the ability to compete? You should ask the coach. Look for signs that he understands what competition kickboxing is about. If all these conditions are met, talk to the coach. He, too, can offer some valuable feedback as to whether your child is ring-ready.

On the other hand, maybe your child has no desire to step into the ring. For example, is he more interested in the social aspects of kickboxing? Does he lack an intense drive to compete? Does he shy away from pressure situations or love playing a variety of sports?

There is no doubt that kickboxing is great for the body and mind; encouraging your child to compete—but only if he wants to—also has many benefits. In competition, your child will learn how to develop the mental strategies, and he'll learn what it means to sacrifice his play time on the weekends as he trains.

Kickboxing Buzz

Sometimes you can find a junior fight that allows the hardcore international rules. Usually these fights are held abroad. The child still must wear shin pads with an instep protector, headgear, boxing gloves, a groin protector, and a mouthpiece. Leg kicks to the upper and outer part of the thigh are permitted; there's no kick requirement. Fight lengths are the same.

Talking to the Coach

Always talk to the coach about the next step—competition—before you take it. It's the coach who can give you an honest assessment as to whether your child is ready to compete. Most coaches won't let a child compete under age 10; 12 is a more realistic age.

Don't take this conversation lightly. Think about the fight and what your child will be doing—hitting someone and being hit. You need to trust the coach; a piece of him is out there with your child as he fights. Your child, after all, is a product of his training. He wants nothing but the best for your child.

Good coaches won't send your child into the ring unless he's physically and emotionally ready. So he'll gradually test the waters, starting with a sparring session.

Pay attention here: How does your child react to the added pressure of full contact sparring? Unless your child has been working at the advanced level, he's probably familiar only with light touch sparring. Drawing back from the coach—who's not going to hurt your child—as they spar is one hint that your child might not be ready for competition. Furthermore, observe how he reacts when a strike lands. Remember, the coach is testing him, looking for signs that he can't physically or mentally handle competition.

Warning Warriors

Parents, you should never force your children to compete; not all kids can mentally handle it. It's scary to step into the ring. Trust that they can enjoy kickboxing at any level and reap its benefits. After talking to the coach, let your child decide if he or she wants to compete.

After a few sessions, sit down with the coach. Both of you should talk about the sparring sessions before talking to the student. Mom and Dad, use this time to ask a lot of questions. You need to feel comfortable with this next step.

Ask to see a video of a junior kickboxing event. A good coach should give you a blow by blow explanation of the fight; have him point out safety measures and tell you why he thinks that your child is ring-ready. As a parent, you need to trust that the coach will always put your child's safety first.

After speaking to the coach, both of you should talk to the child to see if he's interested in competing. Use this time to talk about the sacrifices a pro must make for the sport. For example, stress that he'll will have to work out five days a week, beginning six weeks before the fight date. Is he willing to train on weekends so he doesn't sacrifice his schoolwork? Give up TV? Friday nights hanging out with his friends?

Now, are you ready, parents? You should know going in that preparing your child for the ring takes a lot of time, money, and sacrifice on your

Warning Warriors

If a coach has his students doing a lot of full contact sparring without a competition coming up, pull your child from the program. Your child doesn't need to take this kind of physical abuse. It's just overkill.

part. A young fighter will have to give up his weekends to train five days a week. It's important that you know that this extra training will cost money. Also, competitions are not always in your home state. You may be giving up your weekends to drive your child, and perhaps the other competitors, around the county.

Six-Week Junior Training

Junior fighters, below the age of 15, don't train like adults. The workout lasts about 1 hour; young fighters will spar, and then do focus mitts, bag work, Thai pads, and kicking shields (similar to an adult one-on-one). The difference is that the rounds will last only 1 minute. That's how they'll fight in a real junior competition, as well: 1 minute on, 1 minute off.

Your child won't be practicing in his old class as he prepares for a fight. The intensity level of a normal class is much too slack for the competition. He'll have to focus on his training so that he can mentally prepare for the ring. All outside distractions, parents included, will be removed from the moment he begins training to the end. Finally, he needs to be around other competitors. Attitude is contagious; they think, train, and act the same. Training with other competitors builds a certain camaraderie that helps the fighters to retain discipline when the going gets tough.

Dealing with a Bruised Ego

A coach does the sweating for you, but he can't shield your child against loss—nor would he want to. As a parent, you risk bruising your child's delicate ego by enrolling him in competitive sports. For example, your child may think that he's a failure if he doesn't win. But is all losing bad? Kickboxing is done for the love of the sport, not the love of winning. It's a sport that your kid can compete in and enjoy because he knows in advance that winning is not everything. The point is to improve his own performance and skills. That's the martial arts way; your child is a winner because she got out there and tried. Having the staying power to stick it out is a valuable lesson.

After the initial disappointment of a loss fades, talk to your child about the match. Give him the choice of whether to compete again. After you know where your child stands, you can better suggest a course of action; kickboxing might or might not be it. Find out if he genuinely loves the sport and wants to continue. You might want to tell him that sticking with something demonstrates commitment and dedication; but this is a decision for you and your child.

Your child might not want to compete in kickboxing ever again. In this case, maybe you should suggest another martial art. Again, the coach can help you with these important decisions.

Managing Their Egos

Super kickboxers need guidance, too—even the best national junior amateur competitor. Certainly, you should compliment your child on his successes; make it clear that he's always number one in your book.

Be careful, though—if this praise is repeated too often, you may breed an egomaniac. And that's the last thing this sport needs, another egomaniac. As a parent, you have to find some common ground. Don't overemphasize your child's championship; make it a point to appreciate all his talents (math, poetry, or whatever). Teach your child that competing is a privilege. If you teach your child good values, he will always be a long-standing champion in your book, even if he loses a bout.

Warning Warriors

Don't sign up with a coach who instills a no-lose policy—that's a recipe for major disappointment. His training should represent good sportsmanship, which should be stressed from the first day your child enters class.

The Least You Need to Know

➤ Get snoopy! Snoop around for a gym that is recognized in the community as safe and fun.

➤ A dojo is a gym or training facility.

➤ Kickboxing programs shouldn't accept a child under the age of eight. However, you can start your children in karate as early as age four; it's a noncontact martial art.

➤ Injuries in martial arts account for less than 1 percent; they are very few and far between. In class, your child will only light touch spar.

➤ Junior competition equipment requirements are 12-ounce boxing gloves, headgear, shin and foot pads, a groin protector, and a mouthpiece. Junior bouts consist of three 1-minute rounds, with a 1-minute rest between each round.

➤ Most coaches won't let a child compete under age 10; 12 is a more realistic age.

A Lifelong Career

You're now a kickboxer extraordinaire! Over the years, you've executed a few thousand kicks and punches in some of the most strenuous fights. You've trained moms, motivated the "suits" to get in shape, taught numerous cardio-kickboxing classes, and groomed some tough fighters while bringing home a few trophies of your own.

But the kicks fly no longer. What will you do? Do you say, "Good-bye"? That's a question that can be answered only by you.

It's no secret that these days we can stay fit longer, keep our bodies healthier, and remain competitive into our later years. But your body does eventually slow down. For fighters, you may be sick and tired of the physical abuse. For fitness warriors, you may still want to stay active in kickboxing, but add a more mind-body approach to your weekly workouts. The good news is, you never have to give up kickboxing totally. You can explore the softer side of martial arts. You can still kick, although maybe not as high, to a healthier mind and body.

Calling It Quits

Have you, in an idle moment, had a mental conversation that goes something like this ... "Let's see, my body is still aching from yesterday's workout, and last week, I had a hamstring problem. I really don't want to kickbox today—I'm too tired to kickbox. But it's only a 45-minute workout. Boy, I wish they would remove the clock so I wouldn't watch the time drag on .... My back hurts; no, I can't jump rope. But think about the calorie burn. Oh, I should just do it—if I don't, fat will mysteriously show up around my gut next week ...."

This is a clear sign of burnout, plain and simple. You don't enjoy kickboxing anymore. What was once life's greatest pleasure is now more like an albatross around your neck. But the good news is that the solution is within your training: Go back to kickboxing's roots.

Are you looking in the mirror, shaking your head, saying, "No way am I going to work out!"? If so, it's time to move on. Kickboxing offers three basic elements: physical fitness, self-defense, and the fight game. Guess what: You can get the same training by dabbling in a few of the softer martial arts; think of kickboxing as part of a larger program that will keep you healthy for a lifetime.

You can still train, work on your flexibility, and burn calories. Don't be afraid to branch out—you just have to find something you can throw into your regimen to stay really healthy.

Warning Warriors

Exercise in general can strengthen the immune system, but too much of a good thing can leave you susceptible to illness and injury. Kickboxing is a high-intensity workout. As you get older, you might not want to work out as hard; don't push yourself to exhaustion. If kickboxing makes you sick, think about ways to modify your workouts.

Full Circle

Unlike the traditional "pure" martial arts, kickboxing has been crossbred from several martial arts. Kickboxing gains from all the useful traits of other martial arts while leaving the undesirable traits behind. The end result is an excellent workout, a good self-defense program, and an exciting fighting style.

Kickboxing is taught as a sport rather than a traditional martial art. Besides appealing to all walks of life, it physically challenges you to excel, which is why it has gained an unbelievable amount of momentum in the past few years. Kickboxing is about more than just a physical workout, though; ancient martial arts wisdom has seeped into kickboxing through the years. This combination provides an overall sense of well-being, which will in turn have a positive influence on your physical health. Kickboxing is a step by step process to becoming a better human being.

Just because you're retiring the boxing gloves, though, doesn't mean you have to walk away from the martial arts way of life. The martial arts provide training for life. The lessons learned never turn off: Have respect for yourself and others; do unto others as you would have them do unto you; act with integrity, courtesy, and humility; practice perseverance, self-control, and self-discipline.

Ex-kickboxers can take a more mental approach to health. The martial arts have a language all their own: Call it spiritual growth, a chance to completely control the mind and attain a state of enlightenment through a mind-body connection. But don't expect to understand it unless you can learn to control the balance between the negative and positive forces in your life, known as *yin-yang*. Most traditional martial arts focus on how to achieve this inner peace and harmony with yourself and nature.

> **Words for Warriors**
>
> The **yin-yang** is made of the two opposing forces that make up harmony. These forces complement each other and are dependent on each other. Yin is said to be the negative force: darkness, coldness, and emptiness. Yang, on the other hand, is the positive force: light, warmth, and fullness. You might hear yang categorized as masculine, while yin is considered feminine.

Ancient Times

We'll end this book where the sophisticated study of martial arts began: China. In Chapter 2, "Ancient Art: Sport of Today," we told you when and where martial arts began. The truth is that martial art scholars are torn; nobody seems to agree about the beginning. There is one legend, however, that has withstood the test of time— Bodhidharma. Here's his story:

> Bodhidharma, a monk, is believed to have traveled to Shaolin Temple in China in the early sixth century. He found that the monks there couldn't keep their eyes open after many hours of meditation. Bodhidharma, noted for his harsh training he received in his native India, was annoyed by this lack of discipline; thus, he came up with exercises to keep the monks alert and physically fit. The training he developed emphasized speed, strength, and flexibility; the moves were vigorous and calisthenics-based. These 18 exercises, which evolved into Japan's karate and Korea's tae kwon do, are believed to have been carried to all parts of the Far East by traveling Buddhist monks.

The following list is a sampling of some of the softer martial arts:

➤ Karate

➤ Aikido

➤ Tai chi

➤ Kung fu

➤ Hwarang-do

Kick-Tales

The ferocious spirit of Bodhidharma is legendary. It is said that once, after accidentally falling asleep while meditating in a cave for nine years, Bodhidharma became so enraged with himself that he ripped off his eyelids and threw them to the ground. Tea shrubs grew from where his eyelids lay. After that, the monks of the temples, fearing retribution, drank this tea to prevent themselves from falling asleep.

"Kee-Yah"

Kickboxing roots come directly come from karate. In fact, kickboxing is often called the "modern karate." Although karate is less sports-oriented than kickboxing, it is directly linked to kickboxing: In both martial arts, you use your hands, feet, arms, and legs as weapons and shields. You'll also do similar endurance, stretching, and strengthening exercises. In kickboxing, you're taught to shadow spar against an imaginary opponent; similarly, karate teaches you *katas*, which are dance-like movements that are set against an imaginary opponents. Also like kickboxing, karate calls for not only muscle power, but also strengthened will.

Unlike in kickboxing, however, the emphasis in karate is not on heavy duty conditional drills. Karate is more formal; you must wear the *gi*, which is the white karate uniform, and the belts. The biggest difference between the two is that karate teaches you to use your inner energy, your *ki*.

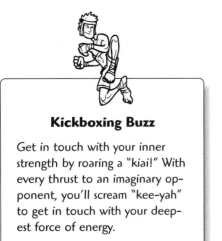

Kickboxing Buzz

Get in touch with your inner strength by roaring a "kiai!" With every thrust to an imaginary opponent, you'll scream "kee-yah" to get in touch with your deepest force of energy.

As you strike, you'll shout, *"kiai!"* (pronounced *kee-yah*). Besides being a murderous shout that is intended to scare off your fighting opponent, the kiai musters up your hidden internal energy. It's more than a shout—when translated, the word means bringing together (*ai*) of spiritual or internal energy (*ki*). Karate teaches that the kiai gets you in touch with your inner power. With a kiai, your strike feels like a burst of generated energy that comes from the core of your being; it's this pent-up energy that breaks boards and bricks. Such feats are not a result of strength alone, but of technique; the kiai is at the heart of that technique and strength.

The Ideal Self-Defense

Aikido is often called the subtle and sophisticated approach to marital arts. Its founder, Morihei Ueshiba, is considered to be one of the greatest Japanese martial artists of all time. He dedicated himself to developing a style of martial arts that is effective but that does not permanently injure your opponent. His vision was for aikido to be the ultimate self-defense; he said, "Aikido is not a technique to fight with or defeat the enemy. It's a way to reconcile the world and make human beings one family."

In aikido, you're taught not to harm your opponent, but to take control of the negative force that is coming at you and use it to gain control of the situation.

Aikido moves are almost always circular, revolving around your center of gravity. You don't grapple with your attacker; rather, you stay focused on making your enemy "turn like a door on a hinge" so that you can get out of the line of attack. You'll learn to use your enemy's force against him. You'll gain control of the attacker through defensive techniques such as wrist, finger, and shoulder locks, and throwing and rolling.

There is no striking in aikido. Instead, you'll work to strengthen the body by bending, twisting, and stretching. You'll work to achieve good posture and good body alignment. The exercises are designed to improve flexibility, stamina, and breathing.

The *ai* in aikido stands for harmony; aikido's philosophy chants harmony with the universe. Students are taught that all things in life fit and work together; violent forces disrupt this perfect union, so they must be neutralized. Aikido's techniques, then, work to restore harmony of the universe. Those who practice aikido don't think in terms of winning a fight; they think in terms of "perfect reconciliation."

Words for Warriors

Aikido's primary concern is a healthy mind and body and a wholesome spirit.

Just as important as harmony is the belief in mental strength. The *ki* in aikido is preached as the core of life itself. Everyone is born with ki—energy. As in karate, aikidoists learn to tap into their ki, using special breathing techniques and meditation. Aikido is said to be, "as a way of life, the final transformation of the martial discipline."

Kung Fu

In China, kung fu means "well done"; it's not an individual martial art, but a term used to describe all kinds of fighting systems in China. Kung fu can also mean skill or ability; something that takes a long time to accomplish or master.

Kick-Tales

Kung fu is, historically, a general name for most of the fighting systems that hail from China. In Japan, karate is the general name for the fighting systems. Today, the term "wu shu" is used to describe all martial arts in China.

Today, there are hundreds of styles of kung fu taught in China. Styles are commonly divided into two categories: external, or hard, and internal, or soft. Some kung fu stresses kicks, punches, speed, and calisthenics; others stress softer, slower, dance-like techniques that develop inner energy.

Words for Warriors

The terms **ki** and **chi** are the same thing; ki is the Japanese word and chi is the Chinese word.

Like the Japanese fighting styles, kung fu also calls for a *chi*, the vital energy that fuels the moves in all living things. The chi is essence of life itself. All styles of kung fu teach students how to connect and use their chi.

Tai Chi Chuan

The softer side of kung fu is tai chi chuan, or tai chi for short. It's based on the ancient saying that "Meditation in motion is far better than meditation in repose." It's symbolized by the half dark, half light circle that stands for the universe (the yin-yang). The exercises, some of which are named after animals, are slow, practiced in a prearranged sequence (like Japanese katas).

Training is usually done in a series of movements: "Embrace Tiger," for instance, moves directly into another specific sequence. Students are taught to use fluid, precise movements as they move from one posture to another, similar to a formal dance in slow motion. Students of tai chi learn to release tension and tightness and get in touch with their chi. Students are taught that the chi is more important than muscular strength. The emphasis is on the strength of the mind, deep breathing, and relaxation—not power or speed.

When you first start, you'll work solo. As you progress, you'll be taught to imagine an opponent. Eventually, you'll work against other students to get fight training. Then, using your chi and the moves you already know, you'll learn a skill called the interpretation of strength, which is the heart of tai chi fighting; you'll learn to sense the negative flow of energy from an opponent, and anticipate his every move. With that intuitive sense, you can stop the move before it's completed. Traditionally, tai chi is not taught as defensive system, but advanced masters are legendary fighters if provoked.

Kick-Tales

Tai chi is the national form of exercise in China. In the mornings at any park in China, hundreds of people line up to do tai chi exercises.

Hwarang-Do

This ancient Korean martial art focuses on healing as well as on fighting. Hwarang-do means, literally, "flower-man-way," or "the way of the flowering manhood"; it started as a hand-to-hand combat system over 1,800 years ago and was founded by a Buddhist monk named Won Kwang Bopsa. His young warriors were said to be the leaders of the country because of their heroic deeds.

For the kickboxer seeking a lifetime challenge, hwarang-do is it. It is unlike any martial art. It's subdivided into four categories:

➤ **Internal power**—You'll learn to control your inner energy, or ki, through meditation and breathing exercises. At an advanced level, you can learn to heal yourself.

➤ **External power**—You'll learn more than 4,000 techniques: everything from strikes to joint manipulation.

➤ **Weapon power**—You can learn how to use weapons.

➤ **Mental power**—You'll learn to develop and control the mind. These exercises are taught to increase awareness and concentration levels, from extrasensory perception to the development of your sixth sense.

This art uses techniques similar to those taught in kickboxing, so you'll feel at ease while learning some of the techniques. But this system also takes martial arts to an elevated level: Hwarang-do students are taught to heal themselves and others by learning acupuncture, and by studying herbal and natural medicines, first aid, acupressure, and bone setting. In this way, hwarang-do presents a lifelong challenge.

Kick-Tales

Zen is often confused for a religion—it's not just that. Zen focuses on meditation to completely control the mind. The ultimate goal is to achieve a state of enlightenment, detached from the physical world. It should come as no surprise that Zen was developed by the Buddhist monks; it traveled to Japan around the thirteenth century and was said to be the foundation of martial arts. Back in feudal Japan, the samurai, or Japanese fighters, studied Zen to prepare them for battle and to face death without fearing it.

Can't Say Good-Bye?

For some of you, staying connected to kickboxing through other martial arts might not seem appealing. Perhaps you thrive on the physical activity, the power and speed. Maybe your competitive spirit craves competition. Walking away from the fight game may be the hardest thing you'll ever do. You know the feeling, fighters; competition is almost as addictive as any drug. The good news is, there are non- or semicontact martial arts that are similar, but less demanding on your body.

Semicontact Martial Arts

Although semicontact fights are primarily for student kickboxers rather than the pros, anyone can compete. It's the easiest step down from competition kickboxing. Sometimes, semicontact is called "sport karate." The moves are the same as in kickboxing: kicks, punches, and blocks. Striking, though, is done on a controlled basis. Semicontact competitions offer a safe environment in which to compete:

➤ It gives students the opportunity to compete at a level where there is a low chance of serious injury.

➤ Semicontact competitions are easy to find; more than likely there will be one in your state every weekend.

➤ It's a great starting place for children.

Competitors can actually be disqualified or penalized for striking too hard. No strikes are allowed to the face under the advanced levels, and even face contact divisions have to exercise control. And points are awarded to competitors who fight clean and land effective strikes with control. Sometimes, depending on where you compete, more points are given for kicks than for punches.

Fouls are given if you strike to the back, legs, or face. Most competition-style tournaments usually range from two to four bouts, each round lasting 1 to 2 minutes. Anyone can compete. There are several categories, which are divided by age, weight, and skill level.

Although semicontact competitions are probably not as thrilling as a pro-kickboxing match, they can reduce the risk of injury. You should also be aware of the following facts:

➤ There are many sanctioning bodies that sponsor semicontact competitions, with various rules and requirements.

➤ Semicontact fighting has very little real life application.

➤ In many cases, controlled martial arts technique has regressed from good technique to "slap-stick" techniques for scoring points.

➤ There are very few state athletic boards that regulate these competitions.

➤ Many of the tournaments are unorganized.

Telephone Ringing?

There comes a time in life when you have to say good-bye.

If you find yourself eating Advil for breakfast to ease your kickboxing aches and pains, it's time to quit.

Old bones might not be the best reason to quit; recurring injury is. Recurring aches, pains, and sprains are a definite sign that it's time to hang it up.

There is an old saying in the fight business: "A tough fighter has a short career and a smart fighter has a long career." In other words, having a lot of tough fights won't preserve your body—especially the brain. It's the fighters who stay in the game a little too long who risk permanent damage. If you hear the telephone ringing and it's not, it's time to say good-bye.

Warning Warriors

Keep in mind that your brain floats in fluid within your head. When you take a hard shot to the head, the snapping back of the head knocks the brain around. Too many shots may cause permanent damage, such as pugilistic dementia.

A Fighter's Farewell

Where do old fighters go? Besides telling a bunch of lies about how good they used to be, many teach kickboxing. Some open kickboxing gyms. Whatever the case, ring experience provides valuable lessons for young fighters—and it keeps former fighters in touch with the sport. You can train young competitors with as much intensity as you've trained yourself.

You can also use your ring experience to give your students that little extra push to help them get closer to their goals. Use your experience to guide your students through their careers and help them to avoid injury and burn out. Old fighters keep the sport going.

Good-Bye

For many fighters, it's sad to leave. For a brief moment, fighters are larger than life—superheroes. It's just you and your opponent engaged in a match, in a fight for survival. Fighting has minimal rules and equipment; it's just man to man, a contest to see whose skills, training, and willpower will triumph. It's the hunger that wins out against another fighter. Stepping into the ring is intoxicating: the lights, the cheering fans, and the smell of sweat.

When you're young, you dream of the big time. It's hard to fathom that one day it will be over. For most fighters, competition is more than just a way to make a living; it helps squash some demons. It teaches fighters a lot about themselves. Competition puts focus in a fighter's life.

Most fighters get to use the world and experience things that many people don't get to experience. So, all young warriors should go for it—don't give up on the dream of fighting. It's time to kick butt.

The Least You Need to Know

➤ When the kicks stop flying, try the softer side of martial arts.

➤ The softer martial arts include karate, aikido, tai chi and hwarang-do.

➤ If you can't give up competing, switch to semicontact competitions.

➤ If you hear the telephone ringing but it's not, it's time to call it quits.

Kickboxing Sanctioning Bodies and Associations

It's show time! You want to join the fierce fighters who make up the kickboxing world. Here's a list of contacts.

Sanctioning Bodies

International Kickboxing Federation (IKF)
9385 Old State Highway, P.O. Box 1205
New Castle, CA 95658
Phone: 916-663-2467
Fax: 916-663-4510
E-mail: ikf@jps.net
Web site: www.ikfkickboxing.com
Contact: Steve Fossum

International Sport Kickboxing Association (ISKA)
P.O. Box 90147
Gainesville, FL 32607-0147
Phone: 352-374-6876

World Kickboxing Association (WKA)
Head office:
63 Gravelly Lane
Erdington, Birmingham, B23 6LR, England
Phone: 44-0-121-382-2995
Fax: 44-0-121-382-5688
E-mail: info@kickboxing-wka.co.uk
Web site: www.kickboxing-wka.co.uk/content.html

Associations

World Kickboxing Council (WKC)
1081 Camino-Del Rio South, Suite 121
San Diego, CA 92108
Phone: 619-296-7000

Karate International Council of Kickboxing (KICK)
3600 Four Season, Suite 335
Chesterfield, MO 63017
Contact: Frank Babcock
Phone: 314-984-8903

The United States Amateur Kickboxing Association (USAKA)
Contact: John Garcia
Phone: 972-562-3590
       972-569-9919

Fitness Kickboxing Videos, Certifications, and Equipment

There are a lot of videos out on the market, these are the ones we recommend. We've also provided a short list of organizations that certify instructors, in case you're thinking about getting certified to teach cardio-kickboxing or kickboxing.

Kickboxing Videos

Cardio-Kickboxing Video
Sport Karate, Inc.
www.wowpages.com/cardiokick
Phone: 1-800-270-5425

Tae-Bo
Billy Blanks
www.taebo.com
Phone: 887-BBTAEBO

The Real Workout
Christina Rondeau
www.rondeauskickboxing.com
Phone: 401-766-5425

Certifications

Box Aerobics
Thomas "the Promise"
Phone: 601-372-8313

Freestyle Fitness Kickboxing
Guy Mezger/Fred Pooladsanj
Phone: 214-954-0022

Power Kickbox
Steve Doss
Phone: 512-447-KICK

The 12th Round
Kurt Pitman
Phone: 972-503-3225

Equipment

For many years, the following suppliers have set the standard in kickboxing equipment. Just call them for a catalog:

Revgear: 1-800-767-8288

Everlast: 718-665-4116

Ringside: 877-4-BOXING

Title: 1-800-999-1213

Century Martial Arts Supply: 1-800-626-2787

Otomix: 1-800-701-7867

Macho: 1-800-327-6812

Index

N

Napoleon, 20
neck wrestling, 240-241
neutral kickboxing stance, 46-47
Norris, Chuck, 23-24
nutritionists, 199
nutrition, 196
 balanced meals, 199
 carbs, 198
 fats, 196-197, 208-209
 proteins, 198

O

offense, ground scenarios, 277-278
offensive front kicks, 51-52, 95-96
 See also rear leg front kicks
oils, 196-197, 208-209
Olympics, 18
omega-3 fatty acids, 197
omega-6 polysaturated fats, 196-197
one-armed dumbbell rows, 131
one-on-one workouts, 9
open guard positions, 273-275
opponents, 220
 fight plans, 199
 headhunters, 211-212
 mind games, 210-211
 strategies, 220
organizations, kickboxing, 241-242
Otomix, 324
overhand punches, 70, 101-102

P-Q

pads, 21-22, 35, 147-148
 foot, 36
 headgear, 36
 shin, 35
 Thai, 38, 118, 214
pains, children, 304
palm strikes, self-defense, 261-262
pancake mitts, 114-116
pancration, 18-20
parrying, 79-80, 165
patterns, aerobics, 171-172
pectoralis major, 64-65
pectoralis minor, 64-65
permission slips, professional kickboxing, 243
petroleum jelly, 164
physical handicaps, 13
physical strength, training workouts, 224-227
physicals, doctors, 243
pilates, 137-138
pivots, 93-94
PKA (Professional Kickboxers Association), 21-22
plans
 child safety, 279
 bear hugs, 282
 communicating, 280
 front chokes, 283
 front grabs, 281
 HELP, 280-281
 side head locks, 282
 wrist grabs, 281
 escaping attacks, 252-253
 self-defense, 283-284
plyometrics, 181-182
police, self-defense laws, 258
positions, self-defense
 closed guard, 273
 ground offense, 277-278
 open guard, 273-275
 standing up, 275-277

power
 hwarang-do, 317-318
 kicks, 49-50
 defensive front, 51
 front, 50
 front leg round, 54
 offensive front, 51-52
 rear leg round, 55-56
 side, 52-53
 turn back, 56-58
 punches, 67
 crosses 67-68
 hooks, 68-70
 overhanded, 70
 spinning back fist, 71-73
 uppercuts, 71
 strikes
 knees, 58
 side knees, 59
 straight rear knees, 60-61
presleep, visualizations, 209-210
prefight, visualizing, 220
presses
 45-degree legs, 134-135
 barbell flat bench, 128
 barbell inclines, 129
 dumbbells, 129
prize money, K-1 Grand Prix tournaments, 245
prizefights, 19
professional fights, 294
 advertising, 296-297
 entrance fees, 297
 locations, 295
 matchmakers, 296
 sanctioning body, 294-295
Professional Kickboxers Association. *See* PKA
professional kickboxing, 242-243
programs
 apprenticeships, coaches, 291-292

R

Y

Z